The Modern Children's Library of Knowledge

BOOK FIVE

THE WORLD OF ARTS AND PASTIMES

How to enjoy Books, the Arts and Hobbies

by

RALPH S. WALKER
M.A.
Professor of English,
McGill University, Montreal

EVELYN CLARK
Former President of the Somerset
Archaeological and Natural
History Society

MARGARET WALKER
M.A.
Formerly English mistress at
St. Margaret's School, Aberdeen

FRANK DAUNTON
A.G.S.M.
Formerly Music Master, Stanbridge
School, Romsey, Hampshire

DENYS KAY-ROBINSON
Diplômé of the University of Poitiers

PIGEON CROWLE
Author of many books on ballet

THE GROLIER SOCIETY LTD.
LONDON

First published 1957
New Edition 1958
Reprinted 1960 (twice)
Reprinted 1963
Reprinted 1964
Reprinted 1966
Reprinted 1969
Reprinted 1970
Reprinted 1971 (with revisions)

ISBN for complete set: 0 7172 7703 8

© *The Grolier Society Ltd., 1971*

Printed in Great Britain by
Lowe & Brydone (Printers) Ltd., London

ALL ABOUT THIS BOOK

THIS is Book Five of *The Modern Children's Library of Knowledge*. On pages 5 and 6 of Book One you will find a description of this Library as a whole, and now you will learn some extra facts about the book you are reading at this moment. This book deals with the world of arts and pastimes, and tells us how to enjoy books, the arts and hobbies.

What do we mean by "the arts"? Usually we mean the arts of painting and sculpture; the arts of singing and music-making of all kinds; the arts of dancing and the ballet; and architecture, too, for that is another art, the art of making buildings beautiful to look at as well as suitable to live in. But poetry is a form of art, like play-writing and story-telling. It is the art of using words to create thoughts in other people's minds. So, you see, all the main arts are dealt with in this book.

Here you will learn about the great stories, poems and plays that everyone reads and hears about, and of the men and women who wrote them. You will learn about famous painters and sculptors and you will begin to understand how they transform what they see into pictures or carve it in stone. You will learn about the world of melody and harmony musicians create from the sounds made by voice and instrument. You will learn about many kinds of dancing and many forms of architecture.

In all these cases something beautiful is being done, something beautiful is being created, and by understanding what it is all about, you yourself can enjoy it. This, then, is the purpose of this book—to tell you how to understand the fine examples in every kind of art through which people express themselves, so adding to the richness of your mind and the enjoyment of your life.

But no one wants all the time to admire what other people have created. Everyone wants to be able to make or do something himself, and a lot of people get a great deal of fun out of having a hobby. There are many hobbies for young and old, and those of the most interest to boys and girls are described in this book. There are things for you to collect, things for you to do, things for you to make. You learn through your hobbies and life is never dull if you have one. Through your hobby you will come into contact with other people having the same hobby, and you will be able to share their thoughts and pleasures.

As in other books in this Library, you will find out these new facts by following the adventures of Billy and Barbara, two young children who go with their parents and friends to all sorts of places, see many exciting things and meet many interesting people.

WHAT THE CHAPTERS ARE ABOUT

COLOURED PICTURES IN THIS BOOK

Hercules holds up the sky for Atlas, while Atlas fetches the golden apples for him.

The Story of Books

Do you ever think what a wonderful world has been opened up to you since you learned to read? There are books about everything, and you have the key to the whole store. Here we shall learn about the books that have been written to stir the imagination and which teach you about the lives, problems and adventures of mankind.

(1)

EVERYONE LOVES A GOOD STORY

"JUST got home in time," gasped Billy, racing his sister Barbara into the porch. Mr. and Mrs. Brown hurried in after them as the big drops of rain began to fall faster and faster.

"Lucky it held off for the afternoon," Mrs. Brown remarked. "Fairs aren't much fun in the rain."

While they were having tea the children didn't stop talking about what they had seen and done.

"Who was the strongest man who ever lived?" Bill asked suddenly, thinking about the strong man at the fair.

Mr. Brown laughed. "I don't know," he replied. "But the Greeks and the Romans would have said Hercules, a son of Jupiter, king of the gods. His mother, however, was an ordinary human being, and when he was still a baby the goddess Juno sent two snakes to kill him."

"Why?" asked Barbara, horrified.

"Because she was Jupiter's real wife, and so she hated Hercules. Well, the baby Hercules just crushed the snakes until they were dead; but when Hercules had grown up and married, Juno drove him mad, so that he killed his own wife and children. As a punishment he was given twelve dangerous and difficult jobs to do,

Bill and Barbara watch the strong man at the fair.

DID YOU KNOW THIS?

The book of maps you use at school is named after Atlas, the giant whom the Greeks believed prevented the sky from falling down on to the earth.

9

Sitting by the campfire, a minstrel tells Greek soldiers the story of one of their great heroes.

Homer, the blind Greek poet who composed the *Iliad* and the *Odyssey*.

which we call the Labours of Hercules. One of these jobs was to pick some golden apples from a tree guarded by a dragon and four beautiful girls. He asked the giant Atlas to do it for him, offering to take his place in holding up the sky while he was away. Atlas came back with the apples all right, but he had enjoyed his holiday so much that he didn't want to start work again. Luckily he was rather a stupid fellow, and when Hercules asked him to hold on to the sky for a moment while he scratched his back, Atlas did so, whereupon Hercules ran away with the apples."

"Who wrote that story?" Bill asked.

Mr. Brown smiled. "It was told long before there were any books and even before anyone knew how to write," he replied. "Mothers told it to their children and men would wander about the country telling this and other stories of the gods and great heroes to the music of the lyre. The Greeks loved these stories, and they would give the singer food and drink and perhaps gold as well if they were pleased with the way he told them. The stories were remembered

10

and passed on in this way for hundreds of years before the great poets began to write them down in their own words. One of these men was the blind poet, Homer, who retold many of them in the *Iliad* and the *Odyssey*, two of the greatest and most exciting poems ever composed."

"What are they about?" asked Barbara.

"The *Iliad* tells how Venus, the goddess of love, promised to give Paris the most beautiful woman in the world if he would give her the prize in a beauty contest with the goddesses Juno and Minerva; how, to fulfil her promise, she helped Paris to carry off Helen, the wife of the king of Sparta, a Greek city; and how the Greeks sailed to Troy to bring her back. There was a siege in which many brave men were killed, but for ten long years the Greeks were unable to capture the city. Then, as Homer tells us in the *Odyssey*, the Greeks thought of a trick. They secretly made a great wooden horse and then they withdrew to their ships, pretending to

ANSWER THIS

What were the labours of Hercules, and how many were there?

The Trojans dragged the great wooden horse into their city.

11

give up the siege. When the people of Troy found it, they were so curious to know what it meant that they dragged it into the city. In the night the Greek soldiers who were hidden inside it leapt out and opened the gates for their comrades to enter and capture the city.

"The man who first thought of the idea, Ulysses, is the hero of the other poem, which tells of his many adventures in sailing home to Greece. The voyage took ten years because Ulysses had offended the sea god Neptune, who did everything he could to stop him from getting home. One of the dangers he passed safely by was that of the Sirens—nymphs whose singing was so sweet that it drew sailors too close to the shore, where their ships were wrecked on the rocks and they were drowned. Ulysses, wishing to hear them, ordered his men to bind him to the mast so that the singing of the sirens would not lure him to jump overboard, while they plugged their ears with wax and rowed safely past. When at last he arrived home, dressed as a beggar, he found many men living in his house as uninvited guests and trying to

Ulysses hears the beautiful voices of the Sirens.

Ulysses returns home

force his faithful wife Penelope to marry one of them. With the help of his son and two trusted servants he killed them all."

"But were all these stories true?" asked Bill. "That one about Hercules couldn't have been anyway."

"Many of them were the first attempts of the Greeks—before the great Greek philosophers (thinkers and scientists)—to explain the world about them. Others, like the story of Troy, are partly true, as archaeologists (men who dig up old ruins) later found out. We call these stories myths and legends to show that they are different from historical stories and scientific happenings, about which more is known."

"Did the Romans tell the same stories as the Greeks?" asked Barbara. "You said something about both the Romans and the Greeks thinking that this fellow Hercules was the strongest man who ever lived."

ANSWER THIS

Why is it that the Roman names for the Greek gods and heroes are more familiar to us than the Greek ones?

The infant Hercules.

"Well the Romans, who were a more practical and orderly people, learnt much of their knowledge, skill and wisdom from the Greeks, and they adopted many of the Greek gods and heroes, giving them new names but still telling the old stories about them. The Romans conquered a great part of the known world, and through their own Latin books, which were for a long time the chief writings studied by the learned men of all European countries, they passed them on to other nations, our own among them. And so the Roman names for the gods and heroes are better known to us than the Greek ones, which is why I used them in telling you those stories. The Greek name for Jupiter is Zeus; for Juno, Hera; for Venus, Aphrodite; for Minerva, Athene; and for Neptune, Poseidon; while Ulysses was called Odysseus by the Greeks; and Hercules, Herakles."

"But what about the first *English* books?"

"The first books written in England were copies of Latin books," Mr. Brown explained,

disguised as a beggar.

"and for many centuries the books of most English writers were written in Latin, not in English. And even when English began to be used more generally for writing it was still mainly employed to translate Latin works. So you can see that the earliest writers of English books certainly learned a great deal from the writers of Ancient Rome."

Odin, the Norse god of war, with his guardian dogs and the two ravens which he sends round the world for news.

(2)

THE FIRST ENGLISH BOOKS

"WERE the Greeks and the Romans the only people who made up stories about gods and heroes?" Barbara asked the following day.

"All peoples have told myths and legends at one time or another," her father replied. "For instance, the Norsemen or Vikings had their own gods and heroes in legend, many of them the same as those of the Saxons and other Germanic tribes. Woden or Odin was their chief god, and from him we get our word Wednesday (Woden's day). Another great Norse

The Valkyries bear dead heroes to Valhalla, Odin's palace of silver and gold.

god was Thor, god of Thunder, from whom we get our word Thursday (Thor's day). It was believed that if a great hero died in battle the Valkyries, warrior maidens, would ride down from the sky and carry him to Valhalla to feast with the gods. One famous hero of these northern races was Siegfried, whom the composer Wagner made the hero of a series of operas. Another was Beowulf, whose story is told in the greatest poem in Old English."

"What's it about?" asked Bill.

"It's a long story about the heroic deeds of a prince who killed two terrible monsters that were terrorizing the people of a foreign country. In his old age, his own country is attacked by a dragon which has made its lair in one of the great burial mounds in which kings and heroes used to be laid in those days, along with their weapons and many other treasures. Only Beowulf and one brave follower dare to approach the dragon, which breathes forth terrible flames, and in slaying it Beowulf himself is killed.

"Although much of the poem is a sort of fairy-tale, real events and people are mentioned in it. Like the early stories of the Greeks, it was

The brave Beowulf and his loyal follower Wiglaf attack the dragon at the mouth of its lair.

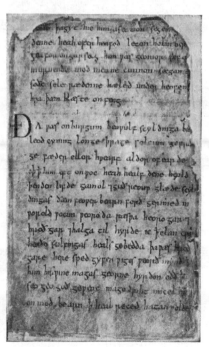

Here is a page from the only manuscript of *Beowulf* in existence. The poem is written in a very early form of English.

15

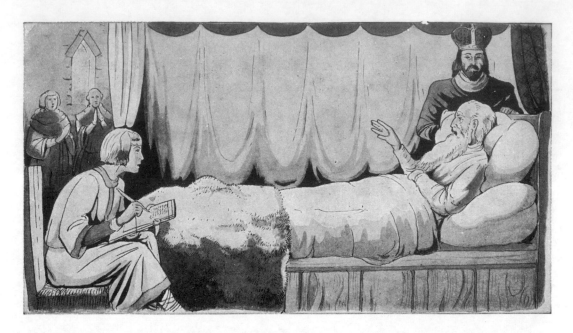

at first handed down by word of mouth. It was probably first written down in the late 7th or early 8th century, but the happenings in it belong to the first part of the 6th century, when many of the tribes which later came to Britain were still on the continent of Europe. The version that has come to us may have been written down by a monk about the year A.D. 1000, because it has references to Christianity in it which could not have been part of the old pagan story, which was set in the days before the peoples of Northern Europe began to be converted to Christianity."

"I should love to read it," said Bill. "It sounds jolly exciting."

Mr. Brown smiled. "It is written in a very old form of our language," he explained, "and is full of words which we no longer use. English was very different in those days and I don't think you would understand one line of the poem unless you read it in one of the translations into modern English."

"What about the early English Christians?" asked Barbara. "Didn't they write any stories about Christian heroes?"

Bede dictating his last book in the monastery at Jarrow where he spent most of his life.

A page showing Noah's ark from the manuscript of a poem that is thought to be by Caedmon.

16

"Certainly they did. After St. Augustine came to England in A.D. 597 and began to convert the English to Christianity, many fine poems were composed in the old English language re-telling stories from the Bible and the adventures of the Christian saints and martyrs. The most famous of the early English Christian poets was Caedmon, a common herdsman of whom it is told that he suddenly received the gift of poetry and was taken before the Abbess Hild to sing his verses on the Creation, as a result of which he was taken into the monastery. Before the invention of printing, many manuscripts (hand-written books) were beautifully decorated with brightly coloured lettering and pictures, and we still have examples of illumination, as it is called, from the times of the early English Christians."

Barbara frowned. "But was all the writing at this time done in verse?"

"Well, the oldest writings that we know of are in verse. One reason is that these old stories were not written down at first, and verse was much easier than prose for the minstrels to remember. But when Alfred became King of Wessex in the 9th century, he encouraged his friends to translate Latin books into Old English, and those, of course, are not in verse. One of these books was the first great book of English history, written by the 'Venerable Bede' in a monastery at Jarrow, in the county of Durham, about 150 years before. Bede himself spent his last days dictating a translation of the Gospel of St. John. Alfred was also responsible for starting the history of England known as the *Anglo-Saxon Chronicle*. He often added pieces of his own to explain the books he translated and bring the information in them up to date. It was Alfred who wrote, as an addition to a Latin history book he was translating, the stories of Wulfstan and Ohthere, the sailors who explored the White Sea and the Baltic in the 9th century."

This chair, now in a church at Jarrow, County Durham, was once used by the Venerable Bede.

King Alfred the Great was a scholar as well as a warrior.

17

"I suppose after this everybody started writing books in English?" suggested Bill.

"Not at all," his father replied. "After Alfred's death there was very little writing in English for about 500 years. Most books were written in Latin or French for a long time after the coming of the Normans to England."

"But my history book," insisted Barbara, "says that in Norman times most people in England spoke only English."

"The answer to that is that most of the people who were rich enough to buy books could speak French, and some of the rich Normans could speak no English, so authors naturally found it better not to write in English.

"But the wars with France during the 12th and 13th centuries made the speaking of French seem something foreign, even to the descendants of the Normans, so that English—although with the addition of many words adapted from French words—was increasingly used by the wealthy classes. Then, for a time, English writings were mainly translations from the French, or imitations of French poems."

"Do you mean to say that there were no English authors good enough to write books of their own?" Bill asked rather indignantly.

"Well, eventually an Englishman did succeed in writing poetry in English which was better than anything the French had written. His name was Geoffrey Chaucer."

"I know," said Barbara. "Didn't he write a poem about some pilgrims or something called the *Canterbury Tales*."

"That's right. In the *Canterbury Tales* Chaucer describes a lively group of English people travelling together on horseback from London to visit a holy place in Canterbury. To pass the time on their journey they tell each other stories, some sad, some funny."

"And what about *his* language?" asked Bill. "Could I understand it?"

Chaucer, the great English poet who wrote the *Canterbury Tales*, was also a courtier and soldier. He lived from 1340 to 1400.

ANSWER THIS

Why is *Beowulf* such a difficult poem to read?

18

CHAUCER RIDES WITH THE CANTERBURY PILGRIMS

ROBIN HOOD AND HIS MERRY MEN MOCK A WEALTHY CAPTIVE

"I think you would find his language easier to read than the Old English of the Anglo-Saxons, but there are still difficulties in it for people who know only modern English.

"Chaucer is called the Father of English Poetry, because although he knew Latin and French, he chose to write in English. He proved (and this had been doubted by many) that English could be used to write great poetry. This was a tremendous encouragement to English authors to use their native language in their writings instead of French or Latin."

(3)

STORIES IN SONG

BILL had set up an archery target at the far end of the garden and was trying out his home-made bow and arrows on it. As Barbara went to pick up the fallen arrows from all round the target, where they had fallen, Bill muttered, "Split a wand at sixty paces! I'd like to see anyone do it ! I reckon old Robin Hood would have a job to hit this target, never mind anything else."

His father stirred in the depth of a deck chair. "I think Robin's aim must have been a bit better than yours, Bill," he teased.

"It's things like this that make you wonder if Robin Hood ever really lived," Bill retorted. "There are so many good stories about him and Maid Marian, and about Little John and Friar Tuck and all the other 'merry men,' and about how he outwitted the Sheriff of Nottingham, that it's hardly possible they can all be true."

"Robin Hood is a character in legend," explained Mr. Brown. "We know nothing about him for certain. He is said to have lived as an outlaw in Sherwood Forest during the 12th century. The adventures of some real man may have started the stories. Richard the Lion-

Bill and Barbara play at "Robin Hood and his Merry Men."

hearted was king at the time, but during most of his reign he was in the Holy Land fighting in the Crusades, and his unpopular brother, Prince John (who later, when king himself, was

forced to sign Magna Carta as a result of his misdeeds) was the real ruler of England. Perhaps people used to imagine that a free and happy life could be lived in the greenwood, and then made up ballads about this outlaw which may have had some truth behind them."

"I like the story of how Robin Hood met Little John," said Bill, excitedly. "One day, as Robin Hood was walking alone through the forest, he came to a stream spanned by a fallen tree trunk. He was just about to set foot on it when he realized that another man had started to cross from the other side. 'Stand back,' he shouted, 'and let the better man cross first.' 'Then stand back yourself,' replied the stranger stoutly. As neither would give way, they fought it out with quarterstaves in the middle of the log, until the stranger dealt Robin such a blow

The stranger dealt Robin such a blow that he fell into the stream.

22

A minstrel singing one of the old ballads on the village green.

that he fell into the stream. But Robin took it in good part, inviting his opponent to join his band of outlaws, and when they learnt that the stranger's name was John Little, they christened him Little John, amid much merriment, for he was a real giant of a man, a good seven feet tall."

Mr. Brown laughed. "Well told," he said.

Barbara had finished picking up the fallen arrows and was now trying to blow Robin Hood's horn, which consisted of a tin whistle with a funnel stuck over one end of it. "What are ballads?" she asked.

"Ballads are merely old poems which were passed down by word of mouth from generation to generation, just as the early stories of the Greeks were, or the sagas of the Norsemen, or our own proverbs and nursery rhymes. Nobody knows who made up the old ballads: they belong to many different times and places. They were sung and recited in olden times by wandering minstrels, and people enjoyed them so much that they came to know them by heart. Ballads like *Chevy Chase*, *Sir Andrew Barton*, and *Sir Patrick Spens* are not very difficult to understand, and they go with such a lively swing.

Friar Tuck, the jovial priest of Robin Hood's band of outlaws.

23

The ballad *Chevy Chase* tells the story of a great battle between the Scots and the English in which the leaders of both armies were said to have been killed.

ANSWER THIS

In what way are the ballads different from most other poems?

DID YOU KNOW THIS?

Many famous poems were inspired by the old ballads. Examples are Coleridge's *The Ancient Mariner*, Browning's *The Pied Piper*, and Cowper's *The Ballad of John Gilpin* —although, unlike the true ballad heroes, Gilpin is anything but a romantic or heroic figure.

The stories are told swiftly too and they are full of exciting adventures. *Chevy Chase* is one of the ballads composed about the stirring deeds on the Scottish border. It is a legend—based on a historical incident—which tells how 'Hotspur,' Percy of Northumberland, went hunting in the Cheviot Hills and there met the Scottish Earl of Douglas. There was a great battle in which, according to the ballad, both Hotspur and Douglas were slain. Here, wait a minute." And their father rose out of his deck chair and went through the French windows into the sitting-room. "I will read you a bit of it to give you some idea of what the old ballads are like."

He came back with a book in his hand and the children listened while he read of how :

"The Percy leanéd on his brand
And saw the Douglas dee;
He took the dead man by the hand,
And said, 'Woe is me for thee!

To have saved thy life I'd have parted with
My lands for yearés three,
For a better man of heart nor of hand
Was not in the north countrye.' "

"Sir Walter Scott made a big collection of border ballads," said Mr. Brown, "and they inspired some of his own story-poems, such as *The Lay of the Last Minstrel*, as well as many of his novels."

(4)

ONCE UPON A TIME

It was a wet Saturday afternoon in late autumn. Outside strong gusts of wind stirred and rustled among the piles of damp brown leaves on the ground; but in the Brown's sitting-room the fire was blazing merrily and it was warm and cosy. Barbara looked up from the rather worn copy of *Grimm's Fairy-Tales* which she had been reading and asked her mother to tell them something about fairy-stories. "*Beowulf* is supposed to be a sort of fairy-tale, but it's not a bit like the stories in this book," she said.

"Well perhaps not, but both those stories and *Beowulf* are folk-tales: they were probably passed down by word of mouth for hundreds of years before anyone thought of writing them down. Then, at the beginning of the 19th century, two German brothers, Jacob and Wilhelm Grimm, already celebrated language scholars, determined to write a big work on the folklore of their country. Europe was troubled by the great wars of Napoleon at the time, but these two extraordinary, solemn brothers refused to be turned from their path by such passing events. With painstaking thoroughness they collected their material together, learning many of the stories direct from the lips of old peasants; and it is as a result of their labours that such wonderful stories as *Tom Thumb*, *Snow White*, *The Golden Goose*, *Hansel and Gretel*, *The Frog Prince*, *Rumpelstiltskin*, *The Goose Girl*, and *The Juniper Tree* have been preserved for the delight of children all over the world."

Jacob and Wilhelm Grimm, the German scholars who collected so many wonderful fairy-tales.

The Frog Prince—the princess's golden ball rolled into the pond and a little frog popped his head out of the water.

"Who wrote *Cinderella*?" asked Bill.

"The story of *Cinderella* as we know it seems to have come from France, where Charles Perrault started the fashion of re-telling the old fairy-tales. In 1697 he published a book which included the story of *Little Red Riding Hood*, and later his son published a collection of fairy-tales which included *Cinderella*. Another famous writer of fairy-tales living in France at that time was the Baroness d'Aulnoy; but many of the tales told by these French writers can be traced back to Italians, among them Giovanni Straparola, a Venetian, who was probably the first European to publish (in 1550) a collection of fairy-tales, which tales included the earliest known version of *Puss in Boots*."

"What about *Andersen's Fairy-Tales*? You haven't mentioned them."

"Well, Andersen's fairy-stories are different in a way, because he made up many of them himself, instead of simply re-writing folk-tales."

The Prince finds that the slipper fits Cinderella's foot perfectly.

"Do tell us something about him." Barbara begged.

"Hans Christian Andersen was born in 1805 in the ancient city of Odense in Denmark. He was the only child of a poor shoemaker who died when Hans was only 11 years old, and he received very little education. Hans wanted to be an actor and an opera singer, and when he was 14 he walked to Copenhagen, the capital of Denmark, thinking that he would soon make his fortune. He almost starved, but eventually he was befriended by the director of the Royal Theatre and was sent back to school for several years at the expense of the King of Denmark. Andersen later wrote many books and became famous throughout Europe. He thought he would be remembered as a great novelist, dramatist and poet, but it is because of his enchanting fairy-tales—stories such as *The Tinder Box*, *Thumbelina*, *The Wild Swans*, *The Little Match Girl*, *The Fir Tree*, *The Red Shoes*,

Puss in Boots, the clever cat who won a fortune for his master.

The Snow Queen, The Little Tin Soldier, The Little Mermaid, The Emperor's New Clothes, and *The Ugly Duckling*—that Hans Andersen's name still lives."

"I suppose you could call *Alice in Wonderland* a fairy-tale then," remarked Barbara, "even if Lewis Carroll did make it all up."

"Yes, but the author's real name wasn't Lewis Carroll at all. It was Charles Lutwidge Dodgson, and he was a distinguished teacher of mathematics at Oxford University during Queen Victoria's reign."

"Gosh! I'd like see *our* maths master telling fairy-stories," gasped Billy.

"Well, Mr. Dodgson enjoyed telling stories, and one hot summer afternoon he took the three small daughters of a friend for a row on the river. The name of one of the girls was Alice, and when, as usual, they begged him to tell them a story, he began to make up *Alice's Adventures in Wonderland*, which was followed later by *Through the Looking Glass and What Alice Found There*. And that is how such extraordinary characters as the White Rabbit, the Mad Hatter, the Dormouse, the March Hare, the Cheshire Cat, the Mock Turtle, the Queen of Hearts, the White Knight, and Tweedledum and Tweedledee were born, and all those delightful nonsense rhymes were written."

The children both began to chant:

> "The Walrus and the Carpenter
> Were walking close at hand;
> They wept like anything to see
> Such quantities of sand :
> 'If this were only cleared away,'
> They said, 'it would be grand!'
> 'If seven maids with seven mops
> Swept it for half a year,
> Do you suppose,' the Walrus said,
> 'That they could get it clear?'
> 'I doubt it,' said the Carpenter,
> And shed a bitter tear."

Hans Andersen, one of whose fairy-tales is illustrated below. The soldier climbs into the hollow tree to find the magic tinder box for the old witch.

An illustration by Sir John Tenniel from *Through the Looking Glass*—the White Knight "rolled out of the saddle, and fell headlong into a deep ditch."

Rip Van Winkle returns home.

Their mother laughed. "You seem to know *Through the Looking Glass* pretty well."

By this time Bill had had enough of fairies and started to sort out the stamps he wanted to exchange at school on Monday, but Barbara still wanted to know more, so her mother told her about Frances Browne, the blind Irish woman who wrote *Granny's Wonderful Chair*; Fiona Macleod, the Scottish poet whose real name was William Sharp and who re-told Celtic folk-tales; George Macdonald, the Scottish preacher and poet; Andrew Lang, the Scottish scholar and journalist who made some of the best collections of fairy-tales in *The Blue Fairy Book* and its companion volumes; Carl Ewald, the Danish schoolmaster; Asbjörnsen and Möe, the great Norwegian collectors of folk-tales; the Italian author Carlo Collodi, whose real name was Lorenzini and who wrote *Pinocchio*, the tale of a puppet; and many others who wrote fairy-tales.

"Then, there is Washington Irving, who was born in the year that America won independence from Britain and is sometimes called the Father of American Literature. Besides his great biographies of George Washington, Columbus and Mahomet, he wrote many delightfully amusing tales, like *The Legend of Sleepy Hollow* and *Rip Van Winkle*, the story of a man who meets a dwarf in the mountains, helps him to carry a keg of liquor to his companions who are playing at nine-pins, and after drinking some of it, falls asleep for twenty years. He returns home to find everything changed, his house in ruins, and himself almost forgotten, and learns that there has been a revolution and that his country is now a republic.

"Another well-known American fairy-story is *The Wizard of Oz*, by Frank Baum."

"I saw the film of that," exclaimed Bill. "It was jolly good."

"Is *Aladdin* a fairy-story?" asked Barbara.

"Yes, I had forgotten about that wonderful collection of tales from the East about beggars, merchants, princes, genii and hoards of treasure hidden in caves best known as *The Arabian Nights*. Besides *Aladdin and His Wonderful Lamp*, most children must know the stories of *Sindbad the Sailor* and *Ali Baba and the Forty Thieves*. The real title of the book is *A Thousand and One Nights*, because a different story is supposed to have been told each night for a thousand and one nights by the beautiful Scheherazade to her husband, the Sultan. This great king used to kill his wives the day after he had married them.

"Scheherazade, who was as clever as she was beautiful, escaped this fate by breaking off in the middle of each story and saving the rest for the next night, when she would also begin another story. In the end the Sultan grew so

No sooner had Aladdin rubbed the ring which the Magician had given him when he sent him into the cave, than a huge Genie appeared.

ANSWER THIS

In what way are Hans Andersen's tales different from the fairy-tales told by the Brothers Grimm?

29

Aesop, the freed Greek slave, tells one of his witty fables at the court of King Croesus.

fond of Scheherazade and her stories that he no longer wanted to kill her. And so it all ended as a good fairy-tale should, and we can imagine that they lived happily ever after."

(5)

ANIMAL HEROES

"WHAT a lot of animals there are in these fairy-stories," Bill remarked later to his mother.

"Yes, animals are often the heroes of folk-tales, and many famous men and women have told stories about them, sometimes in the form of fables teaching moral lessons. One of the earliest of these was Aesop, whose fables—such as *The Frogs and Their King*, *The Goose Who Laid the Golden Eggs*, *The Hare and the Tortoise*, *The Boy Who Cried Wolf*, *The Fox and the Grapes*, and *The Ant and the Grasshopper*—are full of homely wisdom."

"Who was Aesop?" asked Barbara.

"We know very little about him for certain, but according to tradition he was a slave who lived on the Greek island of Samos about the year 600 B.C. He was set free, and later went to

In *Animal Farm* the pigs are masters over all the other animals, and in this scene from the film Snowball is seen preparing the way for the dictator Napoleon.

live under the protection of the fabulously wealthy Croesus, King of Lydia. Aesop was said to be squat and ugly in appearance, but his ready wit and his clever tales must have delighted the lords and ladies of the court. Croesus sent him to Delphi with a large sum of money for its citizens, but Aesop thought them unworthy of the gift, and they were so incensed by his biting remarks that they threw him over a cliff."

Barbara shuddered. "What a horrible death!"

"Another famous writer of fables is the French poet Jean de la Fontaine, who lived at the same time as Charles Perrault, the writer of fairy-tales. La Fontaine did not make up his *Fables* but re-told the stories of Aesop and other writers in sparkling verse so that they became a sort of guide to his own times."

"I don't suppose anybody writes fables now-adays," remarked Bill.

"Oh, yes, they do. Fables have always been popular as a form of writing in which powerful persons or governments can be effectively criticised without actually being named. A famous modern book which is really a long fable is George Orwell's *Animal Farm*, which uses the story of a revolt of the animals on a farm against their cruel master, and their final subjection to the pigs, as a warning against the danger of people allowing their hard-won rights and liberties to be slowly taken from them.

"Some of the delightful stories of Joel Chandler Harris about Br'er Rabbit and other animal characters are fables too. Harris heard them as a boy from the lips of Negro slaves who lived on the plantation in Georgia owned by his employer, and some time after the American Civil War had freed all the slaves, he wrote them down just as he remembered them and invented the character of Uncle Remus, an old Negro slave, to tell them."

"What about *White Fang*?" Bill demanded. "I think it's a jolly good story."

Joel Chandler Harris, who wrote down the stories of Br'er Rabbit.

Uncle Remus, the American Negro slave, tells one of the delightful animal stories of his race to his white master's small son.

31

Mr. Toad "came swaggering down the steps, drawing on his gauntleted gloves"—an incident from Kenneth Grahame's delightful tale, *The Wind in the Willows*.

Toomai of the Elephants—Toomai rides into the forest on Kala Nag to see the elephant-dance.

"Yes, it's one of Jack London's most exciting books; another is *The Call of the Wild*. There are lots of other good stories about dogs, like *Owd Bob*, by Alfred Ollivant, and *Beautiful Joe*, by Marshall Saunders; and fine horse stories, such as Anna Sewell's *Black Beauty*, and *Smoky*, the story of a cowboy's horse, by Will James. There are many other splendid animal tales, like Henry Williamson's *Tarka the Otter*, and *Bambi*, the story of a forest deer, by Felix Salten. And, of course, for younger children there are Beatrix Potter's charmingly illustrated stories about Peter Rabbit and other animals, and A. A. Milne's *Winnie-the-Pooh* books."

"And *The Wind in the Willows*," said Barbara.

"Yes, Kenneth Grahame's tale of Mr. Toad of Toad Hall who comes to grief through his pride and of his faithful friends the Water Rat, the Mole, and the Badger is one of the best-loved of all children's books.

"But some of the best of all the animal stories are by Rudyard Kipling. His *Just So Stories*—about how the elephant got his trunk, how the leopard got his spots, how the camel got his hump, and so on—are a delight to read, and *The Jungle Books* include such wonderful stories as *Rikki-tikki-tavi*, *The White Seal*, *Toomai of the Elephants*, and the stories of Mowgli, the boy brought up by wolves."

(6)

WHEN KNIGHTS WERE BOLD

A statue of King Arthur at Innsbruck in Austria, made by a German sculptor 450 years ago.

BILL and Barbara had just returned from a Christmas bazaar at one of the big shops in town. The whole thing had been made to look like King Arthur's Court, with his Round Table and his famous knights. The children had wandered in and out of castle walls and towers and turrets; they had been introduced to King Arthur and Sir Lancelot, and to Merlin the magician; they had examined the magic sword Excalibur; and altogether they had been quite impressed. Home once more, they hoped to find out a bit more about these wonderful people who had lived so long ago, and their father was doing his best to make things clear to them.

"The fact is, Bill, the stories of King Arthur and his knights are so old that we don't know who made them up or what truths lie behind them. They belong to what is called folklore—that is, a collection of knowledge and fancy remembered by humble people. These people could neither read nor write, so they passed the stories on from father to son by word of mouth. Stories about Arthur had been told for centuries before anyone thought of writing them down."

"Then nobody knows whether he really lived or not?" Barbara sounded disappointed.

"Nobody knows for certain, dear. In the 5th and 6th centuries, after the Romans had left Britain and when the Saxons were pouring over from Germany and driving the Britons westwards into what is now Cornwall and Wales,

33

Queen Guinevere.

Merlin the magician.

the Britons may have had a leader called Arthur who rallied them to check the invasion for a time. Some of the Britons fled across the Channel to seek refuge with their Celtic kinsmen in France, and some of their descendants may still be living in that part of France known as Brittany, where the Celtic language is still in use. These Britons introduced the first stories of Arthur to the Continent."

"Were they Christians in those days?"

"Well, the Britons were Christians, Barbara, but the Saxons were heathens, and Arthur is shown in the stories as a Christian king who fights against the heathen. Long afterwards, in the 12th century, a monk named Geoffrey of Monmouth wrote a wonderful account of the deeds of King Arthur, but he himself did not know how much truth there was in the old stories he had collected and put together. The story of Arthur and his knights grew very popular all over Europe, especially in France. French poets and minstrels retold them and added to them, often introducing French names and new adventures; while Sir Percival became especially famous in Germany through Wolfram of Eschenbach's poem *Parzival*. Later on, in the 15th century, Sir Thomas Malory collected all the Welsh, French and English stories of King Arthur he could find and put them together in an English book. He called it by the French name *Morte d'Arthur*, and this was one of the books printed by William Caxton, the first English printer."

Bill was already doing some shadow fencing against an imaginary enemy knight. He had snatched the poker from the fireplace and was pretending that it was King Arthur's sword, Excalibur. But Barbara still had several questions to ask.

"Isn't there a poem by Tennyson called *Morte d'Arthur*? I suppose he found the story in Malory's book?"

34

Her father nodded. "Yes. It tells the story of a great battle between the knights loyal to King Arthur and the army of the traitor, Sir Mordred, which followed the discovery of Sir Lancelot's love for Guinevere, Arthur's queen. It begins :

'So all day long the noise of battle rolled
Among the mountains by the winter sea,
Until King Arthur's table, man by man,
Had fallen in Lyonesse about their lord. . . .'

Mordred was slain, but Arthur was mortally wounded. He commanded Sir Bedivere, the last of his knights, to return Excalibur to the Lady of the Lake. Twice Sir Bedivere disobeyed his king, for he thought it a shame to lose so wonderful a sword, but at the third command he did his bidding.

'Sir King, I closed mine eyelids, lest the gems
Should blind my purpose, for I never saw,
Nor shall see, here or elsewhere, till I die,
Not tho' I live three lives of mortal men,
So great a miracle as yonder hilt.
Then with both hands I flung him, wheeling him;
But when I looked again, behold an arm,
Clothed in white samite, mystic, wonderful,
That caught him by the hilt, and brandished him
Three times, and drew him under in the mere.'

Sir Mordred rushed at Arthur and smote him with his sword.

The dying king was taken across the lake to the Island of Avalon.

The ruins of Tintagel Castle in Cornwall, where King Arthur is said to have been born.

Sir Galahad rides forth in quest of the Holy Grail.

Then he bore Arthur to the shores of the lake and laid him in a barge in which sat three queens, weeping bitterly, and the barge 'moved from the brink, like some full-breasted swan' and carried him to the fair Island of Avalon.

"Not only did Tennyson get the idea of that poem from Malory, but the ideas for the whole series of poems called *The Idylls of the King*. Many other poets, too, such as Dryden, Morris, and Swinburne, have been fascinated by Malory's book, and have used it to provide material in the same way for their own poetry, and the Arthurian legends have also inspired painters and composers. Wagner composed two great dramatic operas based on German versions of the legends of Sir Percival and of Tristram and the fair Iseult. At Tintagel, in Cornwall, are the ruins of a castle which according to legend was the birthplace of Arthur, and it is this place which inspired Sir Arnold Bax to compose the music, *Tintagel*."

"Why did these stories become so popular?" asked Bill, leaning triumphantly on the deadly poker.

"Well, the legends about Arthur had all the ideals of Christian chivalry—bravery in

36

KING ARTHUR'S SWORD EXCALIBUR IS RETURNED TO THE LADY OF THE LAKE

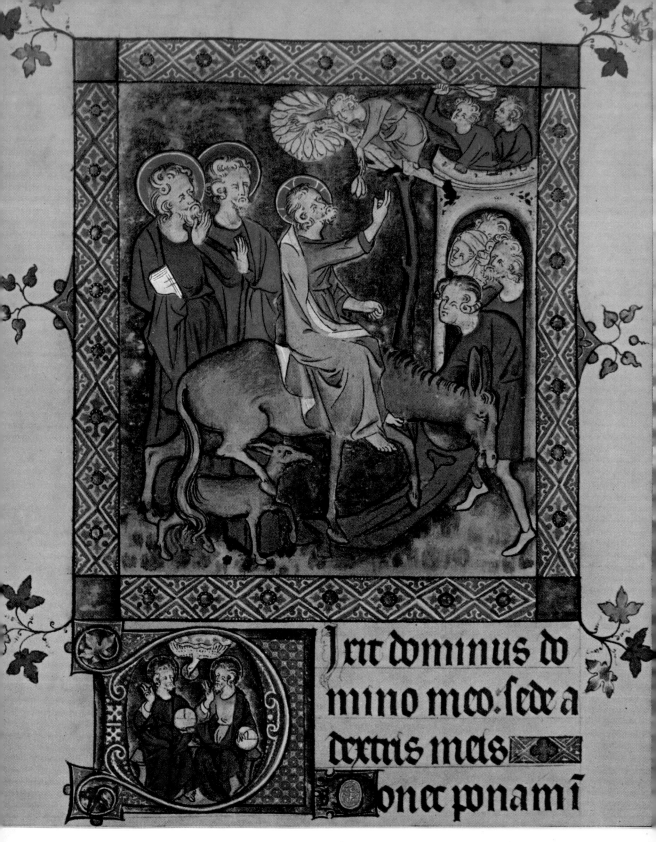

A PAGE FROM AN OLD BOOK OF PSALMS IN THE BRITISH MUSEUM

battle, loyalty to God and one's king, and courtesy towards women."

Among the presents which Bill unwrapped the following morning was a book of stories of King Arthur and his knights, and soon his thoughts were far away among the towers and turrets of Camelot, whence the Knights of the Round Table rode forth on their brave quests, of which the greatest was the Quest of the Holy Grail, accomplished at last by Sir Galahad, the truest and best of all the knights.

(7)

THE BOOK OF BOOKS

BILL and Barbara had just returned from Sunday School and were in a rather quiet mood. Bill still held a Bible in his hand and was turning the pages thoughtfully.

He was trying to remember what his mother had once told him about how the Bible had come to England, and then he said: "Dad, the Bible must be about the oldest book in the world. Why didn't you mention it when we were talking about the early writings before printing was invented?"

"Well," said Mr. Brown, "it *is* a very old book. But it's much more than that. It's different from the others in being not a single book but a whole library of books bound up together. The Old Testament, as you probably know, is made up of many separate books written by different people who lived at different times. It tells the story of the Jewish people from the earliest days and describes their traditions, laws and beliefs, and the experiences they passed through in their search for God. And of course it contains some of the best stories in the world—stories like Noah's Ark and the Flood, Abraham and Isaac, Daniel in the Lion's Den, Belshazzar's Feast, and the stories of Joseph, Moses, Samson, and

ANSWER THIS

How did the legend of King Arthur reach the Continent of Europe? Who is the real Arthur said to have been?

The child Moses is discovered by the daughter of the Pharaoh in a cradle in the bulrushes.

Daniel in the lions' den.

St. Paul, in danger of his life, escapes over the walls of Damascus.

Later, Paul is arrested. The ship carrying Paul prisoner to Rome is wrecked in a storm.

Paul awaits his trial in Rome.

David. The New Testament is in separate books too. The Gospels of Matthew, Mark, Luke and John all tell the story of the life of Jesus Christ. Other books are about the experiences of His disciples in spreading His teaching. *The Acts of the Apostles* makes exciting reading, especially when it tells of St. Paul's adventures."

"Why is the Bible called the world's best-seller?"

"Because that's just what it is. It is a collection of writings which were held sacred by the early Christian church and which still form the basis of all Christian belief and teaching. It is certainly the best-known book in English, for nearly all English-speaking people learn some stories from it while they are still children."

"But," insisted Bill, "isn't it strange that the Bible should be called the greatest book in the English language, because it couldn't have been written in English first?"

"At first sight it does seem strange," admitted Mr. Brown. "But you must remember that the English Bible was so well known and loved by our ancestors that the language in which it was written influenced their ways of thinking and speaking and writing more than the language of any other book."

"What was the Bible's original language?"

"The Old Testament was written in Hebrew, Barbara, and the New Testament in Greek. But the English translation made in the days of King James I which we call the *Authorized Version* has played a great part in shaping English life and thought, and the beauty of its language has made it a standard of excellence for other English writings."

Bill had turned to the beginning of his Bible while his father was speaking, and now he read out part of the text after the title page:

" 'To the most high and mighty Prince JAMES, by the Grace of God, King of Great Britain, France, and Ireland, Defender of the

St. Jerome working on his version of the Bible.

Faith, &c., The Translators of the Bible wish Grace, Mercy, and Peace, through JESUS CHRIST our Lord. Appointed to be read in churches.' I'd often wondered about that part. I suppose that means that this is an *Authorized Version* for the Church of England?"

"That's right. That is what is known as a 'dedication' by the translators to the reigning monarch at the time."

"But surely there must have been other English Bibles before the time of James I?"

"Oh, yes, indeed! It had been translated several times, but not in such a way as to satisfy everyone that the translation was good. You see, the early translators didn't go back to the Hebrew and Greek originals, but used instead a Latin version called the *Vulgate*, which had been made by St. Jerome in the 4th century; but no translation, however good, can ever be perfect, and if you are translating a translation you are bound to be even further away from the exact meaning of the original text."

"Why did they follow the *Vulgate*?"

"I think there were two main reasons," explained Mr. Brown. "First, the *Vulgate* was the version which all the churches used in the Middle Ages; and secondly, there were scarcely any scholars in those days who understood Hebrew and Greek. The first complete translation was made by John Wycliffe and some fellow scholars before the invention of printing in Europe during the 15th century. Wycliffe was a great reformer who condemned those rich priests who were more concerned with wealth and power than with religion. His followers, nicknamed Lollards, used to wander about the country preaching the need for reforming the Church and of looking after the interests of the common people; and it was partly to help his 'poor priests' in their work, and partly because he believed that everyone should be able to know the Bible at first hand, that Wycliffe and

Wycliffe preaching the reform of the Church in an English village.

his friends made their translation. But, as I was saying, their version was not based on the original texts. Neither was that of Miles Coverdale, whose translation was the first complete Bible to be printed in English."

"I suppose every copy of Wycliffe's Bible had to be written out by hand," mused Bill, thinking of the fifty lines he had had to write out at school last week as a punishment. "What a job! And I don't suppose many people can have had a copy."

"No. You had to be very wealthy to own a Bible in those days. And for a long time after the invention of printing, books were still so expensive that when English Bibles came to be placed in the churches for the use of all who could read, they were chained to the lecterns on which they rested, to stop them being stolen."

"Was the *Authorized Version* the first English translation which took into account the original texts, then?"

"No. Almost a hundred years before the *Authorized Version* was published, William Tyndale made a translation direct from the Greek and Hebrew. But like Wycliffe and

Preparing the press and setting up type in an early printer's workshop. The invention of printing was of great importance in spreading knowledge of the Bible.

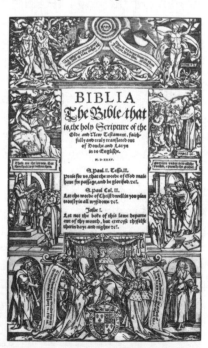

The title page of the first printed English Bible, which was translated by Miles Coverdale.

Coverdale he met with the hostility of the Church, which did not like the idea of unauthorized translations of the Bible. You see, high officials in the Church, like Cardinal Wolsey, thought its influence on the people would be lessened if they began to read these translations.

"As a result of this Tyndale had no encouragement in his work and had to go abroad to complete it. Even there he was followed and spied on, and when he managed to get his translation of the New Testament printed in Germany all copies sent into England were ordered to be seized and burned."

"Do you mean to say that they actually burned copies of the New Testament?"

"Censorship of the printed word is a terrible thing, dear. Many of these books were seized at the ports and in other places, and burned, but copies still kept on coming in, because a great many people were anxious to read them in spite of the law against it. Tyndale himself carried on with his work on the Old Testament, but before he could finish it he was imprisoned and put to death."

"What a wonderful man! He must have been one of the best men who ever lived."

"Well, his work had a tremendous effect, for it spread a knowledge of the Scriptures far and wide through England, and led to a great religious revival there. The Protestant Reformation of the Church was taking place at this time, and a number of other translations appeared, some for Protestant use and others for Catholic use. It was decided to make one as perfect as possible for general use in the Protestant churches, and in 1604, at the king's command, 47 scholars set to work, and seven years later they finished the famous *Authorized Version*, which is still the most commonly used English translation. But it owes much of the beauty of its language to earlier

ANSWER THIS

Who was the reformer who was chiefly responsible for the first complete English Bible, and what were his followers called? Which king ordered the translation of the Bible known as the *Authorized Version* to be made?

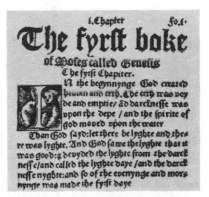

Part of the first page of William Tyndale's translation of Genesis.

William Tyndale is tried and condemned to death.

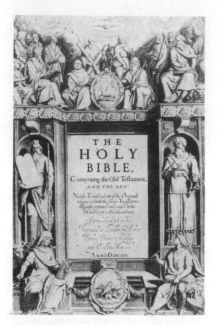

The title page of the original *Authorized Version*, published in 1611 by command of King James I.

versions, including those of Tyndale and Coverdale."

Bill had by this time turned to some of the Psalms and was evidently reading rather slowly and painfully to himself. Suddenly he looked up. "You know, that is just what I find most difficult about the Bible," he confessed. "The language seems to be so old-fashioned that it makes it very hard for me to follow in places. I suppose everybody spoke like that when the *Authorized Version* first came out; but I must say I still can't get used to all these 'thous' and 'thees' and 'yeas'."

"Curiously enough, the translators used language which was far from being the every-day language of the people of King James's day. It had an old-fashioned flavour even then, but the choice of words is such as to give grace and dignity to the whole effect. However, we have a number of modern translations to choose from, written in the language of today, and in some of these, such as that of Dr. Moffatt, for instance, there are places where the sense seems clearer; but many people feel that though the sense is clearer, a great deal of the beauty of the old versions is lost."

A thought struck Barbara. "Does that mean that nothing further has been found out about the New and Old Testament writings since 1611?"

"On the contrary, there have been many important discoveries through the years, most of them around the turn of this century. Among the ancient manuscripts which have been dug up by archaeologists have been a few new sayings of Jesus. A recent translation of the whole Bible, completed in 1970, embodies a great deal of this new material, and is among the most accurate of any yet published. It is called *The New English Bible*, and is the result of a great deal of work on the part of a committee of experts. Although it contains all the latest

Part of the Dead Sea scrolls.

knowledge, it still tries to hold to the beauty and dignity of the earlier language except where the meaning is obscure. In time it may, perhaps, become a serious rival to the *Authorized Version*."

ANSWER THIS

Who made the first complete translation of the Bible into English? What is the name of the Englishman who was put to death for translating the Bible?

(8)

TRAVELLERS' TALES

"YOU said the other day that the translation of the Bible into English had an important effect on the way other English books were written. I suppose you mean books like *The Pilgrim's Progress*? I was looking at it in the school library today and some of the words seemed very old-fashioned," said Billy.

"I was thinking more of the beauty and simplicity of the language of the Bible, Bill, rather than the old-fashioned words. But *The Pilgrim's Progress* is certainly one of the great books it influenced most directly. You see, John Bunyan was a very religious man, and so naturally he knew the Bible better than any other book. When he was young he behaved just as other boys do, getting up to all sorts of pranks. At sixteen he joined the Roundhead forces which were fighting against King Charles I. Then, when he was twenty, he married a young woman who changed his way of life and made him into a devout Christian. He began to preach in the villages to which he went mending pots and pans, for he earned his living as a tinker. But Bunyan was a Baptist, and after the death of Oliver Cromwell and the Restoration of King Charles II, Nonconformists were forbidden to preach. . . ."

"What's a Nonconformist, Dad?" asked Barbara.

"A Protestant who doesn't accept the teaching of the Church of England. But Bunyan refused to stop preaching, and even when he

John Bunyan was imprisoned for his religious views, but continued to preach to his fellow prisoners.

Christian sets out on the perilous journey described by Bunyan in *The Pilgrim's Progress*.

was thrown into prison—where except for brief intervals of liberty he spent the next twelve years of his life—he went on preaching to his fellow prisoners. He began to write *The Pilgrim's Progress* during a later term of six months' imprisonment. This is really the story of a man's search for God, told in the form of a long and dangerous journey from the City of Destruction to the Celestial City, Heaven. Christian, you see, was a traveller through life. First he is warned of the destruction of his city for its wickedness and flees in the hope of being saved. He is almost swallowed up in the Slough of Despond, fights and routs the terrible fiend Apollyon, is imprisoned in the town of Vanity Fair for resisting its temptations, captured by Giant Despair and thrown into the dungeon of Doubting Castle, and nearly drowns in the River of Death, before he is led by angels through the gates of Heaven. It's true the language is a little old-fashioned in places, but *The Pilgrim's Progress* is one of the most exciting stories in literature and it is so famous that it has been translated into over a hundred different languages.

"Another famous but very different Nonconformist writer is Daniel Defoe, who was a child when Bunyan was in prison. His life was full of excitement. As a young man he took part in the Protestant rebellion to overthrow King James II, who was a Catholic. But the Duke of Monmouth's forces were defeated and Defoe had to go into hiding for a time. Later, during the reign of Queen Anne, he was prosecuted for writing a religious pamphlet. He was seized and placed in the pillory, but instead of pelting him with stones and rotten eggs and insulting him, as they did with rogues who were pilloried, the people cheered him and pelted him with flowers. However, he had to spend nearly two years in Newgate Prison, where he started what is now thought of as the

Daniel Defoe, placed in the pillory for making fun in a pamphlet of the persecutors of the Nonconformists, is treated by the people as a hero.

first real newspaper ! Now, Defoe was a writer who also wrote a famous story about a traveller —a very different sort of traveller, however, from Bunyan's."

"I know," cried Bill, "*Robinson Crusoe*—he was shipwrecked."

"Yes," said Barbara. "And we learn about all the things he makes for his home on the island."

"And how he sees a footprint in the sand and rescues Man Friday from the cannibals."

"And then at last a ship comes and takes him back to England !"

"I see you both know all about *Robinson Crusoe*," said their father. "But perhaps you don't know as much as you think ! The idea of *Robinson Crusoe* came from the true story of Alexander Selkirk, a Scottish sailor who, after quarrelling with his captain, was put ashore and spent four years on a desert island. Defoe made all his stories so vivid that many people thought they were true, and so besides being

Robinson Crusoe, as he appeared in an early edition of Defoe's novel.

the father of modern journalism, we also think of him as the father of the modern novel.

"By the way, there's a third traveller's tale that you ought to know about. You've both read *Gulliver's Travels*, haven't you ?"

"Oh, yes !" both the children cried at once.

"I like the bit at the beginning where he's tied up by the Lilliputians while he's asleep, and when he tries to move they shoot arrows at him," remarked Bill. "And it's funny when they try to feed him. . . ."

"What about where he captures the ships of their enemies and pulls them into the harbour ?" Barbara interrupted.

"Well, you may remember that the tiny Lilliputians, who are less than six inches high, are just as ungrateful as ordinary men often are, and on learning that he is to be tried for treason Gulliver escapes and finally reaches home. On his second voyage he visits a land of giants who are more civilized than men; on his third,

Gulliver, fastened to the ground by the Lilliputians, astonishes them by his great appetite.

Jonathan Swift, who wrote *Gulliver's Travels*, lived at the same time as Defoe.

various fantastic countries; and on his last a country where a race of beast-like men is ruled over by talking horses, who are horrified by Gulliver's descriptions of life in England. Like *The Pilgrim's Progress* and *Robinson Crusoe*, *Gulliver's Travels* was not written for children, and in children's versions only those parts which are likely to attract and interest them have been kept in. Swift meant it as a satire or mocking comment upon the governments, political parties, and religious sects of his day, not to mention the follies and vices of people generally. You see, Jonathan Swift was a very brilliant man and had hoped for a high position in the Church, but probably because he was so severe in his criticism of whatever he didn't like, he rose no higher than Dean of St. Patrick's, Dublin. To have to live in Ireland was like being in exile to him, and he became very bitter.

"In the end, his sense of having been unjustly treated grew so great that he went mad."

"How awful!" exclaimed Barbara.

"*Don Quixote* is another favourite children's story which was not written for them, and you would certainly find the full version much too long and complicated, although it is one of the most wonderful books ever written. Like *Gulliver's Travels*, *Don Quixote* is a satire, but a very much gentler one. Don Quixote is a poor Spanish gentleman who has read so many romances about knights and fair ladies that they have gone to his head. He has himself knighted by an innkeeper, and dressed in a rusty old suit of armour and accompanied by his faithful squire, Sancho Panza, he rides forth on a bony old nag to do battle for the honour of the peasant girl he has chosen as his lady. He has all sorts of absurd adventures, tilting at windmills in the belief that they are really giants, attacking a flock of sheep, thinking it is an enemy army, and so on.

"His creator, Cervantes, had as adventurous a life as Don Quixote. He fought against the Turks in the great naval battle of Lepanto, and was later captured by Moorish pirates. Cervantes spent five years as a slave before his family managed to collect enough money together to ransom him. Later he became a tax-collector and collector of food supplies for

Cervantes, on his way home to Spain, is captured by the Moors and carried off into slavery.

Sancho Panza looks on with horror as his master, Don Quixote, attacks the windmills.

49

the great Spanish Armada which was preparing to invade England. But ill-fortune kept on following him. He fell into debt and was put into prison. There the idea came to him of the foolish, brave, noble-hearted Don Quixote, who was to ride through the land righting wrongs, and who rode into the hearts of the people of Spain and then of the whole world."

ANSWER THIS

Which great English writer was a tinker and what is the title of his most famous book? What book do you connect with the name Alexander Selkirk?

(9)

FRONTIER TALES

A game of cowboys and Indians.

BILL crept silently round the side of the house, then, as he reached the back garden, suddenly broke into a gallop, uttering bloodcurdling whoops and brandishing a painted wooden tomahawk. "Bang! Bang!" cried a voice from behind a clump of flowers at the other end of the garden. "I've captured your squaw and now you're dead." A boy of about the same age as Bill emerged, grasping a toy revolver with one hand and Barbara, dressed up in an old woollen blanket, with the other. "Missed me," Bill promptly replied, and charged with his tomahawk. At the very moment when the drama was about to reach its climax, however, Mrs. Brown leaned out of a window and called Bill and Barbara and their friend Kenneth in to tea. By this time it was getting dark, so after tea they had to stay indoors. Bill asked his father if there were any really good books about cowboys and Indians.

"Well, although America has a short history compared with the countries of Europe, it is certainly an exciting one. The early settlers often suffered great hardships and had to fight for their lives against nature and Indians, and very often against each other too. Later, Americans had to fight for their freedom from British control. Later still, they had a civil war between the south and the north. And all the

50

James Fenimore Cooper, who wrote stirring tales of the scouts and Indians of young America.

time they were pushing their frontier westwards to the Pacific, in spite of the hard climate and the fierce resistance of the Indians. You would expect some exciting stories to have come from such a country, and you would not be disappointed.

"One of the earliest Americans to write such stories was James Fenimore Cooper. I'm sure you would like his stories of 'Leatherstocking', the frontier scout. I loved them when I was a boy. 'Leatherstocking' represents the spirit of such great frontiersmen as Daniel Boone, Davy Crockett, and Buffalo Bill. There's *The Deerslayer*, *The Pathfinder*, *The Pioneers*, *The Prairie* and, best of all, *The Last of the Mohicans*, in which the hero is known as Hawkeye. This story is set at the time of the last great war between the British and the French for supremacy in North America. Both sides had Indian allies, and most of the story is concerned with the efforts of Hawkeye and his Mohican friends to save two English girls and their two escorts, an English major and an American schoolmaster, from hostile Redskins. At one

Hawkeye and the Mohicans arrive just in time to rescue their friends from the hands of the Iroquois—an exciting incident from Fenimore Cooper's *The Last of the Mohicans*.

point they are surrounded by Iroquois, but Hawkeye and the Mohicans escape by floating downstream, later returning to rescue the others.

"Another of Fenimore Cooper's novels, *The Spy*, is a tale of the American War of Independence. Although he was born a few years after the war, in 1789, Cooper knew the frontier well, for his boyhood home, in what is now the State of New York, stood on the edge of great forests in which panther, wolf, and Indian still roamed. He also knew the sea, spending some years of his youth as a sailor before he married and settled down as a farmer, and he wrote many exciting sea stories, including *The Red Rover* and *The Pilot*, which is thought to have been inspired by the great American naval commander, John Paul Jones.

Harriet Beecher Stowe, who helped to free the Negro slaves.

Tom is sold by public auction—an incident from *Uncle Tom's Cabin*.

"Of course, many later Americans—like Walter Edmonds in *Drums Along the Mohawk* and Kenneth Roberts in *Oliver Wiswell*—have been inspired by the Revolutionary War. Others have written about the Civil War between the northern and southern states, which for four terrible years split the still young America into two. One of the principal causes of the war was the dispute over the question of whether or not it was right to own Negro slaves, and since most of the slaves worked in the cotton plantations of the South, it was natural that most Southerners should support slavery, while Northerners, who had less or nothing to lose if it were abolished, generally opposed it. One of the most fearless opponents of slavery was Harriet Beecher Stowe. A preacher's daughter, she married a preacher herself and went to live in Cincinnati, which was only separated by the Ohio River from the slave state of Kentucky. Many times Mrs. Stowe must have seen frightened slaves who had fled from the plantations, for her father had been one of those who organized an escape road to the north, and she must have heard many stories of their sufferings. She wrote a novel based on these stories and called it *Uncle Tom's Cabin*. It was not a great book and it gave a rather one-sided view of Negro slavery, because it was the exception, not the rule, for Southern slaves to be cruelly treated, but it was a noble-spirited book that pleaded passionately for the right of all men to be free. It said what many people were thinking, and in five years half a million copies of it were sold in the United States. So great was its influence that Abraham Lincoln himself called Mrs. Stowe 'the little woman who started a great war'."

"I saw a film about cowboys and rustlers last week. Do you know any stories like that, Mr. Brown?" Kenneth asked.

"There are plenty of good tales about the Wild West. You would enjoy Owen Wister's *The Virginian*, about the adventures of a cowboy and the young schoolmistress with whom he falls in love. One of the first men to write about the Wild West was Bret Harte, and you would find some of his stories, like *The Luck of Roaring Camp*, very exciting. Bret Harte worked for a time as a messenger on a stagecoach, and he had gone to California only four years after the great gold rush of 1849, when it was still full of men

Bret Harte, famous for his short stories about the Wild West.

Covered wagons moving westwards to California in the pioneering days of America.

53

Mark Twain, the great American humorist who wrote two splendid books for boys.

Tom Sawyer—Tom and Huck, in the graveyard at night, see three figures approaching.

ANSWER THIS

Who was "the little woman who started a great war"?

hoping to get rich quick, so he knew at first-hand what he was writing about. So did Jack London, in writing of the Alaska gold rush of 1897. Of course, one of the greatest books about the West is *The Oregon Trail*, Francis Parkinson's record of a journey to the Rocky Mountains in 1846, before the building of the great railways across America. Another exciting story, based on fact, is *The Last Frontier* by Howard Fast, which tells of the courage and endurance of a tribe of Indians who set out from their reserve to return to their own country through hundreds of miles of land patrolled by the United States cavalry."

"You haven't said anything about Mark Twain. *Tom Sawyer* and *Huckleberry Finn* are two of my favourite books," said Barbara.

"Mine too," agreed Bill.

"I was just coming to him. Mark Twain was another writer who wrote from first-hand experience. In *Roughing It* he describes his adventures in the West and then in Hawaii; *The Innocents Abroad*, one of the funniest books by this most famous of all American humorists, is about a voyage to the Mediterranean and the Holy Land. Mark Twain, whose real name was Samuel Clemens, was brought up in the sleepy little town of Hannibal, Missouri, where the greatest excitement of the day was the arrival of a steamboat on its way up or down the Mississippi. Like all the other boys in Hannibal, Sam wanted to be a steamboat pilot, and in *Life on the Mississipi* he tells of how this dream came true and he grew to know the great river as only a pilot—whose life depended on knowing its every turn and then allowing for the possibility of its having changed course—could. But although they are not true stories, like the other books of his I have mentioned, you can probably learn more about Mark Twain's boyhood from *Tom Sawyer* and *Huckleberry Finn*, which are two of the best boys' books ever written."

54

MARK TWAIN'S HUCKLEBERRY FINN ESCAPES DOWN THE MISSISSIPPI

THE YOUNG HERO IS RESCUED BY HIGHLANDERS IN SCOTT'S *WAVERLEY*

"What are they about?" asked Kenneth.

"*Huckleberry Finn* is mostly about how Tom's friend, Huck, himself running away from his cruel father, helps a slave to escape down the Mississippi. In *The Adventures of Tom Sawyer*, Tom and Huck, quite by chance, see someone killed in the graveyard at night. If you want to know what happened after that you had better read the book yourself."

(10)

LOOKING TO THE PAST

ONE day Barbara came home from school and told her father that they had been learning about the Crusades to recapture the Holy Land from the Saracens. "Teacher told us that Sir Walter Scott wrote a story about the Crusade that Richard the Lion-hearted went on, but I've forgotten what she said it was called."

"Oh, that's *The Talisman*. A still better story by him, *Ivanhoe*, is set in Richard's reign too, but it takes place in England while Richard's brother John is ruling the country."

"Oh, I remember," exclaimed Bill. "You told us about that when we were talking about Robin Hood."

"That's right. Robin Hood even has a part in this story; but the principal hero is a young knight named Wilfred of Ivanhoe who has quarrelled with his father about his ward, the Lady Rowena, with whom Ivanhoe is in love. One of the most exciting parts of the book is the description of the tournament in which Ivanhoe, in disguise, takes on all comers for the right to name the Queen of Love and Beauty.

"Scott first became famous as the author of exciting poems inspired by the border ballads which he had collected. They were quite long— indeed, rather like novels in verse. Later he turned to writing prose stories, and he was the

Sir Walter Scott, poet and novelist.

The unknown knight unhorses the Templar, Brian de Bois-Guilbert, during the tournament in *Ivanhoe*.

Charles Kingsley, the clergyman and social reformer, who wrote stirring tales of olden times.

first really great novelist to look to the past for his subjects. *Quentin Durward*, one of his best novels, tells of the adventures of a young Scottish gentleman in 15th century France; *Kenilworth*, set in Elizabethan England, is about the tragic fate of Amy Robsart, wife of the Earl of Leicester; but most of his stories are based on events in the history of his own beloved Scotland, which he knew so well from his many 'raids,' as he called them, on horseback into its wildest parts. The first of all his novels, *Waverley*, is about the Jacobite Rebellion in support of Bonnie Prince Charlie. Other outstanding novels are *Old Mortality*, *The Heart of Midlothian*, *Rob Roy*, and *Guy Mannering*, which is set in Scott's own times.

"Scott set the fashion for writing historical novels. He was followed by Captain Frederick Marryat, with his *Children of the New Forest*, a story about Cavaliers and Roundheads, and his tales of the sea, *Mr. Midshipman Easy*, *Masterman Ready*, *Peter Simple*, *Jacob Faithful*, and *Poor Jack*. In his vivid accounts of life aboard ship, naval battles, and shipwrecks, Captain

Amyas Leigh and his men ambush the Spanish treasure train—a scene from *Westward Ho!*

58

Marryat wrote from experience, for he spent twenty-four years at sea himself.

"Among 19th-century authors we must not forget Charles Reade, whose *The Cloister and the Hearth* is one of the most wonderful historical novels ever written. It is a story of medieval times, and takes us adventuring through much of Europe—Holland, Germany, France, and Italy.

"But one of the greatest of the historical novelists who followed Scott was a Frenchman, Alexandre Dumas. *The Three Musketeers* must be one of the best-loved stories in the world, and every boy who has read it must have imagined himself as its swashbuckling hero, D'Artagnan. Scarcely—if any—less exciting are some of his other books, such as *Twenty Years After*, *The Man in the Iron Mask*, and *The Count of Monte Cristo*."

"*Westward Ho!* is one of my favourite books," said Bill.

"Yes, it's a jolly good yarn which captures something of the spirit of the stirring days when the Elizabethan sea-dogs fought on the high seas with the galleons of Spain. *Hereward the Wake*,

D'Artagnan, with his new-found Musketeer friends, Athos, Porthos, and Aramis, clashes with Cardinal Richelieu's Guards—an exciting incident from *The Three Musketeers*.

Alexandre Dumas, creator of the famous "Musketeers."

Kingsley's story of the English outlaw who for several years held out against William the Conqueror on the Isle of Ely, and *Hypatia*, a story set in Egypt and Italy in the days when the Roman Empire was breaking up, are also exciting stories. Charles Kingsley was a clergyman who eventually became a canon of Westminster and Chaplain to Queen Victoria. He was also a scientist, a historian, and a poet. At that time the Industrial Revolution had made many people miserably poor, and Kingsley felt sorry for them and wrote several novels describing their lives. But he is best remembered today for his historical novels, his fairy-story with a moral, *The Water Babies*, and his stories from the Greek myths, *The Heroes*.

"There are lots of other historical novels you would probably enjoy. *Lorna Doone*, by R. D. Blackmore, is an exciting tale of Exmoor in the West Country. It is partly concerned with a rising against James II."

Brigadier Gerard, Conan Doyle's dashing French cavalry officer.

Captain Hornblower, the gallant English naval officer of some of C. S. Forester's stories of the sea.

"Do you mean the one in which you said Defoe took part?" asked Bill.

"That's right. Another book about the same rebellion is *Micah Clarke*, by Sir Arthur Conan Doyle. He wrote, too, several other historical novels, including *Sir Nigel* and *The White Company*, about English knights and yeomen in the Hundred Years' War with the French. But most exciting and amusing of all are his *The Exploits of Brigadier Gerard* and *The Adventures of Gerard*, stories about a cavalry officer in Napoleon's armies.

"Then of course there are *The Scarlet Pimpernel* stories about the French Revolution, by Baroness Orczy; *The Sea Hawk* and *Captain Blood*, Rafael Sabatini's stories of buccaneers; Russell Thorndike's stories of *Dr. Syn*, the smuggler; C. S. Forester's *Captain Hornblower* books, about naval exploits in the Napoleonic Wars; D. K. Broster's stories of the Jacobite Rebellions; A. E. W. Mason's *Fire Over*

England, about England at the time of the Armada, and his story of the British Army in the Sudan, *The Four Feathers*; Eric Linklater's superb tales of the Vikings, *Men of Ness* and *The Ultimate Viking*; and many others. Anthony Hope's adventure stories, *The Prisoner of Zenda* and *Rupert of Hentzau*, read like historical novels, although actually they are entirely imaginary, even being about imaginary countries."

While his father was still talking, Bill went to the bookshelves and took out one of the books. He opened it and started to look at the pictures. "What about *Treasure Island*?" he said.

"Yes, we certainly mustn't forget Robert Louis Stevenson, because he wrote some of the best historical adventure stories ever written. *Kidnapped* and its sequel, *Catriona*, are exciting tales of Scotland after the suppression of the Jacobite Rebellion; *The Black Arrow* is a story about the Wars of the Roses. But *Treasure Island* is the most thrilling of all his boys' stories. You will never forget Long John Silver, the pirate—one of the finest villains in literature."

Bill and Barbara laughed at the idea of a fine villain, but Mr. Brown had taken the book from Bill and was looking for the passage he wanted :

> " 'His left leg was cut off close by the hip, and under the left shoulder he carried a crutch, which he managed with wonderful dexterity, hopping about upon it like a bird. He was tall and strong, with a face as big as a ham—plain and pale, but intelligent and smiling.'

"And here is what young Jim Hawkins overheard Silver saying, when he was hidden in the apple barrel :

> 'Here it is about gentlemen of fortune. They lives rough, and they risk swinging, but they eat and drink like fighting-cocks, and when a cruise is done, why, it's hundreds of pounds instead of hundreds of farthings in their pockets. Now, the most goes for rum and a good fling, and to sea again in their shirts.

Robert Louis Stevenson, who created Long John Silver.

Young David Balfour climbs the tower in his uncle's house—a scene from Stevenson's *Kidnapped*.

61

But that's not the course I lay. I puts it all away, some here, some there, and none too much anywheres, by reason of suspicion. I'm fifty, mark you; once back from this cruise, I set up gentleman in earnest. Time enough, too, says you. Ah, but I've lived easy in the meantime; never denied myself o' nothing heart desires, and slep' soft and ate dainty all my days, but when at sea. And how did I begin? Before the mast, like you!'

"Stevenson was an invalid and had to leave his native Edinburgh for milder climates. He went at length to the warm South Seas, spending three years cruising among the islands of the Pacific before settling in Samoa for the last few years of his life. He was much loved by the natives of the island, and when he died, at the age of 44, they cut a path up the steep side of a mountain so that he could be buried on the top. On his memorial are inscribed these words, written by himself:

'Under the wide and starry sky,
Dig the grave and let me lie.
Glad did I live and gladly die,
And I laid me down with a will.

Two scenes from *Treasure Island*—above, Jim Hawkins hides in the apple barrel; below, captured by the pirates, Jim goes with them to seek the treasure.

This be the verse you grave for me:
"Here he lies where he longed to be;
Home is the sailor, home from sea,
And the hunter home from the hill." ' "

ANSWER THIS

What is the name of the pirate with one leg in the pictures on the opposite page?

(11)

OUR GREATEST STORY-TELLER

"I WANT some more," Bill declared.

The family had just finished their Sunday dinner—or so Mrs. Brown thought.

"That's not the way to ask, Bill," she said. "Oliver Twist was more polite than you and he must have been a good deal hungrier."

When he had finished his second helping, Bill asked : "What did Oliver Twist say?"

"You will find the book in the bookcase," said Mrs. Brown. "Look it up for yourself!"

But after they had gone into the sitting-room Mr. Brown explained that *Oliver Twist* was the story of a poor orphan boy who was born in the workhouse. "In those days orphans were often cruelly treated and half-starved. The boys in the orphanage where Oliver Twist lived were driven

Oliver Twist is taken by the Artful Dodger to meet Fagin and his gang of pickpockets.

Mr. Micawber.

so desperate by hunger that they cast lots to decide who should face the wrath of the masters by asking for a second helping at supper that evening. The task fell to Oliver, and I will read you the description of what happened :

'The gruel disappeared ; the boys whispered each other, and winked at Oliver ; while his next neighbours nudged him. Child as he was, he was desperate with hunger, and reckless with misery. He rose from the table ; and advancing to the master, basin and spoon in hand, said, somewhat alarmed at his own temerity—

"Please, sir, I want some more."

'The master was a fat, healthy man ; but he turned very pale. He gazed in stupefied astonishment on the small rebel for some seconds, and then clung for support to the copper. The assistants were paralysed with wonder ; the boys with fear.

' "What!" said the master at length, in a faint voice.

' "Please, sir," replied Oliver, "I want some more."

'The master aimed a blow at Oliver's head with the ladle, pinioned him in his arms, and shrieked aloud for the beadle.'

As a result of this Oliver was apprenticed to learn a trade, but he was so unhappy that he ran away to London, where he fell in with a gang of thieves and pickpockets led by a miserly old Jew, Fagin, and the brutal Bill Sikes. However, after a lot of complicated adventures, it all ends happily for the young hero, as in most of Dickens's novels."

"Is *Oliver Twist* a historical novel ?" asked Barbara.

"No, Dickens was writing about his own times. He wrote only two historical novels— *Barnaby Rudge* and *A Tale of Two Cities*, which is a very moving story of how a man who has ruined himself through drink gives his life in the French Revolution for the happiness of the woman he loves. Most of his novels are

Mr. Pickwick and Sam Weller

concerned in one way or another with the evils of his own day, but his characters are so wonderfully alive that we do not feel that his books are in the least like sermons, as we may do with the social novels of Charles Kingsley.

"Like Kingsley, Dickens lived during the worst period of the Industrial Revolution ; but unlike Kingsley, he knew from bitter experience what it was like to be poor and hungry and live in the slums of London. His father fell seriously into debt, and eventually he was sent to the debtors' prison, where in those days the prisoners stayed until their debts could be paid —if ever. Charles's mother and the younger children went with him, as was customary, but the 12-year-old Charles went to work in a blacking factory for six shillings a week. Fortunately for him, after three months in prison his father was unexpectedly left some money and was able to pay his debts. Charles went back to school, and then, at 15, became a junior clerk

Charles Dickens.

in a lawyer's office. A few years later he was reporting cases in the law courts. (In *Bleak House* Dickens was later to make a powerful attack on the law's delays, which caused much unnecessary suffering in those days.) Then he became a reporter in the House of Commons. Not long afterwards he began to make a name for himself as a writer, and soon all England was eagerly reading the latest instalment of his latest novel or waiting impatiently for the next instalment, for all of Dickens's books were first published as serials in magazines and newspapers.

"You can learn quite a lot about his life from *David Copperfield*, which Dickens himself liked best of all his books. The unforgettable Mr. Micawber, who always believed that something would turn up to save him, is said to be a picture of his own father. Mr. Micawber summed up his own impossible, irrepressible character in his advice to David Copperfield :—

lodged in the debtors' prison.

' "My other piece of advice, Copperfield," said Mr. Micawber, "you know. Annual income twenty pounds, annual expenditure nineteen nineteen six, result happiness. Annual income twenty pounds, annual expenditure twenty pounds ought and six, result misery. The blossom is blighted, the leaf is withered, the God of day goes down upon the dreary scene, and—and in short you are for ever floored. As I am!"

'To make this example the more impressive, Mr. Micawber drank a glass of punch with an air of great enjoyment and satisfaction, and whistled the College Hornpipe.'

"It has been said that during his lifetime *The Pickwick Papers* was the most widely read of all Dickens's novels. Like *David Copperfield*, this has a scene in the debtors' prison, where the lovable and generous Mr. Pickwick is lodged with his loyal, quick-witted servant Sam Weller.

Nicholas Nickleby, the young schoolmaster, runs away from Dotheboys Hall with the poor orphan boy Smike.

Pip, visiting his parents' grave in the churchyard, is seized by an escaped convict—a scene from *Great Expectations*.

"But besides being a great humorist, Dickens often wrote scenes that were very sad. It is said that the death of Little Nell in *The Old Curiosity Shop* had the whole country in tears."

"I think *Nicholas Nickleby* is a jolly good story," said Bill. "I haven't read it, but Aunt Mary took us to see the film."

"Ah, then you will remember Dotheboys Hall. Well that gives a perfectly fair picture of the worst sort of boarding schools that existed in Dickens's day. Another story I'm sure you would like is *Great Expectations*, which opens with a terrifying encounter between a small boy and a convict."

"Our teacher's been reading us *A Christmas Carol*," said Barbara. "You know, all about the old miser Scrooge."

"That's one of the *Christmas Books*. Dickens wrote a new one every year for five years, until he started editing his own magazine, *Household Words*. He was an amazingly energetic man, and in 1858 he started giving public readings from his books in England and America. At one time

Dickens had thought of making a career on the stage, and had he done so he would probably have become an outstanding actor. This explains the tremendous success of his public readings, but the extra strain they caused him are thought to have led to his early death.

"Many of the scenes in the stories of Dickens are sad, but many are also brilliantly funny, and after Shakespeare, he created the most wonderful gallery of characters in English literature."

ANSWER THIS

Which novel by Dickens is based on his own life and which character in it is said to have been inspired by his father?

(12)

ADVENTURES ON LAND AND SEA

BILL looked up from a book he was reading. It lay open at a picture of two fully-rigged clippers, their sails filled with wind, as they raced for home with cargoes of tea and grain.

"It must have been really exciting being a sailor in those days," he said.

"Yes," his father replied. "But it can still be exciting today, too. Danger can often be found at sea, especially in small boats and although some sea stories are about journeys in sailing ships there are many tales of more recent adventures as well.

"Richard Henry Dana's true record of his life on board an American merchant ship in the 1830s—*Two Years Before The Mast*—and Jack London's story about seal hunting—*The Sea Wolf*—were both founded on the personal adventures of their authors. Most sea stories, whether fact or fiction, are based on actual experiences. In this century love of the sea is seen in H. M. Tomlinson's books, *Gallion's Reach* and *The Sea and the Jungle*, which describes a tramp steamer travelling from Swansea to the Amazon. Nicholas Monsarrat's *Cruel Sea* and Herman Wouk's *Caine Mutiny* show us the courage needed at sea to combat hazardous situations during the Second World War.

The captain of Dana's ship auctions the clothes of a drowned member of the crew, one of the customs of the sea in those days.

"Joseph Conrad is an outstanding writer. At the end of his life he was famous the world over for his books which he wrote in English although he was actually born and grew up in central Poland miles away from the sea. When he was fifteen years old he tried to run away to sea but he was prevented. However, later on he was allowed to go and during the next twenty years while he made his way from ordinary seaman to captain, he came to know the sea in all its moods. His famous tales of man's relationship with the sea in *Typhoon*, *Youth*, *The Nigger of the Narcissus*, *Almayer's Folly*, *An*

Joseph Conrad.

Outcast of the Islands, *The Rescue*, *Lord Jim*, *Victory*, and many other stories are read by lovers of sea-faring adventure everywhere while *The Secret Agent* and *Under Western Eyes* are thrilling stories of spies and revolution.

"Herman Melville, a 19th-century American author, sailed the seas aboard a whaler and from his knowledge of whaling wrote a great story—*Moby Dick*, about a gigantic white whale which is hunted by night and day by Captain Ahab who has sworn to destroy it. Melville's novels, *Omoo* and *Typee*, are founded on his adventures among cannibals in the South Seas, where he found himself after deserting his ship. Later he was rescued by another whaler, caught up in a mutiny and gaoled when he returned home.

"The sea figures largely in many children's stories written in the last century. *The Swiss Family Robinson*, by Johann Rudolf Wyss, is a story also set in the South Seas, which describes how a shipwrecked family managed to survive the disaster and found ways to continue their lives in difficult and unexpected circumstances; while R. M. Ballantyne's *Coral Island* tells of the resourcefulness of boys faced with many difficulties and problems while alone and unaided on the island.

"More recently John Ridgway and Chay

Jimmy, the sick Negro, is passed along the deck from one member of the crew to another during a violent storm--a scene from *The Nigger of the Narcissus*.

68

Blyth, in *Fighting Chance*, wrote the story from log books kept during the 92-day voyage of two paratroopers rowing across the Atlantic Ocean in *English Rose III*, which was only twenty feet long and five feet wide. Both Francis Chichester's *Gypsy Moth Circles the World* and Alec Rose's *My Lively Lady* tell of single-handed voyages around the globe and reveal much of the character of men who attempt this great challenge. Chichester's other adventures, including some in early aircraft, are recounted in *Alone Over the Tasman Sea, Along the Clipper*

Herman Melville.

Above, the last fight with Moby Dick; below, the sailors are captured by cannibals in *Typee*.

Way and *The Lonely Sea and the Sky*, and hair-raising they often are too."

"What about the Kon-Tiki Expedition?" asked Bill.

"Well, that's a true adventure that only happened a few years ago. Do you know, there are lots of other real adventures that you would enjoy, like John Hunt's *Ascent of Everest*, Maurice Herzog's *Annapurna*, Eric Williams' *Wooden Horse*, the record of *Scott's Last Expedition*, 1910 1913 in the Antarctic, together with Apsley Cherry-Garrard's *Worst Journey in the World*, in which he tells his story of Scott's

Sherlock Holmes.

expedition and its end. Another journey under Polar conditions is recounted by Vivian Fuchs and Edmund Hillary in *The Crossing of Antarctica*, while in the *Small Woman* Alan Burgess reveals how an ordinary Englishwoman travelled many miles in China, enduring the hazards of war to reach safety with the children for whom she was responsible.

"The Stone Age race of Bushmen are still little known to most of us and Laurens Van der Post has many interesting facts to tell about the remote areas of Africa and the discoveries made on his journeys in *Venture to the Interior* and *The Lost World of the Kalahari*.

"Rider Haggard's enthralling tales of Africa —*King Solomon's Mines*, *Allan Quatermain*, *She*, and many others, although fictitious, show his keen interest in African life. John Buchan, Arthur Conan Doyle and John Masefield have all written good adventure stories. Two of John Buchan's best books are spy stories, *The Thirty-Nine Steps* and *Greenmantle*, while in *The Lost World* Conan Doyle describes the discovery of an isolated plateau in South America where prehistoric animals still survived."

"I would enjoy that," Bill replied. "His stories about Sherlock Holmes are really worth reading."

"Do you know that Sherlock Holmes is probably the most famous detective in fiction? He first appeared in *A Study in Scarlet*, which is one of the earliest detective stories written. Erskine Childers' *Riddle of the Sands* is a tale of espionage and sinister happenings on a yacht sailing in the Baltic, terminating in an exciting climax on the sands of the North Friesian coast.

"Most of the adventure stories written by Rudyard Kipling were about India, where he was born and grew up. His best known book is *Kim*, the story of a British orphan boy who becomes a follower of a holy man from Tibet. He also wrote *Captains Courageous*, about the

Sir Arthur Conan Doyle.

sea; *Stalky & Co.*, a school story; *Puck of Pook's Hill*, *Rewards and Fairies* in addition to his better known *Just So Stories* and *Jungle Books*."

"Arthur Ransome's adventure stories about children are jolly good—*Swallows and Amazons*, *Coot Club*, *Peter Duck*, and the rest," said Barbara.

Bill agreed, adding "I'm rather keen on Hugh Lofting's *Dr. Dolittle* books because they are such a funny mixture."

"You would probably also enjoy Richard Jefferies' *Bevis*—the exploits of a country boy; and *Emil and the Detectives* by Erich Kastner. *Heidi*, the story of a Swiss girl who lived in the Alps, by Johanna Spyri, and the many stories of Meindert Dejong explain more about the lives of children in other countries.

"Among other children's classics that you should consider are: *Anne of Green Gables*, by L. M. Montgomery; *What Katy Did*, by Susan Coolidge; *Rebecca of Sunnybrook Farm*, by K. D. Wiggin; *Little Women* and *Good Wives*, by Louisa M. Alcott; and *The Railway Children*, *The Story of the Treasure Seekers*, and *The Wouldbegoods*, by Edith Nesbit.

"Written more recently are: Enid Bagnold's *National Velvet*; Eric Linklater's *The Wind on The Moon*; William Mayne's *The World Upside Down*, *Follow the Footprints*, and *Underground Alley*; Mary Norton's *The Magic Bed-knob* and *The Borrowers*; Noel Streatfield's *Ballet Shoes*, *The Circus is Coming*, and *Curtain Up*; Rosemary Sutcliff's *Eagle of the Ninth*, *The Silver Branch*, and *The Lantern Bearers;* and Ronald Welch's *Knight Crusader*."

"What about science-fiction adventures?" asked Bill. "I enjoy those as much as the detective stories and sea-faring exploits."

"In the 19th century a Frenchman called Jules Verne wrote the first science-fiction stories that are still in great demand today. He origin-

Rudyard Kipling, who wrote many fine stories about India, including *Kim*. In the illustration below, Kim, the orphan boy, is going off with the Tibetan priest.

ANSWER THIS

Which world-famous writer in the English language was a Pole?

71

Besides his scientific thrillers, H. G. Wells wrote stories about quite ordinary lives, like *Kipps*, an incident from which is seen below.

ally became known to English readers by having his stories serialised in the *Boys' Own Paper*. *Twenty Thousand Leagues Under The Sea* is the story of Captain Nemo and his submarine, the *Nautilus*, while *Journey to the Centre of the Earth* and *Five Weeks in a Balloon* are two other exciting examples of his work. His adventure story *Round the World in Eighty Days* introduces Phileas Fogg who wins a wager by completing the journey within that time.

"John Wyndham is a writer who is exploring life as we are living it today and then looking at the possibilities for the future. In his *Day of the Triffids* he shows a frightening but possible glimpse of the future, describing what happens to a world overwhelmed by those strange and dangerous plants over seven feet tall. *The Kraken Wakes* concerns the stirring of unknown power from beneath the surface of the oceans and the results of this threat. He has also written *The Chrysalids*, *Trouble with Lichen*, *The Midwich Cuckoos* and *The Seeds of Time*.

"Of them all, H. G. Wells stands out as the author of really original science-fiction. His fantastic *Time Machine* portrays an alarming journey into the future; *The Invisible Man* tells the tale of the exploits of a man made invisible by drugs; *The War of the Worlds* relates how strange Martian creatures invade the earth aided by walking machines which shrivel up all opposition; *The First Men in the Moon* shows H. G. Wells' view of that adventure as he imagined it might be."

"They sound marvellous," Bill exclaimed.

"Much more science-fiction has been written since H. G. Wells created his stories. His scientific training led him to study how people live together in a community and, while he wrote more serious works like his *History of the World*, he also, in *The History of Mr. Polly* and *Kipps*, showed his insight into the lives of ordinary people."

MARTIAN MACHINES STALK THE LAND IN H. G. WELLS'S *THE WAR OF THE WORLDS*

CITIZENS WATCHING PAGEANTS IN THE MIDDLE AGES

(13)

LET'S PRETEND

BARBARA looked at her mother, who was busy sewing a long white dress.

"Will it be finished in time?" she asked.

"Don't worry," Mrs. Brown replied. "I've only got the wings to stitch on now."

"What about the halo?" cracked Bill.

"She'll make a better angel than you would, anyway," Mr. Brown rebuked him.

Barbara was to be one of the angels in a nativity play which her school was putting on the following evening, and she could hardly sit still for excitement.

"Our teacher told us that when people first started acting plays it was because of religion. I wonder if the first plays were anything like the play we're doing," she mused.

"Auntie Mary knows more about the theatre than I do," her father replied, turning to his sister, who was a teacher at a girls' boarding school and was spending the Christmas holidays with the Browns.

"Well, the first *Christian* plays performed in England were probably something like your school play," said Aunt Mary. "But the Greeks used to hold drama festivals in honour of their gods long before that. Like Homer, the great Greek tragic dramatists—Aeschylus, Sophocles, and Euripides—largely used the old myths and legends of gods and heroes for their stories. These three, together with the great comic dramatist Aristophanes, helped to make Athens glorious in the 5th century B.C., and those of their plays which have survived are still occasionally produced. But in ancient Greece drama was quite different from the plays of today. It was much more like a religious ceremony, with a chorus chanting songs describing much of the action of the play; while the principal actors

A Greek tragic actor, dressed up in mask and buskins.

Aeschylus, one of the greatest of the Greek tragic dramatists.

Aristophanes, who wrote some of the world's wittiest comedies, holds up a Greek comic mask.

wore masks as symbols of tragedy or comedy, according to the type of play. In tragedies the actors also wore special thick-soled boots called buskins to increase their height and thereby add to their dignity. Their theatres were wide and roofless, with rows of stone seats, built in the shape of a horseshoe, rising one behind the other round the space where the acting was done. Later, the Romans copied the idea from the Greeks and built huge, roofless, semi-circular theatres of stone or wood."

"There's a picture in one of my books of a very big stone theatre they built in Rome," chimed in Barbara excitedly.

"Oh, that will be an amphitheatre—the Colosseum at Rome, which could seat 45,000 people. Amphitheatres were used for all sorts of sports and shows but they are not quite the same as proper theatres.

"Did the Romans build theatres in England when they settled there?" asked Bill.

"Yes, but they must have fallen into ruins soon after they left the country. One day I will

A play being performed at a festival in honour of the gods in Ancient Greece.

The typical Roman theatre, though based on the Greek theatres, was more elaborate.

take you to see the remains of the Roman theatre at St. Albans.

"In England, centuries before the Elizabethan theatres were built, plays oddly enough were performed in the churches. In those days, you must remember, much of the church service was in Latin, and the priests took to acting some of the central parts of the Bible story at special services in order to make the story clear and impressive. The people liked this and turned up in great numbers, so the churches could not hold them all. The priests then began to act plays in the church porch, letting the people look on in the churchyard. But as time went by the plays got livelier, the actors made up comical scenes, and a good deal began to creep in that wasn't in the Bible. Then the Church ordered its priests to stop attracting the people by such means. They had to give up the plays. But by this time the people loved the Bible plays so much that they started acting them themselves on public holidays and feast days."

"Where did they act them?" asked Bill. "Did they build special theatres?"

This Roman comic actor wears a mask, like the Greek actors.

77

In the Middle Ages, priests would often make up plays telling stories from the Bible. This picture shows one of these plays being performed in a church porch.

ANSWER THIS

In what ways was the drama of the Ancient Greeks different from modern plays?

"Oh no," said his aunt. "The idea of a theatre was almost unknown in England. The little Bible plays were taken up in many towns by the tradesmen and craftsmen of the district. There would be the stories of Adam and Eve, Cain and Abel, Noah and the Flood. Other stories came from the New Testament and from the lives of the saints."

"If they didn't have a church or their own theatre where did they act all these scenes?" asked Barbara.

"Well that varied, too, but mainly it was in the open air at a number of different places in or round the edges of the town. Each trade or profession produced its own play, so that the bakers, the carpenters, and the shoemakers, for instance, each put their own show on; and for this they used double-decked wagons which were known as 'pageants.' A curtain hid the lower deck, where the actors changed their costumes and waited for their turn. The play itself was acted on the upper deck. These pageants were drawn by horses, and they went, one after the other, to the places where the people were waiting to see the plays. Then each moved on when the play was over to make room for the next one following."

"But surely there must have been other plays besides Bible stories and the lives of saints?" remarked Bill.

"The plays telling Bible stories were called *mysteries* and those about saints *miracles*. A third type of play, the *morality*, in which the characters represented virtues and vices such as love and greed, and in which the Devil always played a prominent part, was developed from them."

"And these were the only plays performed in the whole of England at that time?" asked Bill.

"Oh no! You mustn't get that idea. Besides the pageants there were the simple plays of entertainers who wandered from one town or

A masque being performed at the court of King Henry VIII.

village to another collecting what money they could from the people who gathered round to watch them; and folk plays were performed at many village fairs and festivals. Plays of various kinds were also acted in the houses of rich noblemen, and a form of drama called the masque, in which music and dancing played a very important part, became especially popular at court and among the nobility generally. In fact it sometimes happened, in the great houses in the time of the Tudors, that the lord and lady of the house grew so fond of watching plays that some of the many servants of their household became full-time actors."

"You mean that the men who did the Bible story plays were only amateurs, while the full-time actors, like the men of the wandering companies, were all professionals?" asked Barbara.

"Quite right, Barbara, that was the difference exactly. And, as you know, we still have both professional and amateur actors. Professional actors make it the business of their lives to act, and the best of them naturally become expert at it. But actors who act in their spare time just for the love of it are sometimes very good, too."

The Devil in a morality play.

79

"There, finished at last," said Mrs. Brown. "You'll be a pretty enough angel in that, and we're all looking forward to seeing you in the play tomorrow, aren't we, Bill?"

But the only reply was a low groan.

(14)

TO THE PLAYHOUSE

BILL and Barbara, with their Aunt Mary, were standing somewhat impatiently at the end of a long queue waiting for the doors to open at their local theatre, where the pantomime *Jack and the Beanstalk* was being performed.

"Dear me!" murmured Aunt Mary, "I had no idea this show was going to be so popular. I wish I had booked in advance now."

"It's terribly boring just waiting here," Barbara complained. "Do tell us some more about the theatre in the old days, Auntie. I remember that you told us that theatres were built in England in Queen Elizabeth's reign. Was that because the Queen was fond of plays?"

"No, although the famous Elizabethan theatres were all in London. You see, in the 16th century London had been rapidly growing larger and richer, becoming a centre of world trade. This meant that the people who lived in or near London had more time and money to spend on amusements than they had before. Watching plays was a very popular entertainment, and one day an actor named James Burbage had the bright idea of building a permanent place in which his company could act.

"Burbage and his fellow actors had been used to moving about and giving their plays in the courtyards of inns. You see, in those days most large inns were built round a yard which had an entrance for coaches and carriages through an archway from the street outside. Such buildings

This is what London looked like in Shakespeare's time. The cathedral on the far side of the Thames is "Old St. Paul's," later destroyed by fire; opposite

A play being performed in an

are "The Bear Garden" and "The Globe." On the far right of the far bank is the Tower of London. Southwark Cathedral is at the south end of old London Bridge.

Inn-yard in Elizabethan times.

were more often built of wood than of brick or stone. The stable and coach-houses were on the ground floor; the guest rooms were upstairs, and these opened out on to a balcony which ran all the way round the yard. The players would put up a temporary stage in the yard, and the audience stood round it on the ground or went up into the balcony to have a clear view of it from above. The first Elizabethan theatre, a wooden one, was modelled on such an inn-yard. Its stage stuck out into the middle space, and the audience stood round three sides of it, or went up into the balcony and looked down on it.

"It was very successful, and soon others were built. The first building had been called simply 'The Theatre.' Within the next 25 years several others were built, all of them in or very near London. They had names like 'The Curtain,' 'The Rose,' 'The Swan,' 'The Fortune,' and 'The Globe,' the most famous of all Elizabethan theatres, so aptly described in Shakespeare's play *Henry V* as 'this wooden O'.

Bill was suddenly struck by a difficulty. "Auntie, if the stage stuck out far into the centre of the floor, only the people in front could have seen the scenery at the back of the stage.

81

You can see clearly from this drawing of the outside of "The Globe" why Shakespeare described it as "this wooden O."

Romeo declares his love to Juliet, on the balcony above him.

The people standing at the sides would surely have looked straight across it."

"Ah, but at that time scenery hardly existed. A notice was sometimes hung up stating where the scene was taking place and after that you had to use your imagination. People went to hear the actors and see the acting rather than to look at a scene, and the Elizabethan theatre was well suited for that. Of course those early theatres were very different from the theatres of today. For one thing, like the inn-yards, they had no roof over the centre, so the players and a large part of the audience had no shelter from the weather. Another thing that may surprise you is that in the Elizabethan theatre wealthy people would often pay for the privilege of sitting on the stage."

"That must have made it pretty difficult for the actors," Barbara remarked.

"Yes it must have been somewhat distracting at times.

"Another difference was that there was very little of the staging and lighting which help the dramatist and actors of today, and although the costumes at that time were very rich and colourful, they were generally the dress of the day even in plays about earlier periods. In today's theatres, too, as you know, the curtain can cut the stage off from the audience, so that difficult scenes can be prepared unseen, but in Shakespeare's day only the inner stage (the small room at the back used for some scenes) could be curtained off. Also, with the whole audience seated in front of the stage, the modern theatre can use painted back and side scenery.

"Of course, they did use *some* 'props' (as we call them) in the Elizabethan theatre, such as tables and beds, shrubs and tents; and the pillars which supported the roof overhanging part of the stage were often used as trees. They also had trapdoors in the stage floor and sometimes used such elaborate sound effects as the firing of

A PLAY BY SHAKESPEARE IS PERFORMED AT THE GLOBE THEATRE

ACTORS ON THE STAGE AND ACTIVITY BEHIND THE SCENES

backcloth

comedians

principal girl

floodlight

scene shifters

fairy queen

chorus girl

demon king

assistant stage manager

A PANTOMIME IS BEING PERFORMED IN A MODERN THEATRE

Above: **A theatre in Italy during the Renaissance**

Below: **At the playhouse in the days of Charles II**

SCENES IN THEATRES IN ITALY AND ENGLAND IN OLDEN TIMES

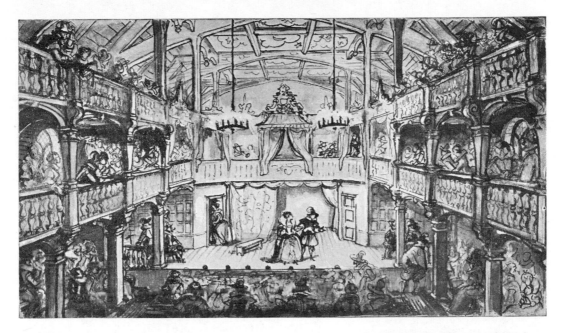

cannons. (In fact this practice led to the original 'Globe' theatre being burnt down in 1613, and it had to be rebuilt.) And then there were two balconies at the back of the stage. The upper one was generally used by the musicians, like the musicians' gallery in Tudor manor houses, while the lower balcony sometimes represented such things as the walls of a city, as well as being used in scenes like the famous balcony scene in *Romeo and Juliet*."

Barbara, who rather fancied herself in the rôle of Juliet, pricked up her ears at this, and was quite astonished when her aunt told her that in Shakespeare's day all women's parts were played by boys.

"There were even whole companies of boy actors," Aunt Mary added.

"How did our sort of theatre come from the Elizabethan theatre?" asked Bill.

"The influence of the Elizabethan theatres I have been telling you about on the development of the modern theatre, with its picture-frame stage, was not very great. We have to go back to the Roman theatre to see the beginnings of our theatre. Now, the typical Roman theatre

Besides the public theatres, there were, in Shakespeare's time, private house theatres, like "The Blackfriars," which is shown here.

Pantaloon, a famous character in Italian Renaissance comedy.

Stage-hands working the ropes for a pantomime fairy in flight.

differed from the Greek theatre in that all the acting was done on a platform stage, and in having an elaborate background of imitation buildings with five doorways. It was this form of theatre that was developed in Italy during the great upsurge of thought and imagination known as the Renaissance, which means literally 'rebirth.' The Renaissance theatres were roofed, and in some of them the doorways led into make-believe streets. As the influence of the Renaissance spread, many of the ideas of this form of theatre were gradually adopted all over Europe, and although they rely more on movable scenery and props than on permanent backgrounds, our theatres still owe much to the Renaissance theatre.

"But 'The Globe' and the other Elizabethan theatres based on the plan of the inn-yards weren't the only type of theatre used in those days. There were also the private house theatres, like 'The Blackfriars' and 'The Phoenix.' As their name suggests, they were rather more select than the public theatres, and people had to pay more to get in. Also, the plays performed in them were more elaborately staged. Masques were especially popular, and Shakespeare's last play, *The Tempest*, clearly shows the influence which they had on the sort of drama being written. Companies of choir-boys acted in these theatres, and later on Shakespeare's company took over 'The Blackfriars' and performed there during the winter months. The private house theatres, which were entirely enclosed and had a stage not unlike that of the ordinary modern theatre in shape (though without its 'picture frame'), contributed greatly to the development of the sort of theatre which is familiar to us."

"Talking of modern stage helps," chuckled Barbara, "it reminds me of seeing *Peter Pan* last year, when they had people flying across the stage. It was wonderful!"

With a revolving stage the next

Bill looked important. "I know how that's done. It's easy. They hook the actors to wires which are hanging down from above, and these wires are then moved backwards and forwards and raised and lowered by machinery at the back of the stage."

"Yes, today's stage has all sorts of machinery to help it work. For instance, in many of the modern theatres the stage itself can be raised or lowered; it can be turned round and divided by means of electric power; and a second stage can be set and raised or lowered into position as the first one is taken away. Many wonderful means of lighting the stage are also used today. As well as the spotlights for drawing our attention to the principal characters on the stage, there are flood-lights for casting a brilliant light over larger areas, and

An actor puts on make-up in his dressing-room before the show.

many other kinds of lighting with which all sorts of colours and effects can be produced."

They had by this time reached the booking office and were relieved to find that there were still a few seats left in the stalls. Soon they were waiting excitedly in their seats, but the curtain still showed no signs of going up. Then the musicians began to troop into the orchestra pit, followed a moment later by the conductor.

"My goodness!" mused Bill. "Wouldn't Shakespeare be surprised to see one of his plays produced in a modern theatre!"

"Yes," said Aunt Mary, "but remember that in spite of all the wonderful inventions and tricks of the trade to help the general effect, no better plays than Shakespeare's have ever been produced. You see, you can't improve the actual play or the acting merely by putting more machinery behind and around the stage. What really matters is that the play itself should be well written and the acting carefully rehearsed. You can find this out for yourselves when you realize that Shakespeare's plays, if well spoken and well acted, can be produced in a school, or

scene can be set, as shown here.

89

a village hall, or in the open air as successfully as in the most up-to-date and wonderfully equipped theatre in the world."

At this moment the lights were lowered, the orchestra struck up, and the children were lost once more in a land of make-believe.

ANSWER THIS

Why did the Elizabethan theatres like "The Globe" take the particular shape they did?

(15)

"ALL THE WORLD'S A STAGE"

Peter Pan fights Captain Hook.

"I THOUGHT that was one of the funniest shows I've ever seen," said Barbara afterwards.

"Well I didn't think it was nearly as exciting as *Peter Pan*," retorted Bill. "That fight between Jack and the Giant was tame compared with Peter Pan's fight with Captain Hook."

"Are there any other famous plays for children, Auntie?" asked Barbara.

"There's *Where the Rainbow Ends.* . . ."

"Oh yes," interrupted Bill excitedly. "I think the dragon kings are wonderful."

"Then there's *The Blue Bird*, a delightful tale of birds and animals and flowers by the Belgian poet, Maurice Maeterlinck. Occasionally, too, we get favourite children's stories like *Treasure Island* being turned into plays. One of the best known of these is *Toad of Toad Hall*, the dramatized version of *The Wind in the Willows*. But it is generally left to the Christmas pantomime, based on such well-known fairy stories as *Aladdin*, *Dick Whittington*, and *Red Riding Hood*, to fill the children's needs as far as the theatre goes."

"I do wish more plays were written for children," sighed Barbara, "or that more writers would write plays which can be enjoyed by both grown-ups and children, like Shakespeare did."

"It's true that there are no dramatists quite like Shakespeare in their appeal, but there are lots of other great writers who have written

90

A scene from *Bartholomew Fair*, a comedy by Ben Jonson.

plays in the English language which you would enjoy. In Shakespeare's own day there was the great tragic dramatist Christopher Marlowe and Shakespeare's friend Ben Jonson. You would probably find some of his comedies amusing. One of these, *Bartholomew Fair*, gives a vivid picture of a London fair, with its ballad-singers and its pickpockets. In later years there were Congreve, Sheridan, and Goldsmith, among others, and in our own time the comedies of George Bernard Shaw have delighted thousands of people. One of the best known of Shaw's plays is *Pygmalion*, the story of how a professor made a Covent Garden flower girl look and speak like a duchess. It was the basis of the musical play and film called *My Fair Lady*."

"Tell us about the plays Shakespeare wrote?" said Bill. "I've seen the films of *Henry V* and *Richard III*."

"There are the tragedies, like *Othello*, *King Lear*, *Antony and Cleopatra*, and *Macbeth*. I think you would like some of the comedies, too, such as *A Midsummer Night's Dream*, *Twelfth Night*, *The Tempest*, *The Merchant of Venice*, *As You Like It*, and *Much Ado About Nothing*, and I'm sure you would also enjoy some of the plays Shakespeare wrote about English kings—

Ben Jonson.

91

Richard II and *Henry IV*, as well as the two kings you mentioned in the films. They are all based on history, though, of course, Shakespeare makes it all come to life and seem much more real than a history book can do."

"What's the difference between a tragedy and a comedy, Auntie?" Barbara asked.

"Tragedies are plays about the serious problems of life, while comedies are gayer and more light-hearted. For instance, *Macbeth*, a powerful and exciting play about the crimes and mistakes which led a great man to disaster, is a tragedy, while *A Midsummer Night's Dream*, part fairy-tale, part romantic love story, and part sheer fun, is a comedy. Shakespeare's plays, even the tragedies, are rich in comic characters, like Pistol, Bardolph, and Fluellen in *Henry V*; Malvolio, the foolish, conceited steward in *Twelfth Night*; and the fat, cowardly, but lovable Falstaff in *Henry IV* and *The Merry Wives of Windsor*."

"I'm going to read all Shakespeare's plays," Barbara suddenly announced.

"I don't think you would enjoy *reading* Shakespeare's plays just yet, Barbara, although you would appreciate seeing almost any of

George Bernard Shaw.

DID YOU KNOW THIS?

The greatest poetic dramatists born in the Elizabethan age (when most poetry was written at court) did not come from the families of nobles or courtiers. Shakespeare's father was a merchant, although he did become Mayor of Stratford; Marlowe's father was a shoe-maker; and Ben Jonson was the son of a bricklayer.

The professor makes notes on the Cockney speech of Eliza Doolittle in Shaw's *Pygmalion*.

them well acted and you would enjoy the stories as retold for children in *Lamb's Tales from Shakespeare*. What you might find very difficult to understand when reading Shakespeare's English would become clear enough if you saw the play performed."

"Yes, I *would* prefer them if they weren't all written in verse," admitted Barbara. "Why did he do it that way, Auntie? Surely it would make people in a play seem more real if they spoke as people really do."

"It's a little difficult to explain," her aunt replied. "You see, just as Shakespeare usually packs into the two or three hours which his plays take to act many more things than could ever really happen in that time, so he manages to pack much more into what his characters say by using poetry than he could have done if he had made them speak in the plain, dull words of every day. Shakespeare uses verse for his most exciting and beautiful scenes, but he doesn't use it for all of them. There are many scenes in which the characters do talk in everyday language, especially, I would say, the comic ones."

"Did Shakespeare write his plays for one particular company to act?" asked Bill.

Falstaff is hidden in a basket in *The Merry Wives of Windsor*.

Henry V addresses the English troops before the battle of Agincourt in Shakespeare's play.

93

The house at Stratford-on-Avon in Warwickshire where William Shakespeare was born.

As you can see from this title-page of the first edition of *A Midsummer Night's Dream*, the play was acted many times by Shakespeare's company before it was first printed in 1600.

"Actually, Shakespeare was an actor in a company called 'The Lord Chamberlain's Servants.' Later, when King James succeeded Queen Elizabeth, they were called 'The King's Servants.' Shakespeare was important to them because of his skill in writing plays."

"But did he write *all* the plays they acted?"

"No. They performed many others besides. But some of his plays were very popular, and they must have done much to give the company its high place in the eyes of Londoners."

"Well how did he become an actor?"

"I can't tell you that. We don't know much about his early life, nor how he came to leave Stratford-on-Avon, where he was born. He seems to have made quite a lot of money as his share of the company's profits, because he bought a large house and some land at Stratford and retired there when he was about 46."

"I suppose he acted in his own plays," mused Barbara.

Aunt Mary stood up with an air of finality. "Yes," she replied, "but not in the principal

94

itania and Bottom in a scene from
A Midsummer Night's Dream

Macbeth and Banquo meet the witches
on the heath—a scene from *Macbeth*

lvolio in love with the Countess Olivia—
a scene from *Twelfth Night*

Mark Antony speaks to the Roman mob in
a scene from *Julius Caesar*

SCENES FROM TWO COMEDIES AND TWO TRAGEDIES BY SHAKESPEARE

ILL-LUCK FOLLOWS WHEN THE ANCIENT MARINER SHOOTS THE ALBATROSS

parts. Those were given to the best actors in the company, like Richard Burbage (the son of the James Burbage who built the first theatre), who acted all the great parts in Shakespeare's plays, and Will Kempe, who excelled in comic rôles. And now it's high time you two little actors ran off to bed—and no nonsense," she warned, as she kissed them both goodnight.

ANSWER THIS

What are tragedies and comedies? Name two of each written by William Shakespeare.

(16)

POEMS THAT TELL STORIES

"I suppose Shakespeare is the greatest poet who ever lived?" said Barbara musingly, when the family were sitting together the following day.

"Yes, he probably is," Aunt Mary replied. "But since the time of Chaucer there have been many great English poets, although some of their verse—for instance, much of the poetry of Milton, Blake, and Byron—would be too difficult for you to understand yet."

"I like poems that tell stories best, like the ballads," remarked Bill.

"There are lots of poems whose style is based on the old ballads," said Aunt Mary. "William Cowper's amusing poem *The Ballad of John Gilpin*, which tells how Gilpin's horse ran away with him, is one example; another is *The Rime of the Ancient Mariner*, in which Coleridge captured much of the vividness and simplicity of the ballads, and something also of the romantic strangeness you find in them. It tells how a sailor stops a guest going to a wedding feast and compels him to listen to the story of a voyage in which he shot an albatross (a bird which sailors believed brought good luck), and the terrible consequences which followed :

> "God save thee, ancient Mariner!
> From the fiends, that plague thee thus!—
> Why look'st thou so?—'With my cross-bow
> I shot the Albatross.' "

"Away went Gilpin, neck or nought,
Away went hat and wig!
He little dreamt when he set out
Of running such a rig!"

Robert Browning, one of whose best-loved poems, illustrated here, is *The Pied Piper of Hamelin.*
"Small feet were pattering,
  wooden shoes clattering,
Little hands clapping and little
  tongues chattering,
And, like fowls in a farmyard
  when barley is scattering,
Out came the children running."

"Another poem which owes something to the ballads is *The Pied Piper of Hamelin*, by Robert Browning. I know very well that Barbara likes that."

"I like the comical way it's told," said Barbara, "but it's sad when all the children are spirited away and the little lame boy is left behind. I like Edward Lear's nonsense poems better, especially *The Owl and the Pussycat*, and Lewis Carroll's nonsense poems in the Alice Books."

"I think *The Hunting of the Snark* is jolly funny, too," put in Bill. "And I like *The Jackdaw of Rheims* because it's comically told."

"That was written by an English clergyman, Richard Harris Barham, famous for his comic stories in verse, the *Ingoldsby Legends*. But there are plenty of good stories in verse which are neither comical nor nonsensical. Browning's *How They Brought the Good News from Ghent to Aix* is the story of a ride on horseback, like *John Gilpin*, but it's all in earnest, and the excitement mounts as the despatch-riders strain to reach their goal. Another verse-story of horseback riding is Longfellow's poem *The Midnight Ride of Paul Revere*, who galloped

from Boston to Lexington to warn the American colonists of the approach of British troops at the very beginning of the War of Independence. Browning's poem is purely imaginary, but Paul Revere is a historical story in verse, like Tennyson's *The Revenge*——"

"I know that one," chipped in Bill. "It tells how Sir Richard Grenville's ship fought a whole fleet of Spanish warships for fifteen hours, before striking her colours, with Grenville himself mortally wounded and only twenty of her crew left alive."

"It does, indeed. And another sea fight is described in Campbell's *Battle of the Baltic*, which is about Nelson's victory over the Danish fleet at Copenhagen. Yet another is *The Coming of the Spanish Armada*, by Lord Macaulay. It tells how England sprang to arms when the warning of the approach of the Spanish fleet flew round the countryside. Scott's *Marmion* is much longer; but it, too, is partly historical, giving a wonderful account of the battle of Flodden between the Scots and the English, in which the Scots' king, James IV, lost his life."

A poem telling of a famous sea-fight is Tennyson's *The Revenge*. The captain of the English ship, Sir Richard Grenville, was mortally wounded in the battle.

Alfred, Lord Tennyson.

The great historian Lord Macaulay wrote a series of poems based on Roman history and legend. The best-known of *The Lays of Ancient Rome* is *How Horatius Kept the Bridge*.

"In yon strait path a thousand
May well be stopped by three.
Now, who will stand on either hand
And keep the bridge with me?"

The burial of Sir John Moore.

"Most of these story-poems seem to be about battles and wars," commented Bill.

"Many poems have been written in praise of warrior heroes. I mentioned these first because they are full of high-spirited action and adventure, and so I know you will enjoy them. Macaulay's *How Horatius Kept the Bridge* is a tale of a battle against great odds in the days of ancient Rome, and a story of a battle settled by single combat between champions is Matthew Arnold's *Sohrab and Rustum*, which has a solemn and splendid ending. Other poems that celebrate the sort of courage that makes a man willing to give his life for his country or his friends are Tennyson's *Ode for the Funeral of the Duke of Wellington* and *The Charge of the Light Brigade*, Sir Henry Newbolt's *Drake's Drum*, and Cowper's *Toll for the Brave*, the story of a troopship going down. Another famous poem by William Cowper, this time about a heroine, is *Boadicea*, about the British warrior queen who rebelled against the Romans.

100

Then there's Charles Wolfe's fine poem written in honour of a British general who was killed fighting against Napoleon's armies in Spain—*The Burial of Sir John Moore*.

"We buried him darkly at dead of night,
    The sods with our bayonets turning,
By the struggling moonbeams misty light
    And the lantern dimly burning.

"There are national songs, too, like *Scots, Wha Hae*, in which Scotland's greatest poet, Robert Burns, celebrates the battle at which the Scots won independence from England. Burns wrote most of his poems in the Scots dialect, but you should not let this put you off, because they are full of homely touches and the language is so simple, as in these opening lines from one of his many beautiful love poems:

"Ye flowery banks o' bonnie Doon,
    How can ye blume sae fair?
How can ye chant ye little birds,
    And I sae fu' o' care?"

"There are so many fairy-tales that I'm sure some of them must have been told in verse," remarked Barbara.

Robert Burns.

DID YOU KNOW THIS?

Did you know the meaning of these words used by Burns in his poems?
bairn = child; gowd = gold;
kirk = church; jo = sweetheart;
brae = hillside; braw = fine;
monie = many; ilka = each.

The monument to Burns beside the River Doon at Alloway in Ayrshire, where he was born.

"A host of golden daffodils;
  Beside the lake, beneath the
    trees,
  Fluttering and dancing in the
    breeze."

"Yes, many have," Aunt Mary replied. "Tennyson's *The Lady of Shalott* is almost a fairy-tale, because the lady lived, you remember, in an enchanted castle. So are Tennyson's other poems about the legendary King Arthur and his knights, with their enchantresses and their magic swords. Matthew Arnold's *Forsaken Merman* is based on a fairy-tale. *Bonny Kilmeny*, by the Scottish poet James Hogg, is a very beautiful poem about a girl who went to fairy-land and came back safely, unlike the little boy in Yeats's *Stolen Child* or the little girl in William Allingham's poem *The Fairies*. And, of course, many famous ballads, like *The Demon Lover*, are fairy-tales.

"But there are also story-poems about real life. I doubt if you would care for Crabbe's grim stories of the lives of villagers, but Wordsworth's *Michael* is a fine story. Among later poets, John Masefield wrote many verse-stories of real life. In *Reynard the Fox* there is a lively account of a foxhunt, and in *Right Royal* of a steeplechase; and there are others which might interest you for he wrote of the sea, and often used a simple ballad form."

"I think *Sea Fever* is a jolly good poem," put in Bill. "Anyway, it makes *me* want to go to sea."

"Are there any poems specially written for children?" asked Barbara.

"You mentioned some yourself by Edward Lear and Lewis Carroll. Then there are the poems of the American author Eugene Field. You probably know *Wynken, Blynken, and Nod*."

"Oh, yes, I like that."

"Robert Louis Stevenson wrote a lot of poetry for children, which was collected together in *A Child's Garden of Verses*. Hilaire Belloc also wrote children's verse in his *Cautionary Tales*—and great fun they are too, if you can stand a grown-up poet getting rather ferocious at the expense of children! Then there are A. A. Milne's Christopher Robin

William Wordsworth.

Keats (left) and Shelley died young, but left us some of the loveliest of all English poems.

verses, *When We Were Very Young* and *Now We are Six*. They are poems almost for the nursery. But even T. S. Eliot, most of whose poetry would be much too difficult for you to understand, has written poems about cats which you would enjoy."

"Most of the poems you have been talking about tell stories; but I like other poems as well," said Barbara.

"Then you must read Walter de la Mare, who has written lots of poems that children have learned to love. And you will like a great many more as you grow older. Poems shape our minds and lives, for they teach us how to feel the beauty of the world and to care for what is most worth caring for. There are some known wholly or in part to every educated man or woman who speaks English—poems like Wordsworth's *Daffodils*, Shelley's *Skylark*, Keats's *Ode to a Nightingale*, and Browning's *Home Thoughts from Abroad*, which speak of the loveliness of natural things, and thoughtful poems like Shirley's *Dirge* and Gray's *Elegy Written in a Country Churchyard*, which express wise thoughts or high ideals in the form of memor-

Thomas Gray was buried in this churchyard at Stoke Poges in Buckinghamshire, of which he had spoken in his beautiful *Elegy Written in a Country Churchyard*:
"The curfew tolls the knell of parting day,
The lowing herd wind slowly o'er the lea,
The ploughman homeward plods his weary way,
And leaves the world to darkness and to me."

103

able verse. Such poems form a very big part of what we inherit from the past, and we shouldn't ignore them because they take a bit more effort to read than stories. What you get easily you tend to lose easily. But what you get with effort often lasts and gives you pleasure for a very long time—all your life in fact."

ANSWER THIS

What is the name of the famous historian who wrote a series of poems about Ancient Rome?

Barbara reads nursery rhymes to Sandra, while Bill constructs a model crane and Aunt Mary knits.

(17)

NURSERY RHYMES

IT was a raw, autumn Sunday evening. Mr. and Mrs. Brown had gone to church with their next door neighbours, the Cliftons, and Aunt Mary stayed at home to keep an eye on Barbara and Bill, and also on little two-year-old Sandra Clifton. Aunt Mary sat close to the inviting fire and started to do some knitting. Billy lay sprawled on the hearthrug, puzzling over a model-making set; and Barbara was doing her best to amuse Sandra by reading to her from an old nursery rhyme book.

Presently Barbara forgot her little audience and became deeply interested in reading to herself. "Auntie!" she called after a while. "Who wrote all these nursery rhymes?"

"Mother Goose wrote them, of course, silly!" scoffed Bill slyly.

Barbara smiled. "I really used to think that at one time because this book is called *Mother Goose's Tales.*"

Aunt Mary laid down her knitting. "Well, there are many collections of nursery rhymes," she explained. "Anybody can copy them out and make a new collection—but they are usually the same old favourite verses. Many of them had been well known to children for hundreds of years before anyone thought of making a book of them."

"I suppose," said Bill thoughtfully, "mothers just remembered the rhymes they knew them-

104

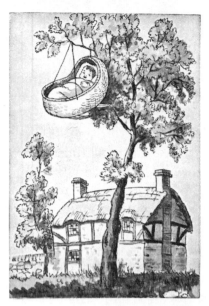

"Hush-a-bye baby on the tree top" is an example of a nursery rhyme which is also a lullaby.

selves when they were children, and used them again when they wanted to keep their own children quiet, or give them something to think about."

"Yes, and the ones kept alive were those most easily remembered, and the ones that babies like best," added his sister.

"Yes, you see although these rhymes were not written out in book form, they changed only very slowly through the years. The earliest things you learn are the ones you remember most clearly, and little children like their songs and rhymes to be repeated in exactly the same way every time."

"But even if these rhymes were not written down for hundreds of years after they first came into use," protested Barbara, "surely each one must have been made up by somebody in the first place?"

"As a matter of fact, they came from all sorts of different sources and times. Some, of course, must have been made up specially for children : lullabies, for instance, like 'Hush-a-bye baby on the tree top.' Others are catchy bits of old songs which were not meant for children at all, but they happened to catch their fancy and so got broken away from the main songs or poems which they had belonged to at first. 'Lavender's blue, dilly, dilly, Lavender's green' and 'One misty moisty morning' are like that."

To the surprise and amusement of them all Sandra's little voice suddenly piped up :

> "Lavender's blue, dilly, dilly,
>   Lavender's green ;
>   When I am king, dilly, dilly,
>   You shall be queen."

Bill had been trying to get a word in edgeways. "I expect the rhymes about the alphabet, 'A was an apple-pie, B bit it,' and 'A, B, C, listen to me,' must also have been made up specially for

"A farmer went trotting" is a game as well as a nursery rhyme.
"A raven cried 'Croak,' and they all tumbled down,
  Bumpety, bumpety, bump!"

105

People used to think they could protect their crops from evil spirits by performing magical dances, and this may be the origin of such nursery rhymes as this:
"Here we go round the mulberry
    bush, the mulberry bush, the
    mulberry bush,
Here we go round the mulberry
    bush,
On a cold and frosty morning."

children—to teach them their letters." He was pleased with his aunt's nod.

"What about all the rhymes that go with the little games people play with small children. You know the kind I mean : 'A farmer went trotting,' 'This little pig went to market,' 'Here's the church and here's the steeple,' and 'This is the way the ladies ride.' I bet all those were made up specially for children," said Barbara.

Bill was not to be outdone. "There are those that go with games for older children too, you know—things like 'Here we go round the mulberry bush,' 'Oats and beans and barley grows,' and 'Go round and round the village.' "

"You certainly both seem to know a tremendous number of rhymes—far more than I do!" confessed Aunt Mary. "But I must say that it's not at all certain that those songs were meant, at first, for children's games. Some of them, and the games themselves, are thought to be very, very old, coming down to us from a time when people believed in evil spirits and thought they could protect their homes and crops by doing magical dances and chanting songs around their fields and houses. If so, the words have certainly changed in the course of time."

"Well," admitted Bill, scratching his head, "the only nursery rhymes that seem to me at all like magical chants are the nonsense ones, with refrains like 'Wisky, wasky, weedle,' or 'Doodle, doodle, Dan !' "

"There are some which aren't quite nonsense," Barbara reminded him, "yet you don't know what it's all about. What made the cow and the dog and the dish behave as they did in 'Hey diddle diddle, the cat and the fiddle' ?"

"I'm afraid I can't answer that one," broke in her aunt, "but it's quite likely that such rhymes once had a meaning for grown-ups which has since been lost. You know the rhyme about the grand old Duke of York ?"

"Yes," replied Barbara promptly :

"Oh, the grand old Duke of York,
    He had ten thousand men ;
    He marched them up to the top of
        the hill
    And he marched them down again."

"Well that is said to have been made up to poke fun at a British general, Frederick, Duke of York, brother of King George IV. The children liked the words and the tune, but didn't bother about the meaning, and so turned it into a nursery rhyme ; the original meaning was soon forgotten. I believe, too, that rhyming riddles like 'Two legs sat on three legs,' 'A riddle, a riddle, as I suppose,' and 'A little round man in a red, red, coat' were first meant for grown-ups rather than for children, although they have now become nursery rhymes."

"Surely," said Barbara, "this type of non-sense rhyme was intended only for children," and she read out one of the choosing rhymes which are recited when you want to pick some-body out to start a game. " 'Eeny, meeny, miny,

"Hey diddle diddle,
The cat and the fiddle,
The cow jumped over the moon;
The little dog laughed
To see such sport,
And the dish ran away with the
    spoon."

"Oh, the grand old Duke of York, He had ten thousand men. . . ."

"Humpty Dumpty sat on a wall,
  Humpty Dumpty had a great fall;
  All the king's horses and all the
    king's men
  Couldn't put Humpty Dumpty
    together again."

ANSWER THIS

Can you name a nursery rhyme which is a lullaby, another which is a children's game, and a third which was not meant for children when it was first made up?

mo, Catch a nigger by his toe.' And here's another : 'Eetle, ottle, black bottle.' " She looked inquiringly at her aunt.

"I wouldn't be too sure even of that Barbara. I've read somewhere that these too are very old rhymes, which may have been used long ago by merchants, priests, rulers, and generals when they had to choose something or someone from among things or people. The words have become jumbled in time, but they show signs of coming from old forms of language no longer in use. 'Eeny, meeny, miny, mo' comes from an old series of Celtic numerals or counting-words, used by our ancestors many centuries ago."

Barbara laughed. It seemed strange to her that children should still be using a language that grown-ups had forgotten.

"There's something else that may surprise you," continued Aunt Mary. "Some of our children's rhymes are found in many different languages all over Europe. 'Humpty Dumpty,' 'Who Killed Cock Robin?' and 'Ladybird, ladybird, fly away home!' are good examples of this kind."

"I wonder who first thought of collecting nursery rhymes to make a book," said Barbara.

"The first collected English edition was printed about 200 years ago. Since then there have been very many collections, both in Britain and in America. And, of course, every year at Christmas-time new ones appear."

Sandra had apparently decided by this time that there wasn't much to interest her in all this, and had fallen fast asleep against a cushion with Mother Goose wedged firmly between her knees. "I think," whispered Barbara, as she gently pulled the book away from the sleeping child, "that babies are luckier today than they were before nursery rhymes got into print. Now they can have these rhymes read to them out of such beautiful books, with such wonderful pictures to look at too."

Let's Look at Painting and Sculpture

Do you know why eggs were important to the early painters? What makes Chinese paintings look so different? What of the sculptors of today, and what are they trying to do? You will find the answers to these and many other questions as you explore with Bill and Barbara the exciting story of art.

(18)

WHY DO WE LIKE PICTURES?

BILLY and Barbara had an Uncle Frank who was an artist. One day when he was visiting their home he remarked that they were old enough now to take an interest in paintings, and if they liked they could come along sometimes to his studio.

They paid their first visit the very next morning. Uncle Frank showed them his brushes and colours and the painting he was working on, and then drew their attention to some of the pictures by famous artists that were hanging on the walls.

"I had no idea paintings could be such fun," Barbara said at the end.

Uncle Frank laughed. "In that case," he said, "it's no use asking if you've ever wondered *why* they are fun, as you call it."

"Well, it's made me wonder now," Bill retorted. "Why *do* people like paintings, Uncle?"

"Perhaps it will be easier," his uncle said, "if we begin by trying to find out why artists paint them. We painters are people who look at something and don't see it just as you or Barbara might. If we look at the face of a person or even an animal we notice every little detail of its

Billy and Barbara love to visit their Uncle Frank in his studio. They watch eagerly as a picture takes shape on the canvas.

109

"An Old Man and his Grandson" by Ghirlandaio, in the Louvre, Paris.

"The Image Pedlar" by Edmonds pictures 19th-century America. (From the New York Historical Society.)

shape and changing expressions. If we look at a landscape or a bowl of fruit, we try to see it with our imagination as well as our eyes. Very often we have an urge to paint it—to let *you* see it as we do. In other words, every picture represents what that particular artist sees in the subject he has painted. Can you both understand me?"

Barbara looked a little puzzled, but Billy nodded eagerly. "Yes," he answered. "That's why different artists all paint the same thing in different ways. We even do that in painting lessons at school."

"Just so." Uncle Frank saw that Barbara had stopped frowning. "It explains, for instance, why a painting is so much more interesting than a coloured photograph. A book would make dull reading if it were just a bare account of the plot. We enjoy books because—even if we don't realize it—we like the way the author unfolds his story, describes his scenes and presents his

characters. In the same way, what we enjoy in a painting is not just the subject the artist has chosen—though we may enjoy that too—but how he has treated it. And that in turn explains why people often go to see paintings they think they won't like, for at least they will have the fun of trying to find out what made the artist treat the subject as he did—what thoughts were in his mind. Indeed, most artists of the past whom we now see to be very great have at some time or other been laughed at for painting as they did."

"Laughed at?" cried Barbara. "What on earth for?"

"Well, the really great artists have never been afraid of trying out new methods and materials, even though these experiments didn't always succeed. But because lesser men were accustomed to seeing their pictures painted in the popular way of their time, any new style was almost always greeted with scorn at first. For example, a very famous Dutch painter who lived three hundred years ago, named Rembrandt, was asked—'com-

The American artist George Bingham painted "Fur Traders on the Missouri." It is in the Metropolitan Museum of Art, New York.

A beggar etched by Rembrandt, now in the British Museum.

111

Rembrandt loved to paint portraits like this head of "Françoise van Wasserhoven," in the National Gallery, London.

ANSWER THIS

Why is it that such a great artist as Rembrandt found it difficult to sell his pictures during his lifetime?

Part of a bull painted thousands of years ago on the wall of a cave at Lascaux, France.

missioned,' we call it—to paint some members of a certain company of soldiers. He accepted the work, but it happened that at the time he was becoming deeply interested in the effects he could get from new ways of using light and shade. So he painted the group in this new manner, and a very wonderful painting it is.

"However, the soldiers were very cross. Some of the faces, they said, were half in shadow, others almost entirely so. Poor fellows, they would have so much preferred a photograph, if only the camera had been invented!"

"And poor Rembrandt too!" said Billy. "I suppose he wasn't asked to paint many portraits after that, was he?"

"He wasn't," said Uncle Frank. "And yet he was one of the greatest of all artists. Remind me to tell you more about him another day when we have more time."

(19)

HOW PAINTING BEGAN

"I WONDER who first thought of painting pictures?" Barbara said to Billy as they entered Uncle Frank's studio the next time.

"Why, the Ancient Egyptians, silly!" her brother retorted scornfully. "They used to paint rows and rows of funny looking people with animals' and birds' heads."

"Those heads," put in Uncle Frank, who had heard what they were saying, "were the signs by which people recognized the various Egyptian gods. And the reason for people being in rows is that the pictures are really scenes which tell stories, just like the film-strips and strip cartoons we have today. But you're wrong if you think they were the first pictures. Men were painting quite wonderfully thousands of years before the Egyptians. Come over here and I'll show you something."

POLISH TRUMPETER BY GÉRICAULT (BURRELL COLLECTION, GLASGOW)

THE FIRST ARTISTS DECORATING THE WALLS OF THEIR CAVES

A wonderfully life-like boar found on the wall of a cave at Altamira in Spain. This is the work of some of the world's first artists.

Part of a South African Bushman painting on rock, probably between one and two hundred years old.

Putting down his palette and brush, he went to the bookcase and took out a large volume. After finding the page he wanted, he held the book out to the children, and what they saw was a big coloured picture of a charging bull.

"I say, it looks almost real!" Barbara exclaimed.

"It does," her uncle agreed. "And yet that was painted long long before men had any of the brushes or colours we use today—long before they wore proper clothes or knew how to build towns, or were civilized at all."

"But how have the pictures lasted all this time?" asked Billy.

"Because they were painted on the hard rocky walls of deep caves, in Spain and southern France. The cave entrances became silted up and it was less than a hundred years ago that the first of them was re-discovered."

"Isn't it dark in the caves, though?"

"Very dark. Yet the ancient artists had only the feeblest of lamps. What is more, many of the pictures are in such a position that they could only have been painted by someone lying down, or sitting on someone else's shoulders."

"What on earth were they painted *for*?" Barbara asked in astonishment.

"No one really knows," Uncle Frank replied. "Probably they had something to do with magic. If you turn the pages you'll see many pictures of animals with spears or arrows

Part of an Egyptian painting in the British Museum, "Inspection of the Cattle belonging to Nebamen."

sticking in them. These were almost certainly drawn to help the tribe's hunters : people thought that if they painted a deer or a boar wounded by a spear it would be easier to go out and spear a real one."

Part of a remarkable fresco of geese found in the tomb of Ra Lotep, at Medûm, Egypt.

"Well then, there were these cave pictures," Billy said, "and a long while afterwards the Egyptian story-strips. What came next ?"

Uncle Frank took up his brush again. "The Ancient Greeks used to paint," he replied, "especially around their beautiful vases. Then the Romans carried out some truly remarkable paintings on the walls of their houses. Have you ever heard of Mount Vesuvius ?"

"Yes !" said both children at once. "It's a volcano in Italy !"

Uncle Frank nodded. "Nearly two thousand years ago it erupted very terribly, burying everything near it deep in lava and ash. Among the rest it buried the Roman city of Pompeii, which then lay hidden for over seventeen

A Cretan vase from Cyprus, made about 1350 B.C., now in the British Museum.

"The Mosaic Standard from Ur, in Babylonia," now

hundred years. Fortunately the ash preserved all it covered, and when people at last began to clear it away they found the old streets and shops and houses, and on the walls all sorts of landscapes, figures and portraits almost as life-like as if they had been painted the week before."

"Did the Romans paint in other cities?" Billy inquired.

"Oh, yes, but their favourite form of picture-making was in what we call mosaic. A mosaic is made up of thousands of tiny pieces of coloured stone arranged to form a picture. But that's another story for a future visit."

This well-preserved Roman mosaic of the first or second century, shows a variety of sea animals. (From the Victoria and Albert Museum, London.)

(20)

HOW PAINTING GREW UP

"PLEASE go on telling us, Uncle Frank," Barbara said, the minute she and Billy were inside the studio on their next visit, "more about how painting pictures began."

"We'd already got a good way from the beginning," her uncle pointed out. "I seem to remember the last thing we talked about was mosaics, or pictures made up of little coloured stones. These continued to be used for decorating Christian churches for about a thousand

DO THIS

Suppose you were designing a page for an illuminated manuscript. Prepare a drawing for this on any subject you like. (See page 119.)

in the British Museum, was made about 4,500 years ago.

"February," a page from the "Very Rich Book of Hours of the Duke of Berry," by Paul of Limburg. It is in the Condé Museum, Chantilly, France.

A section of a recently discovered mosaic pavement from the site of the Great Palace of the Byzantine Emperor at Constantinople.

years—from Ancient Roman days until, well, in some countries almost until the time of Christopher Columbus."

"What made people try something else?"

"Mosaics always limited what the artist could do. You can't make graceful curves or delicate shadows with stones as you can with paint, so that mosaic figures are nearly always stiff and flat-looking, instead of rounded. Mosaic buildings and such-like, too, never look natural, because those in the distance are just as sharp and clear as those in the foreground. In real life, as I expect you've noticed, the farther off anything is, the less clear it is. But for hundreds of years after the end of the Roman Empire everyone had forgotten how to paint. The craft had to be learnt all over again."

"How was that done?" asked Billy. "They had no teachers!"

"In a way there were teachers," Uncle Frank explained. "You two have heard of the Vikings? Well, besides being fierce fighters these sea folk from the North were wonderful carvers; and presently the monks engaged in copying holy manuscripts in the monasteries of England and Ireland began to decorate their work with designs imitated from the stone crosses the

tue retificauerunt animam meam.
Nunquid adheret tibi sedes iniqui
tatis: qui fingis laborem in precepto.
Captabunt in animam iusti: † san
guinem innocentem condempnabūt.

Vikings put up. Then they began to paint figures and illustrate some of the events described in the work they were copying. Presently most of the manuscript books produced in our islands and in France and Germany were being illustrated, or 'illuminated' as it is called, with scenes beautifully painted in glowing colours."

"Why didn't they do that in Italy and Greece?" asked Barbara.

"In Italy and Greece the mosaic method remained everybody's idea of proper art for buildings, and they didn't copy manuscripts so much as they did in northern Europe. Even when men began to paint again they painted as nearly like the mosaics as they could. Then, in about the year 1290, a young Italian named Giotto began to paint in an altogether different way. His scenes were not flat and uninteresting, but real. His human beings were not stiff and artificial, but showed the naturalness of life. Look, I've got a copy of one of his pictures here."

"There's not much scenery," observed Billy, looking at the holy figures that nearly filled the picture.

"Ploughing," a section from the British Museum's Luttrell Psalter. This English manuscript was written and illuminated about A.D. 1340.

This angel of hope by Giotto is in a church at Padua, Italy.

119

Uncle Frank smiled. "You've touched on something very interesting," he said. "At first the artists who began to paint in Giotto's new style were only interested in the figures—they cared little or nothing for the background. Then later painters began to put in trees, and groups of rocks, and castles and cities. Later still other artists tried to make their figures really *fit into* the landscape, instead of merely being in front of it. Presently people began to take an interest in the landscape for its own sake, and for the first time pictures began to be painted *because of* the scenery. But it was still thought necessary to include human figures somewhere."

"Oh, yes," cried Billy. "We have an old picture in the hall at home called 'Landscape With Figures.'"

Uncle Frank nodded. "That's just what I

"St. Jerome in the Desert" by Cimabue. (From the National Gallery, London.)

ANSWER THIS

How did Giotto's paintings differ from those of the earlier artists?

In this section · of Cimabue's "Madonna and Child with Angels," you can see the mosaic influence on the early Italian painters. It is in the National Gallery, London.

mean. And you see, the sort of landscape *without* figures that we're so familiar with today is a fairly new type of art, which at first was hardly thought fit to be called art at all. Later on I'll tell you more about landscapes if you like."

"Yes please, Uncle," Barbara answered. "But before we go, will you say what happened to the people who illustrated all the manuscripts up in the North?"

"Certainly. Their art developed into the great arts of Holland, Germany and Belgium—or Flanders, as it used to be called—in the same way as Italian art grew out of the mosaics. Then, of course, the time came when men travelled about more, and the two great styles of painting began to influence each other, as artists exchanged ideas. It would be hard to say which group learned the more.

"The great painters of Flanders went about their rather soft, dull countryside painting scenes exactly as they saw them. But that is another story which will have to wait," said Uncle Frank, as he bade his visitors goodbye.

120

WHAT THE ARTIST USES

THE next time the children visited Uncle Frank's studio Billy asked almost before they were inside the door: "Are you going to tell us more about portraits, Uncle?"

Their artist uncle smiled at his eagerness. "I'm glad you're so keen," he said. "But before we talk any more about different types of pictures it might be a good idea to think a bit about what the painter actually uses. I wonder how many separate kinds of painting either of you can name?"

Barbara looked thoughtful. "There are oil paintings," she began, "and water-colours. . . ."

"And frescoes," added Billy. But neither of them could think of any others.

"Good," Uncle Frank said approvingly. "And there are two other main kinds—pastels and tempera. Pastels are like crayons and chalks. 'Fresco' is an Italian word meaning 'fresh,' and frescoes are water-colours painted on to a plaster wall while the plaster is still fresh and wet. In tempera, on the other hand, the colour substances—pigments, they're called—are not mixed with water or oil, but with yolk of egg, or something similarly sticky. It's a very old method, and was largely replaced by oil painting, which you may be surprised to hear was invented only about five hundred years ago."

"Who invented it?" Barbara asked.

"We don't know. We do know it was first made popular by two Flemish brothers named Van Eyck. You must remember that in the old days painters couldn't just buy their paints in tubes as we do. They took colouring matter from certain minerals or plants, ground it to powder between two stones, and mixed it with water or egg-yolk. But the Van Eycks found that they could make much better paints

A fine example of medieval tempera painting is "Pallas Taming a Centaur" by Botticelli, in the Uffizi Gallery, Florence.

"Boys Eating Melon and Grapes" is a vivid study in oils by the Spanish painter Murillo. It is in the Pinakothek Art Gallery, Munich.

Sir Henry Raeburn's famous picture of "A Boy with a Rabbit," in Burlington House, London, is a charming picture in oils.

by mixing the pigments with various oils. It was possible to paint finer details, because the colours stayed wet longer on the brush. They could also get brighter touches of light. Today, as perhaps you know, artists use oil paints more often than all the others added together."

"Why do they go on using the others at all?" Barbara wanted to know.

"Oil paints are not always suitable for every subject. Some painters, for instance, feel that they can show rainy skies, or scenes that include a lake or a river, much better by using water-colours, which give a thinner, washier, more watery effect than oils. Again, if a large mural (that's the artist's word for a wall painting) has to be done, the artist may feel that the fresco method is still the best. His choice of paint and his way of putting it on help just as much as his skill in design, or his use of light and shade, or even his selection of colours, to make us *feel* that the picture is a good or a bad one."

"Do colours last for ever?" asked Billy.

Uncle Frank sighed and shook his head. "I'm afraid they don't," he said. "That's where

"The School of Athens" by Raphael, in the Vatican, shows the triumph of Philosophy, with Plato and Aristotle at the centre of the group of scholars.

122

THE CORNFIELD BY CONSTABLE SHOWS THIS LANDSCAPE PAINTER AT HIS BEST. IT IS IN
THE NATIONAL GALLERY, LONDON

THIS BATTLE SCENE IS CALLED *THE ROUT OF SAN ROMANO*, AND IT WAS PAINTED BY THE ITALIAN ARTIST PAOLO UCCELLO.

IT CELEBRATES A CAVALRY VICTORY BY THE FLORENTINES
OVER THE SIENNESE IN 1432 AND IS IN THE NATIONAL GALLERY

A GIRL WITH A KITTEN BY PERRONNEAU, IN THE NATIONAL GALLERY

Probably one of the most famous paintings in the world is "The Last Supper" by Leonardo da Vinci, painted on the wall of a convent near Milan.

knowing something about the actual paints can help us to imagine many old pictures, not as they look today, but as they did when they were new. Some of the world's greatest masterpieces have lost their real colouring as badly as curtains that have faded in the sun. Just behind you is a copy of the best known portrait in all art. It is called the 'Mona Lisa,' and was painted four hundred and fifty years ago by a remarkable Italian named Leonardo da Vinci. It is lovely even now, but how exquisite it must have been before the face faded from pink to yellow, and before the eyebrows disappeared ! And so it is with many other 'old masters,' as we call the works of the great painters. All we are left with is a kind of bad copy, so to speak, of their original beauty, and to enjoy them fully we have to imagine the old artists painting them with the colours we know they used."

"Perhaps if they had tried different ones they'd have lasted longer," Billy suggested hopefully.

"They often did try new methods," Uncle Frank said. "Sometimes, as when the Van

Leonardo's "Mona Lisa" is still lovely in spite of fading. She can be seen in the Louvre, Paris.

127

Eycks tried oils, they were successful. At other times they failed completely. The same Italian who painted the 'Mona Lisa' painted a very, very beautiful fresco of Jesus at the Last Supper; but because he loved experiments he tried using oil paint on dry plaster, instead of water-colours on wet plaster. His lovely painting not only became badly faded, but large pieces flaked off and it has had to be restored. But don't forget, in our clever age we haven't improved on the old masters. We still paint in oils and water-colours, and often not nearly so well."

DID YOU KNOW THIS?

Leonardo da Vinci, in addition to being a wonderful painter and a sculptor, was also a scientist, architect, military engineer and musician. He was left-handed, wrote from right to left, and could break a horse-shoe with his fingers!

(22)

TWO GREAT MASTERS OF DRAWING

ANOTHER day when she and Billy were in Uncle Frank's studio Barbara asked: "Does a painter have to learn to draw first?"

Brush in hand, Uncle Frank paused a moment in his work. "Indeed he does," he said. "No painter was ever great who didn't learn to draw; even modern painters, who sometimes paint such weird-looking pictures, have all learnt drawing, so that each of them *could*, if he wished, draw his subject as clearly as a photograph. It doesn't matter how clever an artist is at arranging the things in his picture, at choosing and grouping his colours; if he can't draw, his picture won't look right."

"Why?" asked Billy.

"Because a knowledge of drawing is for the painter like a knowledge of engineering for the architect. Whatever shape and style of building an architect designs, if his engineering is bad the building will fall down. The reason is that engineering means knowing how a building is really constructed—and in just the same way drawing skill means knowing how the things you want to paint are really constructed. For instance, what do you two find hardest to draw?"

Leonardo's striking "Self-Portrait" in the Royal Library, Turin, gives a good idea of this tremendous genius in his old age.

ANSWER THIS

Can you name the five principal kinds of paintings?

128

This is the famous preliminary sketch or cartoon by Leonardo of The Virgin and Child with St. John the Baptist and St. Anne.

"Human beings," Barbara retorted promptly; and Billy nodded in agreement.

"Exactly—human figures," Uncle Frank said, just as if he'd known all along that this would be their answer. "And why do you find them hardest? Because the human form is extremely complicated. It consists of an outer skin—the only part we can see—covering a most involved arrangement of bones and muscles; and the only way to draw it successfully, or to paint it, is to study this arrangement until you know it so well that when you look at a person you are going to draw you can 'see' the bones and muscles under the skin. This study of the body is called 'anatomy.' "

"Then is every painter an anata— anato—" Billy stumbled over the word.

"An anatomist? Every good figure painter, yes. You remember we talked about the 'Mona Lisa' and 'The Last Supper,' by the same Italian artist? His name was Leonardo da Vinci, and he was one of the most astonishing men who ever lived, for he was almost equally brilliant as a painter, a sculptor, a naturalist, an engineer, and an inventor. Because he knew that to paint he must study anatomy, he studied it as thoroughly as any modern medical student; he dissected—that is to say, cut open scientifically —no fewer than thirty dead bodies, as well as all sorts of animals and insects, and he has left us hundreds of drawings of different bones and muscles and what we call people's insides. In fact, he was so busy with these studies, in addition to a score of others, that he had time to finish very few paintings or sculptures. But we have a large number of the 'try-out' sketches he made, and in these you can see very plainly how his anatomy studies helped him to draw figures in every possible attitude—and, I might add, faces of every possible queerness—without a single one of them failing to look absolutely true to life."

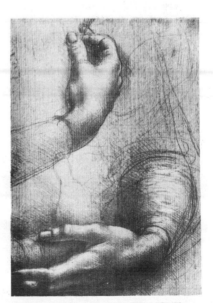

"Study of Hands," another sketch by Leonardo, now in Windsor Castle Library.

129

These three pictures are part of the fresco by Michelangelo in the Sistine Chapel, Rome. They are: "A Libyan Sibyl"; "Jeremiah"; and "God Creating Adam."

"What a pity he couldn't have left more paintings and statues," Barbara said.

"It is indeed," Uncle Frank agreed. "But there was another great artist, some twenty years younger than Leonardo, whose sculptures and paintings, often very large in size, also show most vividly the artist's understanding of the structure of our bodies. This was Michelangelo. Above all he loved painting men, and fine, rugged, enormously strong men they look."

"Did he cut up real bodies, too?"

"He did, yes. You see, in those days artists had no scientific diagrams and plastic models and expert teachers to learn from. They had to find out for themselves; and consequently the impression their mastery of the subject made on other people was tremendous. Michelangelo was more a sculptor than a painter, but if you want to see his best painting —and that means some of the finest pictures of the human figure in existence—you must wait till you can go to the Pope's great palace in Rome, the Vatican. There in one of the chapels you can see Michelangelo's masterpiece covering the whole of the ceiling. You'll find you want to go on and on gazing up at it, and won't even notice the crick in the neck you get from having to stare right over your head! Michelangelo spent four uncomfortable years lying on his back before he finished this wonderful work."

(23)

PAINTINGS AND PLACES

"Christ Driving the Money-changers from the Temple," by El Greco, is in the National Gallery, London.

"WHAT funny paintings these are!" Billy exclaimed. He and Barbara were looking at one of the illustrated books on art in Uncle Frank's studio. Uncle Frank left his easel to glance over their shoulders and see which book it was.

"Ah, El Greco!" he said. "Yes, his pictures do have a style very much of their own: strange, harsh colours, very sharp contrasts between light and shade, and his figures are usually longer and thinner than ordinary living people. There's something strangely exciting about his paintings; we feel we *know* he must have been in a turmoil of emotions all the time he was at work. He was certainly the greatest master of the Spanish School, yet he wasn't a Spaniard at all."

"You mean he was sent to school in Spain?" Barbara inquired. To her surprise her uncle laughed heartily at this.

"The Magdalen," by Tintoretto (Venetian School), is in the Galleria Capitolina, Rome.

131

Typical of the religious art of the Sienese school is this picture of "St. Michael Fighting Satan" by Raphael. It can be seen in the Louvre, in Paris.

An archer from part of "The Martyrdom of St. Sebastian" by the Florentine artist Pollaiuolo. (In the National Gallery, London.)

"I should have explained," he replied. "When artists talk about a 'school,' they mean all the painters who lived in a particular country, or region, or city, and whose styles seem, as a result, to have something in common. Even if the artist lived somewhere else, but painted in the manner of a certain 'school' we say he belongs to it. El Greco was in fact a Greek—his name is simply Spanish for 'The Greek'—but because all his greatest work was done in Spain we always think of him as a 'Spanish School' artist."

"Why," asked Billy, "*should* living in one region give painters' styles something in common?"

"It's due partly to geography and climate. For instance, you wouldn't expect people who live where there is a vast amount of bright sunshine, such as in the south of France, to paint quite like others who live in the duller, softer light that is normal in Holland or England.

"Then another influence on art is history. Think, for example, of Italy. In the Middle Ages Italy was not one kingdom, like England, but a collection of independent cities that developed their own personalities, so to speak.

"Siena, for example, was a quiet, deeply religious city that produced artists who painted devout, restful pictures in which the influence of mosaics lingered long after it had disappeared elsewhere. Florence, on the other hand, though not many miles away, was a bustling city, forever getting involved in wars, and—partly through the desire to invent new war-engines—deeply interested in science. In consequence the Florentine School of artists soon changed the old mosaic style into something utterly different; they became absorbed with the technical side of painting, experimenting with backgrounds, welcoming new problems for the pleasure of solving them. Giotto, about whom I told you, was a Florentine.

132

Bellini, an artist of the Venetian school, delights in showing us the rich colours of the gown worn by the "Doge Leonardo Loredan." (In the National Gallery, London.)

"Then there were the Venetians. Which of you knows what makes Venice different from other cities?"

"I know!" said Barbara proudly. "It's got canals everywhere instead of roads."

"And they use boats called 'gondolas'," added Billy, not to be outdone.

"That's right," her uncle confirmed. "It's built on islands in the sea. Cut off like that from the rest of Italy, the Venetians grew extremely rich by trading with the East; and sure enough, Venetian painting is characterized by rich colours, the portrayal of gorgeous clothes and tapestries, and by a kind of worldly luxury even in religious scenes."

"Was it only in Italy that history affected artists?" asked Billy.

"By no means. Towards the end of the 1400's there began the great religious revolution we call the Reformation. In the northern half of Europe large numbers of people became Protestants—among them the Dutch. Now, the Protestants didn't hold with highly decorated churches, so the Dutch artists found themselves turning more and more to painting landscapes or the interiors of houses, or portraits. Instead of Crucifixions and Madonnas, they were commissioned to paint wealthy merchants and groups of town councillors."

"Hadn't there been any portraits before?" Barbara asked.

"Very few. You did have a few earlier portraits when an artist put in the likeness of his patron, or his lady-love, or perhaps himself, as one of the characters in a crowd scene—trusting to the observant habits of the viewers to make them 'spot' it. Now, however, that the Dutch painters were being actually commissioned to paint portraits, it had a highly interesting effect on their style. But I'll tell you some more about that tomorrow."

"The Rooster and the Jewel" by the Dutch artist Snyders. It is in the Surmondt Museum, Aachen, in Germany.

133

PAINTINGS LIKE PHOTOGRAPHS

In his picture "Boy with Dog" the Dutch artist Ter Borch makes us feel for the patient puppy. You can see this delightful painting in the Pinakothek Art Gallery, in Munich.

"The Shuttlecock" by Chardin is a charming study of young girlhood. (In the Uffizi Gallery, Florence.)

"You were going to tell us, Uncle," Barbara said, as soon as she and Billy stepped inside the studio door, "why painting portraits made a difference to the style of Dutch artists."

"Very well," agreed Uncle Frank, "we'll talk about the Dutch and Flemish painters a little. What I meant to say yesterday was that when a rich merchant or a group of town councillors commissioned a picture of themselves, they expected it to be painted in the way *they* liked, as I told you right at the beginning of our talks. And what they liked was to see themselves on a painter's canvas exactly as they saw themselves in a mirror—except that I suspect they secretly didn't mind if the painter flattered them a little !

"As a result, artists tried to paint not only with great accuracy, but began to pay more attention to all the little details. This came quite naturally to men who painted the little pictures, so full of detail, on manuscripts; but it wasn't until the brothers Van Eyck developed oil painting—as I told you in an earlier talk—that it had become possible to do such tiny 'finicky' work in big pictures without the paint drying too quickly."

"What sort of details, Uncle?" asked Billy.

"Oh, the exact patterns, however small and elaborate, on dresses and tapestries; every little crease and shadow in the folds of a piece of material; the miniature reflection of everything around in the curved surface of a shiny jug, and so on."

Uncle Frank lifted a book off the shelf and opened it for them. "Have a look at some of the pictures in there and you'll see what I'm getting at. Jan Van Eyck himself, the younger of the brothers, clearly took a great delight in

134

FLOWER-PIECE BY VAN HUYSUM, IN THE NATIONAL GALLERY

CHARLES I ON HORSEBACK BY VAN DYCK, IN THE NATIONAL GALLERY

WINTER SCENE BY THE DUTCH ARTIST AVERCAMP GIVES US A VIVID IMPRESSION OF
CROWDED ACTIVITY ON THE ICE. IT IS IN THE NATIONAL GALLERY, LONDON

COURTYARD OF A DUTCH HOUSE IS WHAT PIETER DE HOOCH CALLED THIS PICTURE.
IT IS IN THE NATIONAL GALLERY, LONDON

painting portraits that showed every mole and wrinkle on the sitter's face, or scenes in which you might say that nothing, however small, had been left out."

"Did people in Holland and Flanders paint any more religious pictures at all?" asked Billy.

"They painted quite a number. In fact one of Jan Van Eyck's scenes that I am thinking of is called 'The Madonna of Chancellor Rollin.' Another kind of religious art that became very popular was the painting of wooden altar-screens and panels. You see, owing to the softer sunshine in northern countries the churches there had bigger windows and less wall space than those in the sun-scorched south. That is why northern Europe has few famous frescoes but lovely large stained glass windows, while southern Europe has few notable stained glass windows but many lovely frescoes. So, having less in the way of bare wall to paint on, northern artists became interested in making beautiful altars with altar-screens.

"But in the main the art that developed most fully in the Low Countries was not a religious art. It was made up of landscapes, portraits and 'interiors'—scenes inside houses, shops, inns and so on. Holland especially became famous for interiors."

Their uncle showed them many pictures, by nearly as many different artists, of Dutch rooms and shops, painted three hundred years ago and earlier. They noticed especially the clever way in which a number of artists made use of the light that came through windows and doorways to produce exciting contrasts of brilliance and shadow.

"Look at this lady's clothes!" Barbara cried suddenly, pointing to a colour print of 'Interior of a Dutch Courtyard,' by de Hooch. "They're almost real!"

"Yes," agreed Uncle Frank, looking as he was told, "that's another wonderful thing about

"The Madonna of Chancellor Rollin" is a famous example of Flemish religious painting. The exquisite detail in the robes and columns, and the charming landscape in the background show how careful Van Eyck was to paint everything exactly as he saw it. You will find this superb painting in the Louvre, in Paris.

The artists of the Low Countries were concerned with painting every tiny detail. Van Os does just that in his "Flower Piece." (In the Boymans Museum, Rotterdam.)

"Girl at a Window" by Vermeer. This can be found in the Dresden Art Gallery, Germany.

Dutch interiors. With this new craze for accuracy some artists found they could show not only every fold and detail of pattern, but also make the beholder almost *feel* the different materials of which the objects in the picture were made. And here on this page you are looking at a work by the greatest master of all at that particular effect—Jan Vermeer. Not only do the girl's clothes seem to be made of genuine fabrics, but the tablecloth, the dish, the very glass of the window appear so like the real thing that we imagine if we were to touch the paint it would be bound to feel just like the objects themselves !"

"There are a lot of landscapes in this book too," Billy remarked.

"The Feast of St. Nicholas" by Steen shows a happy Dutch family group of that time. It hangs in the Boymans Museum, Rotterdam, Holland.

"Naturally," his uncle replied. "You expect landscape painters in a flat country."

"Do you? Why?" asked Barbara, her eyes round with surprise.

Uncle Frank laughed. "I'll tell you next time you pay me a visit," he said mischievously.

The Flemish artist Peter Brueghel had a lively sense of humour. This is his "Land of the Idle," which can be seen in the Pinakothek Art Gallery, Munich.

(25)

LANDSCAPE AND SEASCAPE

WHEN they next visited their uncle Barbara was bursting with curiosity.

"Well," she asked, "why *did* the best landscape artists live in flat countries, Uncle?"

"Because of the horizon," replied her uncle. Billy laughed. "You're pulling our legs!"

"Not really," Uncle Frank retorted. "It's just the way I'm putting it. If you go where the country is absolutely flat, like Holland and much of eastern England, what is the thing you see most of? Why, the horizon—the long, dead-

John Constable. (In the National Portrait Gallery, London.)

141

straight line where the sky and land meet. There it stretches, whichever way you turn, and always the same great distance away. The next most obvious thing is usually the sky itself, with its patterns of cloud; nowhere, except out at sea, can you see such a lot of it at once! Finally, there is the sense of *vastness* you get from a landscape so huge, so flat, with trees and rivers and roads becoming smaller and smaller the farther off they are. It's hard to say exactly why, but this kind of scenery has given rise to more fine landscape painters than other kinds of country that you and I think more attractive."

"Landscapes often show lots of clouds," Billy suggested.

"They do. In fact it would be more correct to call some of them 'cloudscapes.' But apart from being interesting to paint, the huge skies of flat countries inspire artists in another way; they produce a particular type of light that is ideal for painting in. Even when the artist decides to depict quite a small scene, with trees or buildings hiding the wide spaces, he still benefits by the special light."

"I think we've got a Dutch landscape picture

One of the most famous landscape paintings in the world is "The Avenue" by Hobbema. The two lines of tall trees give a tremendous impression of distance. You can see this fine picture in the National Gallery, London.

This scene is called "Crossing the Brook," by Turner. It is in the National Gallery, London.

142

at home," Barbara said. "It's over a calendar."

Uncle Frank looked amused. "I fancy I remember it," he said. "It's a copy of a picture called 'The Avenue,' by an artist named Hobbema—a road stretching away into the distance, bordered by two lines of tall, thin trees. Certainly it's one of the best-known landscapes in the world, yet many people today prefer the work of a friend of Hobbema's, Jacob van Ruysdael. If you go to the National Gallery, in London, have a look at his painting of 'The Shore at Scheveningen.' Here is a 'cloudscape' if you like; the sky occupies nearly three-quarters of the picture. But it's a splendid scene."

"Who were the greatest English landscape painters?" inquired Billy.

"The first you need trouble about was Thomas Gainsborough, who lived two hundred years ago—a century after the Dutchmen we have been discussing. Gainsborough said he painted portraits for money and landscapes for love. He lived before the day when most people thought landscapes should really count as serious pictures, and in spite of his fame as a

Thomas Gainsborough, seen here, was better known for his portraits, but he was also an excellent landscape painter. (In the National Portrait Gallery, London.)

Part of a picture called "The Shore at Scheveningen" by Jacob van Ruysdael. It is in the National Gallery, London.

Joseph Turner. This portrait of him comes from the National Portrait Gallery, London. This great English painter loved to paint wild sunsets and fierce storms, clouds bursting into rain and spray tossed from the crests of the waves. Once during a storm at sea he lashed himself to the mast so that he would not be washed overboard while he studied for hours the raging waters.

portrait painter his house when he died was found to be full of unsold landscape pictures, including many that today would sell for a great deal of money."

"Did *he* live in the east of England?" asked Barbara.

"Yes, he was born in Suffolk and most of his landscapes are Suffolk scenes. But a greater artist from the same county is John Constable. I feel sure you've seen copies of some of his celebrated Suffolk and Essex scenes, even if you didn't know they were his. Constable was fascinated by the quality of the light that I've mentioned; where duller eyes saw only solid masses of green or brown, he saw those masses broken up by little areas of brightness, which he expressed in his work by streaks of vivid colour, and here and there even by a patch of pure white.

"Constable lived at the same time as an even more original landscape painter, Joseph Turner. Turner was a Londoner—an exception to our rule, but then he was an exception to almost every rule. Constable's interest in light was nothing to Turner's, most of whose later pictures—especially the water scenes which he loved—are dazzling masses of reds and golds,

"Chichester Channel" by Turner suggests with wonderful simplicity the peaceful evening hour before the sun goes down. It is in the National Gallery, London.

blues and whites, as though everything were seen in a brilliant sunset or through a luminous, pearly mist. The London galleries are the places to see many of his paintings too."

"Did all the later painters," asked Barbara, "try to copy Constable and Turner?"

"Not in England," Uncle Frank answered. "That's the funny thing about it; for in France a whole new school of painting grew up as the result of these two Englishmen. But that, once again, is another story for another time."

Another great landscape artist at this time was John Sell Cotman. This study of him is from the National Portrait Gallery, in London.

(26)

TWO GREAT MASTERS OF THE LOW COUNTRIES

SOME days later Billy and Barbara were again sitting comfortably in their uncle's studio. "You told us earlier about a painter who angered some people who had asked him to paint their portraits, because he put half their faces in shadow," said Barbara. "Do you remember that?"

"I do," her uncle replied. "You mean Rembrandt. And I remember I said I'd tell you some more about him, too. But to make it more interesting I'll tell you at the same time about another brilliant artist, Rubens, who also lived in the Low Countries—that's the old name for Holland and Belgium—during roughly the same period, the early 1600's, but whose fortunes were a complete contrast to Rembrandt's.

"In those days it was still the custom for anyone who wanted to be an artist to go and study in Italy, where for 400 years so many great painters had lived and taught. Rubens accordingly went to Italy, and actually stayed there until he was over thirty, which would be a late age to be a student even today, and was very

ANSWER THIS

What do you think was the main difference between the lives of Rembrandt and Rubens?

This "Self-Portrait" by Rembrandt was painted in middle life and is one of many the artist did. (In the National Gallery, London.)

145

late indeed in a period when diseases allowed few people to live to what we should consider a real old age. When he finally went back to the Low Countries, however, he showed that he not only knew how to paint, but how to make up for lost time."

"Do you mean he painted very quickly?" Billy asked.

"Not so much that, but instead of trying to do all the work himself he employed less clever artists, and students, to help him. If someone wanted a picture painted entirely by Rubens, it was very expensive. For rather less money, Rubens would paint the important parts and leave his employees to do the rest. The cheapest pictures were painted wholly by the employees —working, of course, under their master's close direction and supervision."

"Didn't people mind?" inquired Billy in some wonder.

"They don't seem to have done," Uncle Frank answered. "The fact is, Rubens was so

This study of "A Capuchin Friar" by Rembrandt is a striking example of the use of light and shade. It hangs in the National Gallery, London.

"The Syndics of the Cloth Hall" by Rembrandt. It can be seen in the Rijksmuseum, Amsterdam.

146

excellent that they felt even a picture painted by someone else under his guidance was more worth having than one painted by a less gifted artist with his own hand. Orders poured into his studio."

"Did he only paint portraits?" asked Barbara.

"No, he painted just about everything—portraits, landscapes, religious scenes, illustrations of the great legends of Greece and Rome, sporting views; whatever was ordered. But because he painted what people wanted and in a way that pleased them, you mustn't think he had no real genius or originality. He was the first artist to make a truly successful blend of the North European style of painting and the Italian; perhaps you recall my telling you the very different ways they grew up. For this he deserves the honour paid him, and also the money, for naturally he became very rich—just the opposite of poor Rembrandt."

"Tell us about him now, please," Barbara said.

"Well," Uncle Frank went on, "from the beginning Rembrandt's life was different; for Rubens as a boy had been a page at court, but Rembrandt was a humble miller's son. There was no studying in Italy for him; yet this did not really matter, for by now there were good teachers in his own country, and he quickly learned to paint in Amsterdam. Then, for about ten years, he was nearly as prosperous and successful as Rubens. He married very happily, and it was grief at the death of his young wife, as much as the bad reception of his 'light and shadow' portrait I told you about, that set him off painting as *he* liked, rather than as his patrons did. His experiments helped to take his mind off his sorrow."

"But how did he earn anything?" asked Barbara, dismayed.

"I'm afraid he didn't earn much. All his savings became spent. He had to sell his house,

This fine "Self-Portrait" by Rubens shows off his rich clothes. You will find it in the Imperial Museum, in Vienna.

This delightful picture of a cherub by Rubens is part of his painting "Henry IV Receiving a Portrait of Mary Medici." It is in the Louvre, in Paris.

147

"Saskia as Flora" by Rembrandt. (In the National Gallery, London.)

ANSWER THIS

How did Rubens manage to get so many pictures painted in such a short time?

Hogarth's "Shrimp Girl" is a warm and friendly picture which lives in every detail of the artist's brush. You can see this famous painting in the National Gallery, London.

his own picture collection, even the equipment from his studio. He tramped about the country painting landscapes, and when no one would give him an order for a portrait he painted his own. His friends left him; one after another his family died. But his painting grew ever more brilliant, until at last, at the very end of his life, he was again commissioned to paint a group of officials. This time he took care not to place their faces in shadow, and they were pleased with the work. I wonder how much more pleased they would have been if they could have foreseen that this old, poor, despised artist would come to be looked upon as one of the greatest painters and etchers the world has ever known?"

(27)

SERMONS IN PICTURES

"UNCLE, what does 'sermons in stones' mean?" asked Billy one day in the studio.

"It's a phrase Shakespeare thought of," replied Uncle Frank. " 'Tongues in trees, books in the running brooks, sermons in stones, and good in everything.' Roughly, he meant that someone deprived of books and learned conversation can make up for it by an intelligent study of the world around him. Later, another writer spoke of a 'sermon in stone' to describe the holy effect of a wonderful cathedral. But you can have sermons in pictures just as much as in stones, you know."

"You mean holy pictures of Madonnas and things?" Barbara asked.

"Well, they are included," her uncle agreed, "but I was really thinking of more worldly pictures. After all, what is a sermon? A talk urging people to do good and to avoid things that are wicked. Sometimes a picture, or a series of pictures, simply by showing the thing

148

DID YOU KNOW THIS?

that is wicked, can turn people away from it more quickly than words. And the artist can bring this about in two ways: he can make the wickedness look horrible, so that people become afraid or angry at it, or he can make it look so ridiculous that they are ashamed to be connected with it."

"Have there been many artists who did this?" inquired Billy.

"There have been quite a number," Uncle Frank answered, "but very few really great ones. Generally, you see, a painter who has what we call an 'axe to grind'—a purpose beyond the purely artistic one of painting a good picture—tends to think too much about making sure we grasp this purpose and too little about creating a work of art. Just now and again, however, a painter of genius has managed to preach a sermon and give us a masterpiece."

"Have there been any English ones?" Barbara asked hopefully.

"Yes. One of the two greatest of all was an Englishman, William Hogarth, who was born in London in 1697. Now, this was right in the middle of a long period when London life—as

A "Self-Portrait" of William Hogarth at work before his easel. It hangs in the National Portrait Gallery, London.

This picture by Hogarth, called "The Distressed Poet," gives us an insight into a part of eighteenth-century life. The poet is shown seeking inspiration in a garret; his wife is mending his trousers, the milkmaid is demanding payment of a bill, and the dog is stealing the joint.

"Simon, Lord Lovat," after Hogarth. It may be seen in the National Portrait Gallery, London.

indeed life in many other places—was extremely dirty, greedy, and immoral. Hogarth became well aware of this as he grew up, and being apprenticed to an engraver (that is a craftsman who cuts patterns and pictures with a small chisel on metal, from which prints are taken) and already a keen art student, he hit on the idea of painting a series of pictures showing just what ridiculous pigs so many people were making of themselves, and then having the paintings copied by engravers on metal plates from which prints on paper—engravings, as we call them—could be made in large numbers for sale.

"He held up all sorts of evils to scorn. But although the subjects of his pictures are so vile and ugly, he treated them with such artistic skill that these 'sermon' paintings of his give us quite as much pleasure as the many portraits

150

he also painted. They form a good example of what I said to you in one of our early talks—that a beautiful painting does not require a beautiful subject."

"You said Hogarth was one of the *two* greatest painters of sermons," Billy observed. "Who was the other?"

"The other was a Spaniard born nearly 150 years later—Francisco Goya. He too painted fine portraits, but is probably remembered best for his fierce condemnation of war; for he lived all through the grim fighting in Spain in which the British Duke of Wellington, as he was to become, won his fame against Napoleon. In his anti-war paintings and engravings Goya does not poke fun, as Hogarth did—no doubt he realized his subject was too serious for that—but adopts the other method I mentioned, and shows us various incidents of wartime in all their terror and horribleness. This was something quite new, for hitherto almost every artist had shown war as heroic and glorious.

"Two other evils he condemned by his paintings were the worldliness of the Spanish Church and the empty stupidity of court life."

Part of a charming picture by Goya called "The Swing." It shows an unexpectedly romantic side to his nature. It is found in the Prado Museum, Madrid.

"Children with Dogs" by Goya. This refreshing picture is in the Prado Museum, in Madrid.

"The Bouncing Game" by Goya. (In the Prado Museum, Madrid.)

This jolly sea picture by Christopher Wood is entitled "The Red Funnel."

(28)

PAINTING IN STRANGE STYLES

Paul Gauguin painted this "Girl from Brittany" at prayer.

"UNCLE, what's an 'Impressionist'?" Billy asked. He had noticed the word on the back of one of the art books on the studio shelves.

Uncle Frank considered for a minute the clearest way to explain. "Well, now," he said, "you remember how the English landscape painters Constable and Turner tried—very successfully—to bring a new brightness into their landscapes? In 1870 the Germans invaded France, and a number of young French artists became refugees in England. While here they saw a good many of Constable's and Turner's works, and they became very much interested in the real nature of light and how to represent it in painting. Realizing that the look of a place changes at different times of the year and different hours of the day—indeed, that natural daylight is continually changing—the shadows altering with the sun, clouds passing, mists rising, and so on—they figured out that the way to be realistic is to try to paint a nature-scene *as it looks at a single moment*; or in other words, to capture its fleeting *impression*."

"They must have had to be jolly quick painters," Billy commented.

"Of course, they couldn't paint a picture all in a second, like taking a snapshot," Uncle Frank answered. "But they tried to capture the effect that was there while they looked. They decided, for instance, that a lot of light or 'life' was lost from their colours by blending them on the palette. . . . What colour would you call this cushion cover?" he asked suddenly, pointing to the couch.

"Purple," said both children at once, with no doubt in their minds.

"Learning to Slide"—a happy child study by Staigg. From the New York Historical Society.

The contemporary artist L. S. Lowry has captured the everyday life of a small community quite delightfully in this striking picture of "A Lancashire Village."

This is how one modern painter looks at buildings. The picture is called "St. Mary-le-Port, Bristol," by John Piper, and is in the Tate Gallery, London.

This natural impression of a young child helping herself to the contents of a bowl is an early picture by Picasso, and is called "Le Gourmet." It is in the Art Institute of Chicago, U.S.A.

"All right. Now look at it closely and tell me if it is woven of purple threads."

The children peered, and exclaimed in surprise.

"Why!" cried Barbara. "It's made of red threads one way and blue the other. It's not purple at all, really."

"Just so," her uncle agreed. "These French artists reasoned that if the eye could be deceived with a piece of cloth, so it could with paint; and that instead of mixing red and blue on the palette to make purple, they would paint a red dab and a blue dab—or many of each—side by side and let the human eye do the mixing. By this device—which certainly saved a lot of time—and by using only the main colours of the rainbow, they thought they could really depict a scene as it looked at a particular instant."

"And did they?" Barbara asked.

Uncle Frank took from the shelf the book Billy had noticed, opened it, and handed it to the children. Inside were many colour copies of Impressionist paintings. Despite the small size of the copies the children could easily see the little spots of pure colour that made up each picture; and the general effect was certainly brighter and more life-like than many of the older pictures they had seen. Towards the end of the book, however, they were surprised by the curious shapes and angles given to some of the things.

"They look all out of proportion," Barbara protested.

Uncle Frank laughed. "Ah!" he said, glancing over her shoulder, "you've got on to that strange artist Van Gogh." (He pronounced it 'Van Goff.') "That's because Van Gogh sees the things he paints in a way we find unusual at first. But the really queer thing is not his way of painting—it's that after a little you find you are seeing the things the same way he does, so that his method no longer looks odd at all.

154

Van Gogh loved to paint quaint bridges; his use of brilliant, even crude colours gives us a sense of the strong, bright contrasts in sunny Provence

in this Self-Portrait Van Gogh uses streaks of bright green and yellow and orange in building up the face; and blue broken by spots of orange in the background

THE BRIDGE (ABOVE) AND SELF-PORTRAIT (BELOW) BY VAN GOGH

TODAY'S ARTISTS

PAINT

TODAY'S SCENES

All these paintings are reproduced by permission of the Peter Stuyvesant Foundation, London

BUSES BY ALLEN JONES

ROCKY MOUNTAINS AND TIRED INDIANS BY DAVID HOCKNEY

YORK WAY RAILWAY BRIDGE FROM CALEDONIAN ROAD BY LEON KOSSOFF

TROUT FOR FACTITIOUS BAIT BY R. B. KITAJ

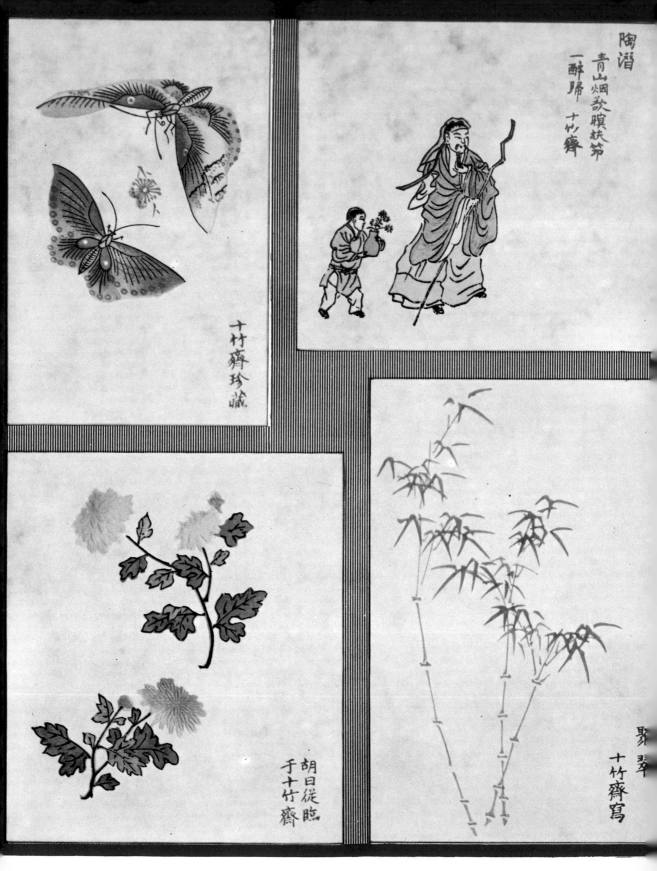

FOUR PICTURES WHICH SHOW THE DELICACY OF CHINESE ART

"Later on certain artists thought the Impressionists were paying too much attention to the surfaces of things and forgetting their solid structure. About this time there was a fashionable scientific notion that all substances were really composed of crystals—like salt or sugar. So these artists fancied they could produce an effect of solidity by avoiding all curves and keeping to straight lines and flat surfaces such as all crystals have."

"What a funny idea," murmured Barbara.

"Yes. Not many people now agree that the Cubists, as they came to be called, succeeded. But today we have artists trying even stranger methods, still harder to understand. Yet if you always remember what you learned on your first visit here—that every artist paints to show us how something looks *to him*—at least you will be able to understand that modernistic painters are merely trying to see familiar objects in new and perhaps more truthful ways."

ANSWER THIS

Why did the Cubists differ from the Impressionists and how did they try to show us their ideas in their art?

"The Sleeping Poet" by Marc Chagall conjures up a dreamlike —almost Noah's Ark-like—farm yard.

(29)

WIIY CHINESE PAINTINGS LOOK DIFFERENT

"Is Europe the only place where people paint pictures?" Barbara asked her Uncle Frank.

"Of course not, silly!" Billy exclaimed. "There were the Ancient Egyptians, and the Babylonians, and——"

"That'll do," his uncle interrupted, laughing. "You're quite right, but I don't think it's exactly what Barbara means. The old races you're talking about were not European, but they all lived close to Europe, round the Mediterranean Sea, and it was out of their civilizations that ours grew. I fancy your sister is thinking of the many other parts of our large earth, and the answer to her question is, No, Europeans are not by any means the only people to have practised painting. There have been

This clever Chinese silk painting of a fish comes from the Museum of Asiatic Art in Paris.

great artists in Persia, India, and among the Arabs of the Middle Ages whom we fought in the Crusades. And on the other side of the world there were painters among the races that lived in North and South America before Columbus sailed there. But perhaps the foreign painting best known to us is that of China and Japan. I should be very surprised if you two haven't seen at least one or two Chinese or Japanese pictures somewhere or other."

"Yes, we have," Barbara admitted. "But they were so tremendously different from all the pictures you've been showing us I quite forgot them."

Uncle Frank smiled. "They *are* tremendously different," he said, "and I'll tell you a few of the reasons why. In the first place, instead of being painted on canvas or wood or copper, they are painted on paper made from rice, or on specially prepared silk. Secondly, only water-colours and inks are used—no oils or tempera. In the old days the inks were often made by a secret process handed down in one family. And thirdly,

A good example of the delicacy of the brushwork of some of the earlier Chinese artists can be seen in this quaint little picture of a wise man and child on a donkey, from a series of letter-papers.

you must remember that Chinese and Japanese paintings were not made to be framed and set permanently on view, like ours, but were either pages in an album or long scrolls, kept rolled up and only unfurled and displayed for short periods in a place of honour during a celebration, or for the pleasure of art-loving guests. The nearest they came to permanent display was when the Japanese developed a liking for painted folding screens."

"I think it's a shame they should be kept rolled up," Billy remarked. "I've seen some jolly nice Chinese pictures."

"I'm sure you have," Uncle Frank agreed. "But I still haven't come to the end of the reasons why they look strange to us. It isn't only that the Chinese used unfamiliar materials and shapes. They had a very different method of painting as well. In Europe, for several

These lifelike birds come from an ancient Indo-Persian silk painting.

160

centuries, every artist has worked by the rules of what is known as *perspective*. Briefly this means that not only do things look smaller the farther away they are, but all parallel lines—like railway tracks or the opposite sides of a table—appear to get closer together the farther away they go from us. If you're not clear what I mean, just look out of this window and see how the road seems to taper as it goes away.

"Well, the Chinese and Japanese painters have very seldom used our rules of perspective. Their way of showing distance is simply to place the more distant things higher in the picture, and of course the result appears rather odd to us."

"That's like a willow-pattern plate," Billy said, remembering the blue and white design on his grandmother's tea-service.

"Yes, willow-pattern is a good example. It shows how this method makes many Chinese scenes look as though you were seeing them from the roof or halfway up a mountain. Imagine how strange our European pictures would look

Chinese penwork can be seen to advantage in this landscape with figures.

An attractive woodcut by Hiroshige, a Japanese artist who lived from 1797 to 1858.

"Geese by Stream," painted by the 15th-century Chinese artist Lin Liang. (From the British Museum.)

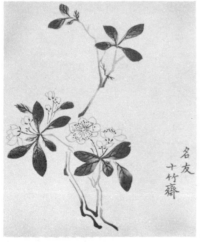

Beauty and economy of line are seen in this delicate Chinese flower study.

ANSWER THIS

Why did the Oriental artists so often draw only the tops of their mountains?

if they seemed to have been painted from the top of a church tower."

"Chinese pictures," Billy said thoughtfully, "show a great many mountains."

"They do," agreed Uncle Frank. "Our discovery that most of the best landscape painters lived in flat countries certainly doesn't apply in the Far East. And if you've noticed the mountains you must have noticed, too, how often only the tops are drawn, as if the lower slopes were hidden by mist. There's a highly interesting reason for that. Just like some of our artists today, the old Chinese and Japanese artists were much less concerned with showing a thing as it looks to the eye, than with finding its inner meaning. This led them to invent a sort of short-cut system—depicting only as much of their subject as was necessary to make it recognizable, and leaving out the rest. They worked with certain simple brush-strokes. Some of these strokes actually had names, like 'cow's shoulder' for the wrinkles on a mountain or 'crab claw' for a bunch of pine needles. So you see, there are many reasons why we should find Chinese and Japanese paintings different."

This old Persian design is called "Four Horses." Can you see why? (This picture is reproduced by courtesy of The Museum of Fine Arts, Boston, U.S.A.)

PICTURES THAT MAKE US LAUGH

This is how General de Gaulle appeared in a cartoon.

"WHAT a funny drawing of General de Gaulle," exclaimed Barbara one day as she picked up an old newspaper. She was looking at the drawing you see on the left.

"Yes, it is," said Uncle Frank. "It's a caricature."

"What's a caricature?" said Billy.

"This is," said Barbara, showing it to him.

"Yes, but what does it mean?"

"Oh, a caricature is a drawing of a person done in such a way as to make us laugh."

"But it's very like him," said Billy.

"Yes, indeed," said his uncle. "It is by a caricaturist who is also a good artist. Such caricatures are never so exaggerated as not to bear a real resemblance to his victim." (And perhaps if the children had seen the photograph below on the right, they would have marvelled even more at the likeness.)

"But, of course," went on his uncle, "the secret of the art of the caricaturist *is* to exaggerate. If you have big ears he will always give you big ears. If you are inclined to have a longish nose, he will give you, unmistakably, a long nose. If you are a bit of a dandy in your dress, you will be more dandified than you ever thought yourself to be. If you are small, you will be very small; and if you are big and broad and shaggy-haired you will all but roar like a lion. And if you have the tiniest suggestion of a piggy face, it will not be overlooked. In fact the good caricaturist pounces on those features which are anything but your best features and comically exaggerates them. Everyone of us can be caricatured for we all have little weaknesses."

"There are often drawings like that in Daddy's newspapers," said Billy.

Here is a photograph of General de Gaulle. You can see how, in the drawing above, the artist emphasized his most prominent features.

163

Mr Micawber makes a speech in a scene from *David Copperfield*, illustrated by Phiz.

A "Reversible Face" from *Oho!* by Rex and Laurence Whistler. Turn this drawing of Cinderella by Rex Whistler upside down and you will see the Fairy Godmother.

"Yes indeed. Many papers employ a caricaturist to draw politicians who are 'in the news.' Usually he shows them doing something quite silly or even impossible, which he uses to show how their real-life actions appear to him. This kind of sketch, in which the actions of the characters are more important than their portraits, we call a cartoon."

"Weren't there any caricatures or cartoons before we had newspapers?" Barbara inquired.

"Oh yes. Our friends Goya and Hogarth were brilliant cartoonists and caricaturists as well as fine artists. Goya, in fact, is probably the cleverest cartoonist who has ever lived. But some of the unknown men who did so much carving in our churches in the Middle Ages were good caricaturists long before even Hogarth—although I must admit that not every medieval picture that we find amusing was meant to be so! And farther back still, some of the vases decorated by the Ancient Greeks show scenes that are first-class cartoons. The first caricature, in fact, was probably drawn by a cave-man on the wall of the cave !"

"Really !" cried Billy, impressed. "But I thought funny pictures were always *drawn*, like the ones in *Punch*. Now you say they include paintings and sculptures and even Greek vases."

Uncle Frank laughed. "Why not ?" he asked; and going over to a shelf, he took off it a little clay statuette that the children had never seen before. It showed a tall, thin man with a fierce moustache and a scraggy neck, wearing a battered top-hat and long-tailed coat and standing in a defiant attitude with his hands in his trouser pockets. "I've only just bought this," Uncle Frank explained. "It's a copy of *Ratapoil*, one of my favourite caricatures, made about a hundred years ago by a Frenchman named Daumier. Ratapoil wasn't a real man, but just Daumier's mischievous idea of any typical member of a certain political party. For some years his wife hid the figure for fear the party's supporters would come and smash it in their annoyance !"

"I suppose you have to be grown up to know what cartoons *mean* without having to be told," said Barbara, looking rather glum.

One of the best caricatures ever made of George Bernard Shaw is this one by Ruth, because it shows something of his character as well as his outward appearance. Compare it with the photograph of Shaw on page 92.

This famous cartoon by Honoré Daumier, called "Le Bon Argument," makes fun of a lawyer presenting his client's case in a French law court.

"The Mad Hatter's Tea Party"—one of the illustrations by Sir John Tenniel to Lewis Carroll's *Alice in Wonderland*. It shows Alice, the March Hare, the Dormouse, and the Mad Hatter having tea.

"The sort that deal with politics and grown-up subjects, yes," her uncle admitted. "But," he added cheerfully, "there are plenty of cartoons that are just funny exaggerations of scenes you can understand for yourself. If you don't believe it, just remember what I've said next time you look at the pictures in *Alice in Wonderland*!"

ANSWER THIS

How do cartoonists get a likeness of the people they are drawing and at the same time make us laugh?

(31)

WHY MEN MAKE STATUES

A Mexican god. (In the National Museum of Anthropology, Mexico.)

"I SAY—are you making a statue?" Billy asked one day. He and Barbara had gone to their Uncle Frank's studio, as they had so often done before, to watch him paint. But this time his easel and canvases were laid aside and the artist was busy chipping away at a large block of stone.

"Yes, I am," Uncle Frank answered. "But you needn't look so astonished, both of you. I'm not the first artist to have gone in for sculpture as well as painting. Remember our old friends Michelangelo and Leonardo da Vinci? Not that I'm anything like as good as they are," he added modestly.

"But if you can paint well," Barbara said, "why should you *want* to make statues?"

Uncle Frank put down his chisel and began

166

to fill his pipe. "Ah, now you're bringing us right to the heart of the matter," he said. "Why, indeed, do we bother to make statues? It's untidy work, it's slow, it takes up a lot of room, and as often as not the finished article is too heavy to be easily moved like a picture. On the other hand, a piece of sculpture has one thing—or perhaps I should say three things—that no painting ever has: namely, two sides and a back! Have you ever thought how even the cleverest *picture* only shows you one flat surface whereas even a bad statue is at least something you can walk all round?"

"Why should you want to walk all round it though?" Barbara persisted. "I've never heard of anyone being disappointed because they couldn't walk all round a painting."

Uncle Frank and Billy laughed at this. "Quite true," Uncle Frank admitted. "But having two sides and a back makes one big difference even if you look at a statue only from in front, as you do a painting—the statue has *real shadows*. Of course painters use shading or

This statue of the Egyptian Pharaoh or King, Rameses II, is now in the Egyptian Museum at Turin, Italy.

The lions of Naxos marble, Delos, date from the time when Delos was the religious capital of the Greek islands in the Aegean Sea.

dark colour to indicate shadows, but the sculptor's pleasure lies in using the real shadows as the painter uses his colours."

"Is that why statues are never coloured?" Billy inquired.

"One of the reasons, though it is not quite true to say that sculpture is never coloured. The Ancient Egyptians coloured many of their figures, and you yourselves have probably seen examples of coloured medieval sculpture in churches. Furthermore, it may surprise you to know that many of the beautiful Greek statues were originally coloured. But another reason why in general we don't like coloured sculpture is that it hides the beauty of the material used. And that, by the way, is another cause of our having sculptors—they enjoy showing off the loveliness of their material. No painter ever painted because he wanted to show off the loveliness of a piece of canvas or a plastered wall!"

"I thought all sculpture was done in stone," said Billy in some astonishment.

Part of an ivory carving 12 inches high showing the "Adoration of the Magi." It is probably English, done about A.D. 1100. You can see it in the Victoria and Albert Museum, London.

"Seated Cat," Egyptian, made about 400 B.C. (In the former State Museum, Berlin.)

"Oh, dear me, no!" said his uncle. "But even plain stone can give you a feeling of strength and dignity that it would be a shame to hide underneath paint. However, in addition to stone, sculptors have used wood, ivory, jade, bronze, clay, and several other materials."

"But bronze is metal," Barbara objected. "Isn't it too hard to carve?"

"Yes. Sculpture, you see, is really of three sorts. There is the sort that includes stone, ivory, wood, and jade, all of which are carved. Then there are plaster and clay (including china clay), which are shaped or modelled in a soft state—like plasticine—and afterwards hardened; and finally there are metals, gold, silver, lead, aluminium and bronze. Bronze is the most used, and is treated like this. First the sculptor makes his statue very carefully in clay or perhaps wax. When this is hard he coats it with plaster, which also hardens. Then he cuts the plaster away in sections, sticks them together again, and has a hollow plaster *mould*, as we call it, the inside of which is shaped exactly like the statue. The bronze is made liquid by heating and then poured into the mould. When it has cooled and hardened the plaster is once more cut away, and there is the bronze statue! It's really very similar to what a cook does when she makes a blancmange or jelly 'shape,' except that she has an aluminium or plastics mould instead of having to make a plaster one.

"If the statue, or it may be a group, is too complicated to be cast in one mould it is made piece by piece, and the pieces are then joined up. Finally the sculptor finishes off the work by cutting or scratching in some of the finer details with a sharp tool. So you see, sculpture can mean other things besides chipping pieces off a lump of stone!"

"Head of a Negress," in Italian marble, done in the 16th century. This head is in the Victoria and Albert Museum, London.

(32)

TELLING STORIES IN STONE

THE next time the children called at Uncle Frank's studio he was again at work on his statue.

"It must take a very long time, chipping away all that stone," said Billy. "Making a bronze statue sounds much quicker."

"It is as a rule," Uncle Frank admitted. "But just as, in painting, oil seems right for some subjects, water-colours for others, and pastel or tempera for others again, so in sculpture some things can only be made really satisfyingly in strong, solemn-looking stone, while others, for example, where there are flying garments or long, thin bits sticking out on their own, are better in bronze because it does not get broken so easily. Even with stone, some subjects that look right in rough granite would

"The Horse." Italian Renaissance, 15th-century bronze. The design was taken from a draft by Leonardo da Vinci. It belongs to the former State Museum, Berlin.

169

"Great Fountain of Neptune" made by Ammanati in 1576 in the Piazza della Signoria, Florence.

not be nearly so pleasing in shiny marble, and some marble subjects would never do in granite. The Ancients found that out quite early."

"Sculpture must be terribly old," Barbara said thoughtfully. "How did it start?"

"It's so old," Uncle Frank replied, "we don't really know. Probably a queerly-shaped bone or pebble or bit of wood reminded some early cave-dweller of a human figure or an animal, and he began to look out for others. Then one of his descendants—for this kind of progress took place unbelievably slowly—had the bright idea of improving the likeness of one of these objects by cutting it a little with his hunting-knife. And gradually, over further generations, this notion of 'improvement' developed until the improvers—the first sculptors—cared less and less about any original likeness in the objects they worked on, and in the end were ready to carve *any* piece of stone or bone or wood to the shape they wanted."

"Why did they like to make such shapes at all?" Barbara asked.

"Like the early cave paintings I told you about, it was all connected with magic at first, and then religion. Most of the ancient peoples made statues of gods and goddesses long before they made them of mere human beings. But one rather exciting early use of sculpture was for the telling of stories. You remember our talking about the Ancient Egyptian picture-stories that are like modern film strips? Sometimes the Egyptians carved their stories instead of painting them; and when the Greeks, and later the Romans, came along they made this method into one of great beauty."

"You mean there were rows of little statues, like toy soldiers?" Barbara asked.

Uncle Frank smiled. "Not quite," he said. "You see, there's more than one type of sculpture. First, there are statues and groups

This grim-faced head belongs to General Gattamelata and is part of a horse-and-rider statue in Padua, made by Donatello.

170

Part of the sculptures from the frieze on the Temple of the Parthenon at Athens. It was carved under the supervision of the famous sculptor, Phidias. This is part of the collection known as the Elgin Marbles, in the British Museum.

that you can see all round, like the one I'm at work on here. They're called sculpture *in the round*. Then there's the kind you often see bordering the doorways of medieval cathedrals, where the figures are nearly round, but remain attached at the back or base to the stone they are cut from. These are called sculpture in *high relief*. Finally there are carvings that are raised only a little from the surface of the surrounding stone—just enough to make the shadows we have found are so important—and these are said to be in *low relief*. The designs on a new coin will give you a very good idea of what low relief looks like."

"I should think low relief is the easiest to tell stories in," Billy remarked.

5th-century fountain in the shape of a carved head in Rome.

171

A good example of low-relief work is this powerful figure of an Assyrian god.

"It is," Uncle Frank agreed. "The most famous in the world was carved more than two thousand years ago in Greece, where it formed a decorative band all round the top of the most beautiful temple in Athens, the Parthenon. When a strip-picture goes all round the top of a building like that we call it a *frieze*."

"What story did it tell?" inquired Barbara.

"Actually it didn't," Uncle Frank admitted. "It showed a great procession instead. But some reliefs told chapters of real history. One of the Roman emperors, Trajan, had the story of two long military campaigns recorded in relief on a stone column that still stands in Rome. The record winds round and round the column in a spiral band over two hundred yards long, with one hundred and fifty-five separate and beautifully carved pictures !

"In Christian times most stories told in relief were scriptural ones. The most wonderful was

This is a reconstructed model of the Parthenon as it may have looked over two thousand years ago. Enough remains of the original building to erect accurate models like this one in the Metropolitan Museum of Art, New York.

the work of an Italian artist, Ghiberti, who died 500 years ago. His masterpiece was not a frieze or a column, but a pair of doors for the Church of St. John the Baptist in Florence. The doors are made of bronze, and divided into ten panels, each representing a scene from the Old Testament. So lovely is the work that Michelangelo said the doors were worthy to be the gates of paradise."

"I suppose they took ages to do!" exclaimed Billy.

Uncle Frank nodded. "It's hard to believe," he said, "but these two doors, together with another pair—also bronze—that Ghiberti had made just before them, took him *forty-nine years*. Next time you think carving on stone is slow, just remember that!"

The bronze doors which Ghiberti made for the eastern entrance of the Baptistery, Florence.

(33)

THREE REMARKABLE SCULPTORS

"UNCLE," said Billy, "have there been more sculptors than painters in the world?"

"What an impossible question!" Uncle Frank laughed. "I can tell you one thing, though: that in European art we know far more painters' names than sculptors'. That's because much more sculpture than painting has survived from ancient Greece and Rome, and in very few cases do we know who did the sculpting; nor do we know who did most of the medieval carving that decorates our churches and cathedrals. But we know who painted nearly all the pictures that have come down to us through the ages."

"Don't we know the names of *any* ancient sculptors?" asked Barbara.

"Oh, yes, some of the Greeks, for example, because we can read about them in Greek writings. But although classical Greek sculpture is the most beautiful the world has ever known,

The statue of Zeus at Olympia was the work of Phidias and was regarded as one of the Seven Wonders of the World. It may have looked like this.

173

"Moses" is one of Michelangelo's majestic masterpieces. It was made for the tomb of Pope Julius II.

Michelangelo's gigantic statue of "David" suggests both confidence and watchfulness.

there are only one or two statues that we can definitely say were made by a particular artist."

"What about the procession carved all round the Greek temple, about which you were telling us last time," Billy said. "Doesn't anyone know who made that?"

"Ah, you mean the Parthenon and its famous frieze. Yes, we do know that the frieze and the other Parthenon sculptures were designed by a certain Phidias, who was born about 500 years before Christ. But like Rubens the Flemish painter, Phidias made his work go farther by also employing other sculptors to work for him, so that it is impossible to point to any one figure and say it is by the master's own hand. Unfortunately the figure that we know from history that he *did* fashion with his own hand has disappeared. This was a tremendous statue of the goddess Athena made to occupy the inside of the Parthenon. Imagine a figure as tall as six real men one on top of the other, her face, arms and feet of shining ivory and her dress covered with pure gold!"

"It must have been wonderful!" Barbara gasped. "How did it disappear?"

"It was thrown down when Christianity replaced the pagan religion, and then all the valuable gold and ivory were stolen. The same thing happened to an even greater statue that Phidias made of Zeus, the father of the gods, at a place called Olympia. So marvellous did the ancients think this figure of Zeus that they included it among the Seven Wonders of the World."

"Was Phidias as great as Michelangelo?"

"It's a matter of opinion, but *I* think so," Uncle Frank answered. "Phidias was the greatest sculptor of the ancient world, and Michelangelo of the medieval world. You remember how strong and muscular Michelangelo's painted figures are? His sculptured figures are just the same, especially later ones. Look, you see this

174

PETER PAN BY GEORGE FRAMPTON IN KENSINGTON GARDENS, LONDON

THIS CHARMING SCENE OF *THE NATIVITY* IS THE WORK OF A FAMOUS FLORENTINE, LUCA DELLA ROBBIA. IT IS MODELLED OUT OF GLAZED TERRACOTTA AND MEASURES OVER FOUR AND A HALF FEET ACROSS (IN THE VICTORIA AND ALBERT MUSEUM, LONDON)

little statue?" He pointed to a carved figure standing on top of the bookshelves. "That's a small copy of a statue of Moses that Michelangelo designed for the tomb of a pope. Even in this tiny size it looks striking, but the original is enormous—much bigger than life-size—and I don't think anyone could see it and not feel awed. It's a bit like the feeling you get in the presence of someone you know is very famous or important. And that's the impression most of Michelangelo's sculptures give you."

"Does anyone make statues like that now?" inquired Barbara, her eyes on Uncle Frank's own half-finished effort.

Uncle Frank saw the glance and smiled. "Great artists are as rare today as they have always been," he answered. "And like painters, modern sculptors try out such queer new styles that it makes comparison difficult. However, leaving aside the *very* modern stylists, there is one sculptor of the present time about whom you should know. His name was Jacob Epstein, and even he was much too 'modern' for some people! This is because, like El Greco the painter, he often made his figures very long and thin; or on the other hand he sometimes made them very squat and thick-limbed. But there's no doubt that his figures *are* impressive, whether they're in stone or bronze. You may like them or hate them, but you can't see one and merely feel bored. Quite a number of his works are to be seen in London, some of them decorating the outsides of buildings; so next time you have the chance, ask your Dad or Mum to point some out to you, and then see what *you* think!"

"I wish you'd tell us about the *really* modern sculpture," said Billy.

"I will with pleasure, next time you come. And I'll tell you one thing now to be getting on with. In spite of what I've just said about queer *new* styles, modern sculpture isn't always quite as new as you suppose!"

This splendid bust of Cunningham-Graham shows you very clearly Epstein's rugged technique.

"Madonna and Child" by Epstein. This more than life-size statue is attached to the wall above the entrance to the Madonna and the Holy Child Convent in Cavendish Square, London.

MODERN SCULPTURE ISN'T SO NEW

This Cypriot terracotta statuette of a man riding a long-necked horse was probably modelled nearly two thousand years ago. It is in the Metropolitan Museum of Art, New York.

"You don't seem to have got very far with your statue !" Barbara said to her uncle when she and Billy paid their next visit to the studio.

Uncle Frank pretended to look indignant. "Well, I like that !" he protested. "When I've almost finished it, indeed !"

Certainly it did not look finished to the children, for although the stone had been shaped to the vague outlines of a human figure, there were no separate arms, legs, face, or any detailed features. Uncle Frank began to explain.

"We've had a chat or two about modern painting," he said, "so it ought not to surprise you that there is very modern sculpture as well. When I spoke about Epstein I told you there were sculptors with even stranger ideas. Do you remember how we found that modern painting began with the impression made on a group of

Henry Moore gazes thoughtfully at his famous "Reclining Figure." It took him eight months to make and caused quite a stir when it was first shown.

young French artists by the work of Constable and Turner? Modern sculpture too can be said to have been started by one man. He was a Frenchman named Aristide Maillol, and he died only a few years ago. He felt that sculptors were trying to copy reality much too closely, without using their imagination; their statues, in fact, were becoming as uninteresting as those paintings that are no better than coloured photographs.

"So Maillol tried to go back to the sort of sculptures that were made in ancient Greece and even earlier times. As a result, these statues, which are nearly all figures of women, are graceful as women should be, but strong and vigorous-looking instead of unexciting and rather 'flabby.' Naturally they made a great impression, especially on other sculptors, who began to study with fresh attention the work not only of the early Greeks, but of the Egyptians, Indians, Chinese, African Negroes, and the ancient peoples of Central and South America."

"Did all these countries do sculpture in the same way?" Barbara asked.

"No, though it's surprising how often their efforts resemble one another. But in the new craze to follow Maillol's example and return to a type of sculpture that really showed how the sculptor saw his subject, people felt that all the early work we still consider beautiful or great could teach them something. Which was true."

"Did they just copy?" asked Billy.

"Not at all; each sculptor tried, and still does try, to bring his own way of seeing and thinking to his work. But it is amusing to find how often pieces of statuary we think of as very modern might have come from the same workshop as other pieces carved or moulded hundreds of years ago in India or darkest Africa or Mexico. I can show you what I mean."

Moving across to the bookshelf, Uncle Frank took out two books and handed them to the

A graceful study in stone called "Girl with Guitar" by Mestrovic. It is in the Tate Gallery, London.

Rodin's famous statue of "The Thinker," in the Louvre, Paris.

179

"Sarah" is a skilfully modelled head in bronze by Frank Dobson.

children. One book was called *Sculpture in the Ancient World* and the other *Sculpture in the Twentieth Century*. "Look at the pictures in these," he went on, "and see how many modern works you can match, so to speak, with those made by ancient or *primitive* races, as we call the less experienced and educated ones. You'll find quite a lot of similarities, for even when sculptors had become used to Maillol's ideas and started to think out others of their own, most of them still took the primitive sculptures for their models and followed the same rules."

"What sort of ideas did they have?" Barbara inquired.

"Well, they would say to themselves, 'Sculpture shows the *shape* of a thing. Therefore why not try to express *just* the shape of a human body or an animal or whatever it is, without diverting the attention with any details? Or if certain shapes can give pleasure just because they're shaped the way they are'—and they can, you know—'why not try sculptures that are *only* pleasant shapes, without any other meaning?' This is the sort of reasoning that has led to most of the present-day sculpture that appears so queer to many people."

"Why, here's a lady with no middle!" exclaimed Barbara suddenly, staring at one of the pictures in the Twentieth-Century book.

Her uncle bent to look. "Yes, that's by Henry Moore," he said, "perhaps the best known of all the triers of new ideas. Moore has reasoned : 'we are more-or-less hollow inside, so why not let a statue show the same contrast between the solid and hollow parts?' You may think Moore's ideas really *must* be new. Yet he was one of the keenest students of primitive sculpture, especially African and Mexican, and his ideas owe a lot to those early artists. It is often said there are few things in this world that haven't been tried somewhere before, and that's certainly true of sculpture !"

In contrast to the above is this bronze head of a Queen Mother of Benin, in Southern Nigeria, in the 16th century. The high head-dress bent forward, is traditionally worn by women. (In the British Museum.)

180

The Story of our Buildings

OUR distant ancestors needed shelter from the weather and wild beasts almost as much as they needed food and drink. How did they get on? They progressed from caves to covered-in pits and thence through buildings that grew more weatherproof, more skilful in construction, more convenient to live in, until there developed a real home, often a thing of beauty as well as a place of comfort.

(35)

A ROOF OVER ONE'S HEAD

IT was Billy's birthday, and he was looking at the pictures in Uncle Frank's present—pictures of the kinds of dwellings in which men lived hundreds of years ago.

"It's a wonderful book," said Billy.

"Yes," cried Barbara, "it's lovely! But oh, uncle! Do tell us why people lived in such funny places."

"Some of the early people," replied their uncle, "lived in rock shelters, open caves with an overhanging roof. The climate was warmer than it is today, and man's home was already made for him. Later, because the weather grew colder, he went to live in caves above or below ground. Some people in Spain, Italy and Africa live in them still. Then early man later made himself pit dwellings—small or long trenches for warmth and safety. They weren't much to look at but they served their purpose."

"A sort of hole in the ground with a roof," said Bill.

"That's just about it—a roof made of trunks of trees or brushwood, which he could cut down for himself."

"What other kinds of houses did the people make?" asked Barbara.

Long ago, before they had learned to build themselves proper homes, people used to take shelter in caves like this one.

181

For hundreds of years many Red Indian tribes have lived in tents made from poles covered with the skins of animals. Besides being easy to put up, these tepees or wigwams, as they are called, could be taken with them as they wandered across the prairies.

"Rings of fairly large stones, mixed with smaller ones. We saw them on Dartmoor last year. Sometimes they were covered with earth with an opening for the door, and a pole in the middle to which wickerwork or brushwood was fastened and held in place by the stones. In Scotland, two well-built houses have been found, without a central post, roofed by boughs wedged into the walls and then covered with turf and bracken. The part of the walls resting on the ground was made of bigger stones than the rest to keep them firm."

"When were these houses made?"

"Between fifteen hundred and two thousand years ago, many of them, and today in parts of Africa, people are still living in similar ones."

"What a long time ago," said Barbara. "Tell us what other kinds of houses people had then."

These stone huts shaped like beehives were built by a tribe of Celts more than a thousand years ago. On the right is a Celtic cross, which shows that by this time the Celtic peoples had been converted to Christianity.

Scattered about the countryside in Britain you can see rings of stone like this.

182

"In some parts of North Africa, people still live in caves which they have cut out of the ground, with rooms opening from a central court or hall. Some of the Red Indians in North America make their houses of poles lashed together at the top and covered over with skins —a pattern that is very old indeed. People who live away from towns in lonely places do not change their habits very much, and you will often find the same kind of houses being built for hundreds and hundreds of years."

"Why are houses so different?" asked Bill.

"Partly because of the materials; in a stony country, stones would be used. When wood was plentiful, that was the material. Think of the climate too. In a hot country like Africa, it might be cooler to live in underground caves; in Greenland, which I will tell you about presently, a snow hut would be kept very warm if it were sealed up with snow blocks. In those days, people were afraid of possible enemies, so the dwellings were usually in groups, so that people could help each other in time of danger."

Here is a hut with a landing stage built on the banks of the River Amazon in South America.

This native hut in Papua in the Far East is made from grass and sticks, and provides welcome shade.

183

The Eskimo's igloo, seen here, is used only as a temporary shelter. It is built entirely of blocks of ice and snow, and is stiflingly hot inside.

ANSWER THIS
Peoples in different parts of the world often live in very different sorts of houses. Why is this?

This happy gipsy family in Granada, Spain, lives in a house carved out of the cliff.

"Here is another picture of a little round house," Bill said, turning over the pages, "with stone walls and windows, and a place for the door between two big stones. Here's a lot of houses together, built like a village."

"How could they move such big stones?"

"By all helping, or by rollers up a slope. These houses are still to be seen in Cornwall, grouped round a paved courtyard. There is plenty of stone there."

"Here's a picture of an Eskimo's hut in Greenland. It says it is made of snow," said Barbara, "and the Eskimo lives in it still, as he did in the old days."

"Greenland is a very cold country in the winter," said her uncle. "There's very little but ice and snow, and the Eskimo uses them to make a temporary shelter."

"How does he make it?"

"The snow becomes hardened by the cold winds, so that the Eskimo can cut it with a knife —square blocks of frozen snow instead of blocks of stone. He builds himself a round house called an *igloo*, shaped like a beehive. He can make one in an hour, for the snow never melts. The walls become frozen and solid. He puts a pole in the middle of the hut, and lays one block of snow on the top of another, with part overhanging the one below and gradually builds up a dwelling rounded on the top, with a block to seal the opening. People in Britain roofed their stone buildings in that way. They too are called beehive huts."

."Does the Eskimo live there all the year round?" asked Bill.

"In the spring, he can make himself a deerskin hut, and in the autumn he can dig out a hut in a bank and cover it with earth and logs."

"How cosy!" said Barbara.

"Yes indeed, for at night he covers up the small entrance with skins, leaving just a little window in the roof filled with parchment

184

instead of glass, for in those Arctic regions, it is never dark in the summer and autumn, but in winter there is no daylight at all."

"The people always seemed able to find what they wanted to build their houses with," said Bill.

"That is why they were so clever. They had to make the best of what they had," replied his uncle. "In Bolivia, a country in South America, the early peoples, too, lived in stone houses, as some of them still do today, and as people did in England and elsewhere. In different parts of the world, in past times and even today, they used materials like wood and stone that they could find for themselves. In a country called New Guinea, the people live by growing food plants—coconuts and bananas and sago, and by fishing. Their houses are of wood, built on piles or wooden stakes in the swamps where their foodstuff grows. They place tree trunks across the piles or posts, and make wooden walls and roofs, joined together by wooden pins or bolts. They have lived like that for centuries. All over Europe, including Britain, people once lived in houses in, or above, lakes or swamps. Tomorrow we will go and see the site of one of these and I can show you what I mean."

"A house in a lake!" cried Barbara. "What is it like?"

"Wait and see," replied her uncle.

Here is a model, made for the Somerset Archaeological Society, of a British home of two thousand years ago. The village built by a tribe of Ancient Britons on a marshy island in the middle of a shallow lake at Glastonbury, in Somerset, is thought to have been made up of huts like this, and the picture below will give you some idea of what the village may have looked like in those days.

From bridle bits found at Glastonbury we know that the people of the lake village kept horses; and from reaping hooks (on the right), that they grew corn for food.

LIFE IN A LAKE VILLAGE

"I AM going to see the place where people lived about two thousand years ago," said Uncle Frank, the next morning after breakfast. "Would you like to come?"

"Oh, yes!" cried Bill and Barbara in one breath.

"Are we going to see houses in a lake?" asked Bill.

"You will see the site of such a village," said his uncle, pointing to a big field as they went along. As they drew nearer, they could see a little wooden hut, and a wide trench dug in the ground, in which people were apparently digging for something.

"Here's Mr. Green, who is in charge of the digging."

"Please tell us what you are looking for," said Bill.

"Two thousand years ago," said Mr. Green, "this field was a shallow lake. People of those days, called the Iron Age people because they found out the use of iron, had their winter quarters on the hills over there. In the summer, they drove their cattle down to pasture here, and built themselves houses in the water."

"Built them!" cried his listeners.

"Yes. You see those low mounds over there? They are the sites of houses covered over with soil after the people had left them, or died, and the lake dried up. We cut trenches through the mounds, and find the things they have left behind. Look here!" He pointed down into the trench. "Do you see those tree trunks sticking out of the black earth? They are the foundations of the houses. Imagine small round or square enclosures, with a foundation of wood and stones piled up, and a clay floor, some as much as sixty feet wide, the walls made of split tree

The villagers were skilled craftsmen, and made many fine pots and bowls decorated with beautiful patterns, like those shown here.

trunks, sharpened at the ends to keep them firm in the ground. One of them is lying over there."

"I see," said Barbara.

"Holes for upright posts were dug here and there to support the roof of brushwood thatch which rested on the walls, and when finished, the dwelling probably had a pointed roof."

"Weren't there any windows?" asked Bill.

"No. The people of that day did not seem to mind about darkness; the door would let in some light."

Although they had learned the use of iron, the villagers still made many articles of bronze, like this bronze bowl.

ANSWER THIS

Why do you think many people in those far-off days built their homes in the middle of lakes?

These beautifully decorated bone combs were probably used for weaving by women who lived in the lake village.

"What is that big pile of clay?" asked Barbara, lying down and leaning over the edge of the trench, pointing as he spoke.

"The hearth or fireplace, round which people gathered in the evenings to tell stories. If the clay sank into the rather damp floor, they piled another layer on top, and so on, until you may get as many as six or seven clay layers, one above another. If the floors sank, they were built up in the same way with brushwood and clay. That lady is just digging up a piece of the pots they used. They dropped their beads or their broken pots in the ashes, and it is usually beside the hearth that you find them. Miss Bent : let these people do a little digging with you; there is some more pottery over there."

"Why did they drop their things about?" asked Barbara.

"They were careless, I suppose. The hearth was the centre of the house, where everyone met after their work was done. Then things fell into the ashes, and were preserved, as we find them today."

Miss Bent handed a little trowel each to Bill and Barbara as they jumped into the trench beside her. "Dig very carefully," she said.

They dug as she did, and brought up several pieces of pots.

"Oh!" cried Bill, "there's a pattern on this piece, dots and circles."

187

"And mine's got squares and circles on it," said Barbara.

"Come into the shed," said Mr. Green, "and I will show you other things we've found. Bring your pieces of pot with you, and we will wash them and bring out the pattern."

He showed them how to wash the pieces, and then put them carefully away with many others, some patterned and some plain. They found pierced coloured beads, too, made of clay.

"For necklaces," suggested Barbara.

There were one or two amber ones as well.

"Did they find amber here?" asked Bill. "I thought you only found that by the sea."

"It was brought by a merchant from another country, perhaps France or Spain, who exchanged it for things that the people here made —bone needles, weaving combs, and so on. Trade between different countries was beginning at that time. They exchanged goods instead of paying money for them, though sometimes they used metal bars in exchange, like these."

"What's this?" asked Barbara, pointing to a kind of comb, beautifully decorated.

"That's a weaving comb," said Mr. Green. "The women wove, judging by all these loom weights that we've found, and they probably dyed the stuff, using woad for blue, and lichen for yellow colours. Then they sewed them with needles like this and fastened them with pins and brooches, called fibulae, like these."

"What did they eat?" asked Barbara.

"We find bones of some of the animals—oxen, sheep, birds of various sorts, cranes and ducks. They grew corn, and made it into flat scones. Pieces of them have been found here. They ground the flour by putting the ears of corn between two stones, called querns, sometimes round like these, or long and shaped like saddles, and so called saddle querns. They turned the stones round and round, or to and

Corn was grown on the mainland, and after it had been reaped and carried across the lake in boats, it was ground into flour and made into scones.

A woman of the lake village spinning wool in preparation for weaving into cloth.

188

fro, and so ground the wheat into flour. A boatful of corn was once dug up over there; it must have sunk on the way to the village."

"What was the boat like?" asked Bill.

"Here's a picture of it—flat bottomed, cut from a tree trunk and hollowed out—the same type of boat that the people who live on the marshes today still use. People went from one village to another by water, but they also made a raised road, called a causeway, to take them to the shore of the lake."

"They must have been very clever to make so many different things," said Bill.

"Yes, cleverer in many ways than people today. They used the materials they had—wood, clay, and stone—and made iron reaping hooks for cutting corn, pruning hooks, files, harness rings, bridle bits for their horses, and bars. We have seen their hearths, and they probably started their fires by rubbing two pieces of wood together. It is likely that some of the houses

The people of the village probably relied partly on killing wild animals for their food, and here is a hunter drawing his bow.

were burnt down. They were artists, too, not only drawing charming patterns on their pottery and woodwork, but inventing these patterns themselves. They made the pots you see, wooden bowls, and other vessels. They were what we call today 'self-supporting.'"

"Tell us what people in other countries lived in lake villages," said Bill.

"The ancient people in Ireland and Scotland lived in somewhat similar islands, called crannogs, in lakes, as places of safety from their enemies, but they were differently made from these huts."

"Do tell us about them."

"A circle of stakes was driven into the bed of the lake, then filled in with material brought from the shore in boats. If the bottom of the lake was soft and peaty, the builders made a kind of raft of tree trunks, wickerwork or brushwood, that floated on the surface. The raft was sunk with stones to the bottom of the lake, and

This woman is modelling clay into pots which will then be made ready for use by heating them beside the bonfire in the background.

made a firm foundation for the island. A fence of sticks was set up around it, and houses or enclosures of wood built upon it, and perhaps a causeway to reach the land, built zigzag so as to confuse unwary strangers. You see they were different from these huts—really little islands in a deep lake, not in shallow waters like these. In Switzerland and Austria, where these lake villages are especially common the people of that time lived in houses built on wooden platforms resting on poles right above the water."

"What fun!" said Barbara. "I should like to live in a house like that."

"We must be going now," said Uncle Frank. "This afternoon we want to see a castle where people lived in later times. Thank Mr. Green, children; he has given us a very interesting morning."

"Thank you very much!" cried Bill and Barbara together.

Here is a smith of the lake village making iron tools and weapons. Although the things he made were clumsy by our standards, they must have been in great demand.

Here you can see an artist's reconstruction of an Austrian lake village as it may have looked to some of the very early Europeans.

(37)

SECRETS OF THE CASTLE

"Do tell us something about castles, Uncle Frank," said Bill. "I've got to write about one for homework, and I really don't know anything about them."

They were standing by a ruined castle—just some walls and one tower left.

"Let's see what we can find out," said his uncle. "Do you know what castles were for?"

"Places of safety, but I don't know *exactly* what that means," said Bill.

"When the first castles were built nearly one thousand years ago," was his uncle's reply, "wars were very frequent since they could break out between rival barons as well as between rival kings. Nowadays wars are more terrible than then because of the weapons that have been invented, but the rich people—lords and barons, as they were called—made war on each other with their private soldiers, so that the owners of castles never felt sure that some neighbour was not coming to attack them. Those were the richer men; the poor people had little to lose, and were usually safe in their thatched huts. When castles were built at the time of the Norman Conquest, or just before,

The great castle at Bodiam, in Sussex, with its wide moat, was built in the days of the warring barons, when a rich man might only feel safe behind his own stout walls.

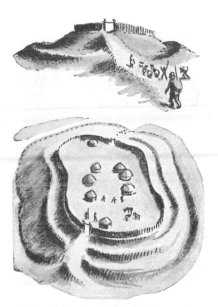

These pictures of a hill fort in prehistoric times suggest the origin of the stone castle, as in the photograph above. When there was danger of attack the cows and other animals would be driven into the stockade on the hilltop.

191

A central tower known as the keep was the most strongly fortified part of the medieval castles.

Here are the twin towers which form the gateway of the castle, with the iron gate called a portcullis raised and the drawbridge lowered to allow entry.

it was not difficult to make a fairly safe place of defence. A round mound of earth was piled up, flat on the top, with stakes round it like a fence, and a deep ditch below. It was, and still is, called by a French word *motte*. There was often a bailey or court of horseshoe shape within the fence or palisade, and also a look-out over the courtyard."

"Why," cried Bill, "here are the remains of it. Do you see? There's the ditch——"

"And I believe that's the mound!" exclaimed Barbara.

"Now we are in the courtyard," said Bill.

"What comes next?" asked Barbara.

"After that, keeps or stone buildings were built as places of safety. The whole fortress then became a tower and castle. It was usually built on a hill, like this one. After the Crusaders (you've learnt about them, I expect, Bill) came back from the Holy Land, they brought other ideas about castles with them. The next kind to be built in England had several walls and yards within the outermost wall, which was protected with square or round towers. Here are the ruins of that, I believe. There was a keep, or chief tower——"

"That tower over there," cried Bill.

"Yes. It was regarded as the strongest part of the fortress, and in case of a siege, the place of refuge for the defenders. Round it were specially strong fortifications, as there are in this case, all within the outer walls of the whole fortress."

Uncle Frank drew a plan. "Now you can see how it all was," he said.

"The castle must have been very strong," said Barbara.

"Yes. But because men are always improving on their work, the castles went on changing—developing, as it is called. Instead of always being on hills, as at first, they were often on flat ground, and the ditch was filled with water.

THE CASTLE IN OLDEN DAYS WAS A SYMBOL OF PROTECTION FOR ALL THOSE PEOPLE WHO LIVED AND WORKED NEAR-BY

THE QUIET BEAUTY OF SALISBURY CATHEDRAL

The inner walls of the fortress were strengthened; curtain walls, or places for the men-at-arms to keep watch, were built on the inner sides of the walls, and slits for spy holes placed here and there, so that the guard on duty could see enemies approaching. Look ! You can see where the curtain wall was, and the moat."

"Yes—and slits for arrows, weren't they, for the men to shoot through?" Bill was quite excited.

"All these precautions were very useful," went on Uncle Frank, "until the cannon was invented."

"What happened then?" asked Barbara.

"Towers for guns were placed at the angles of the castle, and earthworks were built against the walls. But gradually the castle fell into ruins, or was partly destroyed by firing, or became the peaceful home of some great lord or baron."

"You haven't yet told us about dungeons," said Bill.

"I am coming to that. From time to time, prisoners fell into the hands of the lord. Under the castle, with hardly any light at all, no proper windows, damp floors, and perhaps only entered by a hole in the floor through which prisoners were lowered on a rope, or by narrow winding stone stairs, were the *dungeons*, in which they were kept perhaps for years, badly fed and neglected, so that they often died. Here's the way into them."

"Let's come and look," said Bill.

"How dreadfully dark," murmured Barbara, as they went down some steep steps into a dark room with no windows.

"How did people get into the castle?" asked Bill as they came up again.

"The front of the castle was the most strongly fortified part of all. It was usually flanked by two towers——"

"There's a bit of one over there !" interrupted Bill.

Many of the castle walls contained slits like these, where the bow-men inside could aim in safety at the enemy.

Well below ground were the dungeons, where prisoners spent a miserable existence.

Part of the impressive battlements of Caernarvon Castle as they can be seen to this day in North Wales.

"One on each side, with a small courtyard between. Watch was closely kept on all comers. On these towers were soldiers, and if strangers were seen approaching, they would lower a *portcullis*, or metal grating, in front of the great wooden door, studded with nails, by which you usually entered the inner parts or precincts of the castle. The portcullis prevented enemies from entering, unless they could batter it down. There was also a drawbridge over the moat by this gateway."

"I think these are the stones that the drawbridge rested on," said Bill.

"This drawbridge could be lowered or raised," said Uncle Frank, "by the castle guards. And when you remember that there would be soldiers manning every turret as well as the main entrance, you will see that the whole castle was well defended. Well, Billy, have you got all that down?" asked his uncle, laughing.

"Not quite," admitted Bill, "but I have made a lot of notes, and I shall remember a good deal, I think. Thanks very much, Uncle; you've made it so interesting for us."

A fine view of Herstmonceux Castle in Sussex. It was built in 1440 but has since been completely restored.

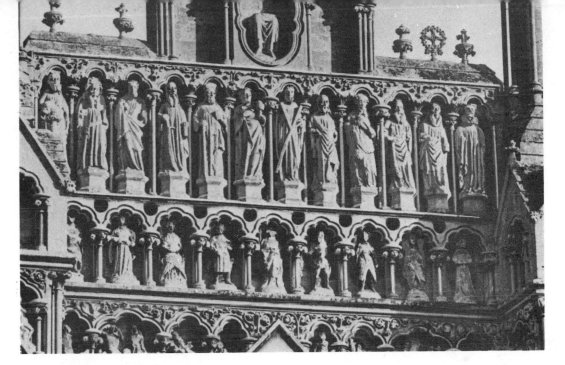

An interesting close-up of the Twelve Apostles carved on the west front of Wells Cathedral. This building was started in the 12th century under the supervision of Bishop Jocelyn.

This statue of William of Wykeham can be seen on the west front of Winchester Cathedral.

38

EXPLORING A CATHEDRAL

"WHAT a wonderful church," cried Bill in admiration.

He and Barbara were looking up at the carved figures on the front of a cathedral, angels and saints, knights in armour, crowned kings, ladies in flowing robes, and above them the figure of Our Lord.

"Tell us all about it, Uncle Frank," said Barbara.

"A cathedral is a church which contains the seat or throne of a bishop," said Uncle Frank. "Not only in England, but in other countries is this so. This one was founded a thousand years ago as a Norman church, and later on parts were pulled down or fell down, and others were added in the Gothic or later styles. This cathedral is full of all kinds of lovely work, for the best builders and carvers were employed in the building of it. Sometimes a monastery was attached to a cathedral, but this one was run by ordinary clergymen (not monks)

197

who were called canons. A church is nearly always built facing east and west. Now we are at the west front."

"There are two little square towers above the figures along the front of the church," said Bill.

"And a big tower in the middle of the church, with a row of little windows with round tops on each side," added Barbara.

"The tower is the only part left of the earliest church. Now we will go through the big west door below the carved figures into the *nave*. What do you see here?"

"Pointed arches along each side and pillars with round carved tops," said Bill.

"There is another passage behind them," added Barbara.

"Those are the *aisles*, so that you can walk round the church."

"And a little passage above the pillars, with pointed arches too, and big windows above."

The nave usually extends from the entrance to the choir or chancel.

"The passage is called the *triforium*. The line of windows is the *clerestory*, to let in light. You see the roof of the nave is curved and is of stone, with stone ribs coming from between the windows," Uncle Frank told them.

Barbara was looking at the pillars. "Here are carved leaves and flowers," she said, "and faces and a bird—and a man's head. Why are they like that, Uncle?"

"The carvers saw that the tops of the pillars, which are called *capitals*, could be carved with many different things, such as flowers, people's faces, and so on—by which they could make their work as beautiful and interesting as possible for the House of God."

They were walking down the nave now, towards a great stone arch crossing it from side to side.

"The work in the nave is called *Early English* or pointed," said Uncle Frank. "This arch is part of the tower of the earlier church which you saw outside."

Part of a carved capital in Wells Cathedral, showing a bird and other quaint figures.

198

"It has a zig-zag pattern round it," said Bill.

"Yes—the chief Norman ornament, called *chevron*. You see there are three other Norman arches, making a square enclosure in which we are standing."

"And there is a passage each side, going east and west, with windows at the ends. Such lovely patterns in glass and stone!" exclaimed Bill.

"Tell us about the windows, Uncle Frank."

"Norman windows are round and set in very thick walls; you saw them just now in the tower. The Gothic or pointed styles had pointed windows and arches. At first, they were tall and narrow but as the builders became more skilled, the walls became thinner and the windows bigger, with stonework in patterns, supported by little *shafts*. In the later Decorated style, the patterns became more beautiful and filled with coloured glass, showing stories from the Bible."

"There's Noah and the Ark in that one," cried Barbara. "He has a bright red cloak."

On the left is a typical Norman window, with a rounded top. On the right you can see the Gothic pointed type. The simple zig-zag moulding round the first window can be seen in a number of small village Norman churches.

Part of a beautiful stained glass window in Canterbury Cathedral.

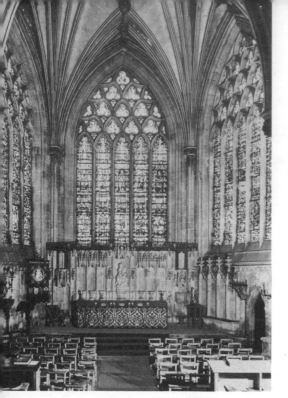

A view of the Lady Chapel in Wells Cathedral.

Coventry Cathedral, completed in 1962, is one of England's new cathedrals.

They came now to a great carved wooden screen between the choir and the nave.

"There are grapes and birds and windows, all in wood, and it has a wide top. What is it for?" asked Barbara.

"For processions on Saints' days, when the choir would sing up there," said Uncle Frank.

They went into the choir, with carved seats on either side. Beyond, behind the altar, was the Lady Chapel, dedicated, as their uncle told them, to the Mother of our Lord, with great windows filled with coloured glass, and a splendid stone roof.

"This chapel has openings on all sides," was Bill's comment, "and a stained glass window in each."

"I think these are figures of saints," said Barbara.

"I want to show you some other things," said their uncle.

He led them through the choir and down one of the aisles into a great square hall. The windows were lovely, like the others, and round the walls

below them was a band of carving with little figures, single and in groups.

"There's Joseph and his Brethren," cried Bill.

"Look, Uncle! Adam and Eve, and here's Daniel in the lions' den," exclaimed Barbara. "Fancy Bible stories carved in stone! What was this room used for?"

"The clergy of the cathedral, the dean and the canons, held, and still hold, their meetings here. It is called the *chapter house.*"

They now crossed the south transept, and went into a wide passage outside the cathedral which, with three others, was built round an open space of grass and trees. It had a carved roof overhead and big windows without glass.

"These are the *cloisters,*" said Uncle Frank. "They were used by the clergy for rest and study, and sometimes they were buried here, and, if a cathedral belonged to monks, they would come here to read or write, or sit in the sun."

"How do the walls stand up?" asked Bill, looking up at the great building.

"The walls of the Norman buildings were very thick," said his uncle, "and the roofs curved or barrel-shaped, but in the later styles they became thinner, and needed to be held up by *buttresses,* especially as the windows were so big. Buttresses were of many different kinds, some flat against the wall, but some of the later ones, which you can see from here, were called flying buttresses. Their curved tops rested against the wall between the clerestory and the vault or roof. The end of the buttresses received the push or thrust where the vault and wall met, and so held them up, two things pushing one against the other. Do you understand?"

"I think I do," said Bill rather doubtfully. "But thank you, Uncle. May we go back and look about a bit now? There are so many things I want to see again, don't you, Barbara?"

A magnificent alabaster panel on a tomb in Wells Cathedral.

Two different kinds of buttresses used for supporting walls. The one on the right is called a flying buttress.

39

THE BEAUTY OF GREEK BUILDINGS

This type of pillar, carved like the statue of a woman, was frequently used by the Greeks to adorn their temples. It is called a *Caryatid*. This example has been worn by wind and rain over the centuries.

BILL and Barbara were looking at a picture book of different countries.

"What is Greece like?" asked Bill. "Here's a picture of a temple, and another of a theatre. Do tell us about them, Uncle Frank!"

"Greece is a country of mountains and islands, warm and sunny. Thousands of years ago their buildings, many of which remain today, were some of the most beautiful in the world. The Greeks were great artists, and their buildings seem to reflect the beauty and sunshine of their country. Look at this temple," went on Uncle Frank.

"What is a temple exactly?"

"A place dedicated to the worship of different gods or goddesses. They were long walled buildings, with pillars built into the walls, open at one end, with a porch. The roof was sloped on either side, with a ridge along the top, and ended in a gable called the *pediment*. Below the pediment were the *cornice*, the *frieze*, and the *architrave*, resting on the tops of the pillars. You can see them in this picture. There are three styles or orders in Greek architecture. In the *Doric* order, the pillars have tops rather like stone cushions; the *Ionic* are curved like rams' horns round the tops of the pillars; the *Corinthian* is much more decorated with carved flowers and foliage."

"What are the lines down the pillars?" asked Barbara.

"Flutings or carved grooves. You see that the pillars taper and get smaller towards the top. The temples are set on stone floors, with steps leading into them."

"What were they built of?"

"The earliest may have been of wood—small, square rooms probably copied from the Greek houses of that time, the front or porch having only one pillar on each side. Then a porch was made by a wall across, with doors in it, and the building was lengthened. Later, the temples were built of the stone of the country, then of marble. Probably they were painted inside and out with pictures of the gods and goddesses to whom the temples were built or dedicated. There was also another kind of pillar used in the porches of temples—a beautifully carved figure of a woman, called a *Caryatid*, holding up part of the roof on her head. In one temple in Athens, the chief city of Greece, Caryatids are used in the porch instead of pillars."

"How are the temples lighted?" asked Bill.

"I am glad you asked that. Lighting was important, for inside the walls were, as I said, probably carved or painted, and had to be seen. Lamps were used sometimes; sometimes there were windows; sometimes light from overhead was let in by an opening called a clerestory between the roof and the walls."

This Greek lamp in the form of a greyhound's head holding the head of a hare in its mouth, may at one time have been used to light a Greek temple. It is now in the British Museum.

These columns show on the left the three orders or styles of Greek architecture, and on the right the two orders used by the Romans.

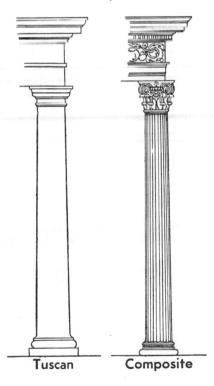

Doric   Ionic   Corinthian   Tuscan   Composite

A statue of a Greek comic actor.

"What were the theatres like?" asked Barbara.

"They were splendid buildings, open to the sky, and often placed on the sides of hills, sometimes overlooking the sea. The seats for the audience were arranged in a semi-circle of tiers or rows, one above the other. Below was a round, level enclosure called the *orchestra*, for the dancers, musicians, and perhaps some of the actors. Although the theatres are all in ruins today, we know something of how they were used. In some we can still see the real stage, or *proskenion*, on which the main actors appeared. It is a high stone platform above and facing the *orchestra*. There were great writers in early Greece, and their plays would have been acted in these theatres. The Greeks valued the poets and their work, and theatres are the largest of their public buildings. The Romans who came after them were also great builders, but their work is less beautiful."

Here is a typical Greek open-air theatre, perched on a hillside, just as it might have looked in the days when Euripides was holding his audiences spell-bound with his latest tragedy.

40

WHAT THE ROMANS LEFT US

"Do you remember going to St. Albans last year," asked Uncle Frank, "and seeing the ruins of the great Roman city of Verulamium?"

"Yes," said Bill, "but there wasn't time to see it all. You said you would tell us about it and other Roman cities."

"We are going to see one now," said Uncle Frank. "It's not very far away."

"You told us that the Romans conquered this country—Britannia, as it was called—nearly two thousand years ago," said Bill as they drove along, "and that there were a great many more cities in other places."

"Yes—especially in their homeland of Italy. The Romans were different from the Greeks— warlike, but fine builders, fond of comfort and splendour. Rome is full of fine buildings such as temples and baths——"

"Baths !" interrupted Barbara.

"We will go and look at one."

They had reached the site. Before them was a wall built of rubble and flint, with little red bricks between these materials.

"You find these bricks in most Roman buildings. Here is a bath——"

"With a lovely pavement at the bottom," said Bill. "Why, the bath has a stone wall and steps round it."

"Look !" said Uncle Frank. "There are the walls of the furnaces that warmed the baths, in which the Romans sat for hours in warm water. Then they would go from room to room until they cooled off."

"I see," cried Bill. "Those must have been the furnaces over there !"

"They were called *hypocausts*," said Uncle Frank. "Some of the baths were merely steam baths, called Turkish baths."

Apart from their magnificent public buildings the Romans built simple dwellings which were neat and useful.

A public Roman bath was also a place of entertainment where you might find shops, a library and even a theatre!

205

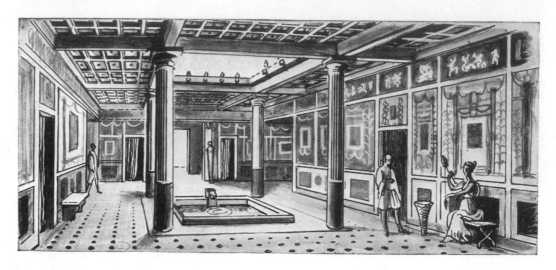

The inner courtyard of an attractive Roman house.

This typical Roman head represents the god Jupiter, and is now in the Vatican Museum.

"I know, Daddy has them sometimes," said Barbara.

"Look at that funny stone head over there, with curly hair," Barbara went on.

"Yes, the Romans often carved such heads and strange figures of their gods. That may be Neptune, the sea god."

They went along a paved street. "Do you see these ruts?" asked Uncle Frank. "They were made by Roman chariot wheels. Now we are in the *forum* or market place."

"Look at all the ruins," cried Bill. "And what's that, Uncle? Little buildings with counters in front—are they shops? They're all along the side."

"Yes. And look over there." Uncle Frank pointed to some tall pillars.

"What are those?"

"Part of a temple. It's all in ruins, but you can see the plan."

"It's rather like a Greek one, isn't it?"

"The porch was in front, and one or two pillars are left."

"Look! What's that big arch for?" asked Barbara.

"The Romans were the first people to introduce the arch into general use. You know how common it became many centuries later in Gothic architecture, Bill."

"Yes," said Bill. "In churches, wasn't it, Uncle?"

"Yes."

"How was the arch made?"

"It is difficult to explain, but I will try," said his uncle. "The arch was formed by a curve of brick or stone so arranged that half of the curve pushed against the other half, and supported it by its thrust or push. It was very widely used in Roman buildings. The great halls or *basilicas* often ended in an *apse*, or roofed arch. The windows and doorways were arched, too. When a king or emperor won a great victory, an arch like this one, decorated with figures and foliage, was dedicated to him. The arch became the chief feature, we may say, of Roman architecture. They also built graves for their dead, often arched over, too, or with pillars in the front, like the Greek temples, and temples and palaces and great round *amphitheatres*, as they were called, for sports of all kinds. But they were a cruel people, and the amphitheatres were often used for shows in which slaves fought with wild beasts. The Colosseum in Rome was a huge building seating thousands of people. The seats were arranged in

A Roman arch. These were often built to commemorate some military triumph.

ANSWER THIS

Who was Neptune, and how did the Romans honour him and keep him in mind?

A Roman forum in its simplest form, that is, a market place. The Great Forum at Rome grew into a splendid centre of magnificent buildings.

On the right is an inside view of the conduit through which the water supply passed along the top of this mighty aqueduct from the melting hill snows to the city of Rome.

A typical Roman street scene.

The carved end of a Roman sarcophagus, or coffin.

tiers, one above another. Behind the seats were arched galleries."

"I can see bits of them up there," said Bill.

"The Romans were the greatest builders ever," said Uncle Frank. "The remains of their cities are all over the world—in North Africa, Italy, Spain, Britain and even India. When they conquered a country, they began to build roads. There is one thing for which they are specially famous : huge bridges or *aqueducts* across valleys, built as a series of arches carrying channels to take water from place to place. There is a splendid one called the Pont du Gard in France. Perhaps one day you will travel and see some of these wonderful Roman buildings. I have pictures of some of them at home which I will show you."

"Are there any houses here?" asked Barbara.

"There is one over there. Come and look at the mosaic floor made of little bits of coloured stone, fitted into a pattern. The house will have had stone or brick walls—you can see a bit of one still standing, plastered and painted inside—several rooms on the ground floor, and a veranda or *loggia* with pillars. The roof was tiled; there was a *pediment*, as the Greeks called it, with figures over the portico or porch, held up by four pillars. Now we must go home. You've seen enough for one day."

"It's all very interesting," said Bill.

41

THE TUDOR HOUSE

Part of the Tudor houses which still survive in the Suffolk village of Lavenham.

Another view of the picturesque village of Lavenham, showing how well kept these old houses are.

UNCLE Frank took Bill and Barbara to visit a friend of his. They went under a big archway into a courtyard round which was built an old grey stone house.

"Please tell us about your house," said Bill, as their host met them.

"This part is the oldest," he said. "It was built in the reign of King Henry VIII, at a time when it was fashionable for rich people to travel and to bring back new ideas of building and decoration and comfort to England, where people were still living in cold, draughty castles or fortified manor houses."

"We've seen some," said Bill.

"The comfort and beauty of the houses built at that time was greater than anything known in England before."

They went through a screen of carved wood and entered the Great Hall.

"The Great Hall is the most important room," said their friend. "There are many rooms instead of only a few, as was common before this

This minstrel gallery overlooks a spacious hall in a Surrey mansion.

A fine staircase at Clandon Park in Surrey.

period. This great hall was used for entertaining. You see the *gallery* above the *screen*, where the minstrels used to play."

"What a splendid carved wooden ceiling," said Bill, looking up.

"Why are some of the windows so high up?" asked Barbara.

"To light the carved patterns on the ceiling. You see the walls and the great carved stone fireplace—all kinds of different patterns were used for decoration."

They went through a door at the far end of the hall and up a winding stone staircase built round a single stone pillar.

"This is a *newel* staircase," said their host.

"With the stairs fitted into the pillar," said Bill. "Are the stairs always made of stone, sir?"

"No, later they were often of wood. You will see some presently, but when these houses were built, people were more interested in having larger rooms, and did not trouble much about the stairs and passages leading to them. They liked to be private as well as comfortable, and had many more rooms, although some of them were small."

They were now in a narrow passage. Their host opened a door into a small panelled room.

"Why, it opens into another!" cried Barbara, running ahead, "and there are others, too, opening out of each other."

"And the windows have little panes of glass and stone pillars between them," said Bill.

"*Mullions*," said his friend.

"What lovely needlework on the walls—and curtains to that big bed," said Barbara.

"Yes, those embroidered hangings, as they are called, were made by the ladies who lived here. Now we will look at the newer part of the house, built in the reign of Elizabeth I."

He opened a door into a wide corridor, with yet another carved stone fireplace, and several

210

LITTLE MORETON HALL, CHESHIRE, AN EXAMPLE OF A TUDOR BUILDING

HORSE GUARDS, LONDON, A BUILDING ERECTED IN GEORGIAN TIMES

doors. At one end, a wide wooden staircase with carved banisters led down into another large panelled room below. It had a moulded plaster ceiling decorated with flowers and birds.

"I didn't know a house *could* be so beautiful," said Barbara.

(42)

THE GEORGIAN HOUSE

"I WANT you to see some houses built between the reigns of George I and George IV," said Uncle Frank. "I know the lady who lives in this one. Let us go in."

"What fine long windows these are, two on each side of the door," said Bill. "And with a straight parapet above."

"I think you must have been reading it up in your book of architecture!" said his uncle.

A lady welcomed them into a narrow hall with stairs at the end, and a room on either side with pale green walls, furnished with charming furniture of polished wood, made by a man named Chippendale, the lady told them.

"Look at the plaster garlands on the walls," cried Barbara.

"And figures and flowers, and vases round the fireplace," added Bill. "We've not seen anything like that before, Uncle."

"The work of the brothers Adam, who built this house. They were famous architects, whose houses are always beautifully decorated and proportioned."

"Look at the plaster *frieze* below the ceiling," said Bill.

They had walked up the staircase on to a square landing, with carved marble fireplaces and plaster friezes in the bedrooms opening from it.

"I love those low windows with square panes," sighed Barbara.

Part of the beautiful Adam decorations in the dining-room of a London house.

Part of the wall and ceiling in the music room of the same house.

"Towns were being planned more carefully at this time than ever before," said Uncle Frank, as later they walked down the street, looking at various types of houses. "The chief architects were Vanbrugh, Gibbs, Kent, the Woods of Bath (father and son), Chambers, Soane and the Adam brothers. Their work was very light and delicate, never too much decoration, but all of charming design. Notice the pretty fanlights over that door."

"And tall windows opening on to a balcony," said Bill.

"And look how pretty the ironwork is," cried Barbara.

Another house had four storeys, as Barbara pointed out, the windows separated by small pillars.

"And a low gable on the roof like the Greek temples," said Bill. "A pediment, isn't it?"

"Yes. At this period Greek designs were being introduced in English buildings," replied his uncle.

They went to see a great house, with a large portico or porch, supported on Corinthian pillars, as Bill quickly noticed, with steps from the front door dividing into two.

The north front colonnade at Stowe school in Buckinghamshire, showing the graceful lines of its 18th-century architecture.

A closer view of part of the same colonnade of this famous school.

They also visited a row of beautiful houses arranged in the form of a crescent, "all joined together," as Barbara observed, the upper storey decorated with pillars between the windows.

"And all the owners share alike in the beauty of that curve," said Uncle Frank.

ANSWER THIS

Can you name two architects who became famous for their buildings during the Georgian era?

(43)

HOW OUR GREAT-GRANDPARENTS LIVED

DID YOU KNOW THIS?

Although Victorian architecture is generally condemned today for being too ornate, the furniture of the period is already beginning to enjoy a certain value as antiques.

"I AM going to call on a very old friend of mine," said Uncle Frank.

The house they went to was one in a row of dingy brick buildings, each with a basement— "a storey below the ground where the kitchen was," said Uncle Frank—and a row of steps leading to the front door.

"What big bow windows, and—yes—four storeys altogether, and a roof with gables; it *is* ugly," was Bill's whispered comment to his sister, before they went in.

An elegant Victorian bedroom, from a design produced in 1882.

An imposing Victorian building is this headquarters of the National Liberal Club, in Whitehall Place, London.

The hall they entered was papered in dull red, though not much of it was visible, it was so covered with pictures, almost touching each other. They followed their uncle into a room in which sat a very old lady, in a black dress and white cap.

The high walls of the room were covered with pictures, painted fans, and china plates. All the chairs and tables were heavy with dark coverings, the fireplace hung with green curtains. Above was a wooden framework with panels of glass and little shelves holding ornaments of china or silver.

Uncle Frank chatted with the lady for a time and then said : "May I show the children your house? We have been studying architecture lately, and this is such a perfect example of the 19th-century house."

"Yes, do," replied their hostess. "I have lived in this house all my life. It belonged to my parents, and has never been altered."

Bill and Barbara went on tiptoe looking at everything. There were many small tables, one arranged with little silver ornaments, and one big one by the bow windows, all covered with books and china and small vases of flowers. A blue tea-set was arranged on the mantelpiece. Every available space was covered with ornaments.

"There is nowhere to put anything down," whispered Bill. "And how dark it is, with blinds drawn half-way down the windows."

The lady took Uncle Frank into another room, and Bill and Barbara were left alone.

"What an ugly wallpaper," whispered Barbara, "red and green roses—and look at the carpet—blue and pink leaves ! I've never seen anything like it before."

"And great big chairs covered in red silk," said Bill.

Presently they went into the dining-room. It was also a very lofty room, "with a black marble

A typical Victorian parlour could have looked something like this, with its over-decorated furniture, and the inevitable aspidistra in the corner.

This elaborate Victorian couch is just large enough to seat a very small child. You can see it in the Geffrye Museum in London.

mantelpiece," as Bill told his uncle afterwards, "and red velvet curtain to the windows, and *such* big furniture—great chairs covered in leather, and a great table in the middle of the room."

"That house was built in the reign of Queen Victoria," said Uncle Frank when they came out, "at a time when people were making a great deal of money, and loved to fill their houses with furniture and many ornaments. In Georgian times, the furniture was made by hand, by craftsmen; in the later period, it was often machine-made, heavy and ugly."

(44)

BUILDING TODAY

A row of houses built among the existing trees and shrubs so as to give the feel of living in the country. It is pleasant for the city worker to be able to get home to different surroundings.

UNCLE Frank was driving Bill and Barbara along a country road towards the town.

"That house over there seems part of the fields," remarked Bill. "The walls and the roof match the colour of the ground, almost as if they had grown out of it. Why is that, Uncle?"

A modern bungalow.

Compare the older type of windows (above) with the airier lighter version (below).

"Because it is built of wood and stone, the roof thatched with straw—things taken out of or from off the ground itself. Now look at those new houses !"

"Why are they so different ?"

"The parts are ready-made, turned out by thousands from the factories, concrete blocks, steel window frames, roof tiles, and so on. The people in days gone by, when that old house was built, used the materials that came to hand, and built it themselves. That is one of the chief differences between old and modern buildings."

"Why don't they build like that now ?"

"They still do in a few places, but so many houses were destroyed in the last war, and there are so many more people in the world than ever before, that new houses have to be built quickly for them to live in, and be as near to their work as possible. A few years ago," went on Uncle Frank, "I was in the Shetland Isles, and went to see a village hall of wood that the people themselves had built, the parts made and fitted together by hand, making a delightful modern building, but built by old methods, well-proportioned and well-planned. Let's look at some buildings of a different kind."

He stopped the car, and they got out.

"Here's one of the new housing estates," he said.

"What nice little houses, built two and two," said Bill.

"With big windows," added Barbara.

"Windows are a special feature of building today, to let in as much light and air as possible. These houses were built of brick, the doors and window frames all ready to be fitted together. Look at that factory over there ! Those walls are made of concrete, a mixture of crushed stone, sand and water, which hardens quickly when lime or a substance called Portland cement is added to it. The Romans used lime for their concrete in building bridges, and aqueducts to

218

carry water from place to place, but in most modern buildings Portland cement is used instead, as it hardens more strongly and quickly. You see those upright supports—they are part of a steel frame which will hold up a building just as the frame of bones holds up a human body. In this building, which will be fourteen storeys high, the steel skeleton goes up first and all the other materials—concrete, brick or tile—are hung on this strong frame.

"American *skyscrapers* are very tall buildings indeed, soaring up to as much as a hundred storeys. They rest on enormous steel columns sunk deep into solid rock."

"What are they for?" asked Barbara.

"The very tall skyscrapers are used for offices. In New York the law also forbids any building to go *straight* up for more than a certain distance above the street. This allows light to get to the lower storeys.

The Chrysler building in New York towers over its neighbours.

"Are there any skyscrapers in Britain?" asked Bill.

"Not as tall as those in America. The use of great quantities of glass and steel for lighting and strength are helping to produce different kinds of building from any known before. Look at that new school. The wall facing us is almost like a glasshouse, the windows so large that they fill nearly the whole of it. The walls and the pillars at the entrance are all made of concrete, strengthened inside by upright steel rods. Now I want to show you a brick building."

A new school built to a new design.

They were soon looking at the curving wall of a great hall ("Where the work of the city is planned," their uncle told them), crossed by three lines of large windows, a fine porch in the centre, and one on either side of the ground floor. The whole frontage was very plain and simple.

"I like it," said Bill.

This is the shopping centre of a new town. Notice that it is for shoppers only, since there is no roadway for cars or other traffic.

Blocks of modern flats like these are helping to solve the problem of over-populated areas. These estates boast many advantages, from automatic laundries to children's playgrounds and community centres.

As they came out, Bill pointed to a building ten storeys high, built round three sides of a courtyard. Some of the rooms had balconies outside the windows, all of which were large.

"What is that?" he asked.

"A new block of flats. People have been moved there from the poorer parts of the town where housing was very bad. You see there is a nice playground for the children, and baby's pram can be put out in the sun on the balcony."

"I suppose that is one of the main things an architect has to think about," mused Billy. "What a lot there is to designing a good building!"

Uncle Frank nodded. "Bill," he said, "you've touched on a most important feature in building throughout the ages. To be successful as architecture a building must be suitable for its purpose. From the smallest garage to the largest cathedral, ability to serve its purpose well and truly is the absolute essential. However beautiful a building may look to the eye, if it is ill-adapted to its purpose it is a useless building. Think of all the buildings that have served men from the lake village huts to the modern school, and you will see that every time their designers did their best to keep this one fact in mind."

The Music-Makers

Do you ever listen to music? Of course you do—you know very well what it sounds like. But have you ever wondered how it all started? Why did people begin to sing? Do you like "classical" music as much as "pop," and would you call them both *music*?
Let's find out what Billy and Barbara think of it all.

A lyre like this is a world-wide symbol for music.

Billy blew hard against the blade of grass.

(45)

MUSIC WHEREVER WE GO

A LITTLE puff of wind shivered through the new leaves, caught Mr. Wells's hat, and sent it dancing merrily along the grass in front of them.

"I'll get it!" cried Billy, as he raced ahead. Barbara giggled.

The two children had just finished a music lesson and were walking over the heath with their teacher on his way to catch a bus home. It was a bright spring day and the wind seemed to be singing little songs to itself as it chased the butterflies over the gorse bushes.

"I just love this breeze," laughed Barbara, "don't you, Mr. Wells?"

Her teacher was too busy brushing down his hat to reply. Barbara went on chattering gaily. "Do you know, I can almost hear it playing a tune sometimes. I wonder if music was invented like that."

Mr. Wells stopped suddenly. "I'm sure you're right, Barbara. Just think of it! Long before there were any people in the world there must have been music of a kind—the music of nature."

"You mean the wind whistling about through the grass like this?" asked Bill as he blew hard against a blade of grass held between his thumbs. It made a not very tuneful squawk.

221

"Not only the wind, Bill, but there was the roar and hiss of the waves on a rocky beach for instance. There would also be the angry grumble of thunder following those flashes in the sky, and the pitter patter of raindrops which would sometimes sound like a million tiny drum beats."

"I can hear these leaves around us now making a noise," said Barbara as she bent her head to listen.

"And water over stones too," added Bill eagerly, pointing to a nearby stream. "That makes quite a sound of its own, doesn't it?"

Mr. Wells smiled. "It certainly does. A famous English poet called Coleridge knew that too. He once wrote a long poem about the adventures of a sailor, and in one verse he describes the sound of water hurrying through the woods.

> A noise as of a hidden brook
> In the leafy month of June,
> That to the restful woods all night
> Singeth a quiet tune."

"But what about animals and insects?" asked Bill as they walked on. He hadn't thought of music in this connexion before.

Mr. Wells stopped again under a huge oak. "Just listen," he said. From a bush nearby rose the clear piping of a blackbird. "I think that's real music!" murmured Barbara as they followed the path down into a grassy hollow.

Next time you pass by a swiftly flowing stream listen carefully, and you will discover that the water has a music of its own.

222

"A great many famous musicians and poets have given us some wonderful songs through listening to the birds. The lark has always been a favourite. The great Austrian composer, Franz Schubert in a few minutes wrote the happy music for Shakespeare's 'Hark, Hark the Lark,' and later an Englishman, Henry Bishop, made a lovely use of the flute to copy the bird's notes in his 'Lo Hear the Gentle Lark.' But many birds have had songs and tunes written about them, especially the nightingale, the blackbird, the wren, the dove and the swallow."

"I can understand birds being used as models," said Bill, "but what about insects?"

"These too have been used Bill. Right now I can think of wasps, bees, grasshoppers and cockroaches."

"Yes, but these are all nature's sounds," Barbara pointed out. "What I want to know is, how did man-made music start?"

Mr. Wells was puffing a little as he climbed up the far slope. "You've heard your baby brother playing with the cat, haven't you? He says 'miaow' and tries to copy its cries to talk to it. I dare say each of you has often barked back at a dog. Well, the first human beings must very early have begun to copy all the sounds around them, first with their voices, and later with very simple instruments."

"What kind of instruments, Mr. Wells?"

"Probably the human whistle was the nearest they could get to a bird-call at first, Barbara.

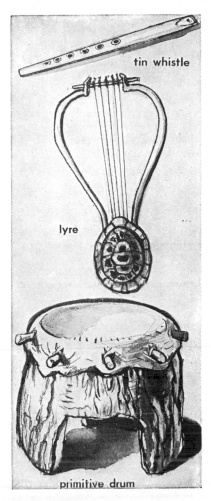

Three of the instruments which were among the earliest made by man for creating sound. They are still played today, even though their form may have changed.

Each of these insects has had music written about it. See the next page.

But the wind blowing through a hollow pipe or reed, the plucking of a tightened string against a hollow box, or the beating of a piece of skin over a frame all helped man to imitate the many sounds of nature.

"However, some people believe that dancing is the oldest art. You see, primitive man probably danced to try to influence the gods, spirits and demons of nature. It is difficult to dance in silence, as you may have already found out, so trying to dance to the voice possibly produced the first singing.

"Then there's the very interesting story of the orchestra, but that will have to wait until next week, when we have seats at the concert hall—remember? See you on Thursday," he shouted hastily, for they had reached the road just in time to meet the bus which was to take Mr. Wells home. With a wave of his hand he jumped on and was gone.

Here are the pieces of music written about the insects on the previous page.
"The Grasshoppers' Dance" by Bucalossi.
"The Flight of the Bumble-bee" by Rimsky-Korsakov.
"La Cucaracha" (Spanish for cockroach)—a famous marching song used by Mexican revolutionaries in 1916.
"The Glow Worm" by Lincke.

An orchestra performing in the Royal Festival Hall, London. This great concert hall is remarkable for its acoustic properties. It is panelled in wood for resonance, and is so well insulated against outside noise, the very busy railway line just outside is never heard at all.

THE ORCHESTRA

DO THIS

Ask somebody to take you to an orchestral concert, and when you are there see if you can recognize the various instruments and learn where their players sit. Below you see two most important stringed instruments of the orchestra, and the various instruments which make up the percussion section.

BILLY and Barbara were having an exciting evening out with Mr. Wells. To begin with they had eaten a marvellous high tea, which had been rounded off with the biggest ice creams the restaurant sold, and now they were sitting in the concert hall, full of excitement as the orchestra tuned up ready to begin the concert.

"I've just counted the number of men, and, do you know, there are eighty-six of them," said Billy.

"Yes, there's usually about that number in a symphony orchestra," answered Mr. Wells, "and sometimes more."

"Almost half of them seem to be violinists. Why do they have to have so many?"

"Well, the violin doesn't make nearly so much noise as a trumpet or trombone, so they have a lot of them to keep an even balance of sound. Actually they're not all violins, though they look like them. About a dozen of them are violas, which are a bit bigger. It's difficult to see the difference from here, but the violas play lower notes than violins. The cellos play lower still of course they're the big violins which the

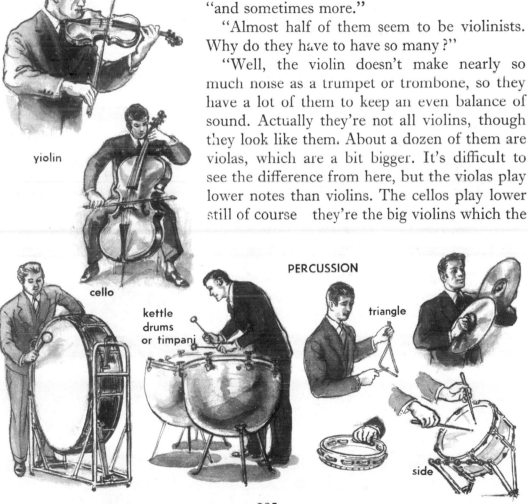

STRINGS

violin

cello

PERCUSSION

kettle drums or timpani

triangle

side

225

French horn

trombone

Two brass instruments which are
difficult to play.

men are playing between their knees. Then at the back, on the right there, are the double basses (or, simply, basses), which look like enormous violins, and play the lowest notes."

"Do the violins all play the same notes?"

"No. The violins themselves are divided into two groups, each playing their separate part. Those five groups, first violins, second violins, violas, cellos, and double basses make up what is called the 'string section,' and you notice they are spread right across the front so that they are nearest the audience."

All this time Barbara and Billy had been leaning forward in their seats looking at the orchestra as the players continued to take their places, tune their instruments and practise bits of tunes.

"I'd like to be that man at the back," said Barbara, "with all the drums round him. It must be great fun banging those."

"You mean the timpani player. Yes, I think you would enjoy playing those. They are the three timpani, or kettle drums as we sometimes call them. They are the only drums which can be tuned to definite notes. You see those other two men just nearby, they have lots of drums to look after too—the side drum, bass drum, and so on. Then they've got cymbals, a xylophone, a gong, and can you see the triangle hanging on a stand too? There are many other instruments these chaps play. All those instruments which you bang belong to the 'percussion section.'"

"How many sections are there altogether?"

"Apart from the strings and percussion there are two others, the brass and the woodwind."

"The brass is easy," said Billy. "I can see three trumpets, and just behind them are three trombones—you know, the instruments with the slide they pull in and out. There's a funny big brass instrument, open at the top; it must send its music straight up into the air. I don't recognize that!"

trumpet

tuba

Two more of the brass section.

clarinet

flute

cor anglais

oboe

piccolo

bassoon

The woodwind section.

"Ah ! That's the tuba, which plays the very low notes in the brass section."

"There are some more brass instruments just in front of all those," said Barbara. "Four of them. They look rather like enormous snails from here."

"They are the four French horns which have a warm, mellow sound. The part of the instrument into which the players put their hands is called the bell. The concert will be starting any minute now, so take a quick look at the woodwind section in the middle towards the back there. There are two flutes—see them playing their instruments across the front of their mouths. One of them is playing the piccolo at the moment—that's a small flute. A flute player is expected to play the piccolo as well. Then there are two oboes, two clarinets, and the three big instruments are bassoons."

227

The conductor in action.

The great German composer, Wagner.

While Mr. Wells was talking a man holding a violin threaded his way through the orchestra, and after bowing to the applause of the audience, sat down in the seat right at the front of the violins on the left.

"Who was that?" asked Barbara.

"That's the leader of the orchestra. He always comes in on his own."

"Is the leader always a violinist, or could he be a trumpeter or an oboe player?"

"The leader is always a violinist, and he sits at the head of the first violin section right by the conductor. It's a much more important job than most people think——"

Mr. Wells got no further because there was a tremendous burst of applause. There on the platform was the conductor, looking very smart indeed in his white tie and tails, and bowing in all directions from his rostrum. Soon the applause died down, the conductor raised his baton, and as he brought it down the orchestra burst into the overture to *The Mastersingers* by Wagner. The hall was full of rich and beautiful sounds for the next ten minutes.

When the piece was over, and the conductor had bowed to some more applause, a new person appeared, and immediately the audience started clapping again. Barbara and Billy had been so busy watching the various players blowing, scraping and banging that they hadn't really noticed a large grand piano just by the conductor's rostrum. The man who had just come on now took his seat at the piano. Taking a quick look at the programme they read, "Piano Concerto in A Minor by Grieg."

The timpani player started a roll on one of his drums. It got louder, then there was a crashing chord from the orchestra, and the pianist played a lot of very grand-sounding chords up and down the piano with both hands. It was an exciting start, and although this piece lasted quite a long time—there were in

228

TYPICAL ARRANGEMENT OF A MODERN SYMPHONY ORCHESTRA

CHOPIN COMPOSING HIS FAMOUS *REVOLUTIONARY STUDY*

fact three pieces, or movements, as the programme called them, joined together—the
audience was completely spellbound by the
sound of the piano and orchestra, sometimes
playing together, sometimes playing separately,
and occasionally almost fighting each other.

During the interval Barbara said, "That
pianist had a wonderful memory. Did you
notice that he had no music to read from at all?"

Mr. Wells didn't seem to be surprised.

"Pianists usually play concertos from
memory. Often conductors don't use any music
either, but you notice our conductor has his
scores on the desk in front of him. The score
shows everything that the orchestra should be
playing, but the players themselves only have
their own part in front of them."

"The conductor's score must be pretty
difficult!"

"It is, and to conduct properly is a very
difficult job. It's not just a matter of beating
time and telling the instruments when to come
in. Most of them know that all right anyway.
The conductor has to rehearse and direct the
players to get the best possible effects.

"Up to about a hundred years ago orchestras
didn't have full-time conductors such as there
are now. The first violin, the leader, would set
the orchestra going, and in the days when a
piano or harpsichord was used as a regular
instrument in the orchestra, not just for a
concerto like the one we've heard, the pianist
would direct the orchestra while he played.

"But orchestras were much smaller then. Our
big modern symphony orchestra is a very
recent invention, you know. It got to its present
size only during the last century. Before 1600
there were hardly any orchestras worth talking
about, and most of the instruments we use now
hadn't been invented then."

"It must cost a lot of money to run a big
orchestra like this one!"

Pietro Mascagni, an Italian composer, is famous for his opera
Cavalleria Rusticana. Here he is
as the cartoonist saw him conducting his own music in 1893.

ANSWER THIS

How does a conductor's score
differ from that of the players
in an orchestra?

Mendelssohn's manuscripts were
always neat and clear as you can
see from this copy.

"Believe me, it does. Each player is an expert musician who has had long training on his instrument, and therefore has to be paid a good salary. Really we get wonderful value for the little money we pay for our tickets. But we won't get our full value if we don't get back quickly; they are just tuning up for the second half of the concert."

ANSWER THIS

How did the orchestra manage in the days before full-time conductors were used?

(47)

THE PIANO

"WHAT a thrilling piece of music! What is it called?" asked Barbara next morning.

"It's called the *Revolutionary Study*, Barbara, and it's by Chopin. You see, Chopin was Polish, but he left Poland as a young man and settled in Paris. While he was living in Paris he heard that Warsaw, the capital of Poland, had been taken by the Russian armies —that was in 1831—and he was so angry that he wrote that furious piece of music to express his feelings. At least, that's the story told about it, and the nickname *Revolutionary Study* has stuck to the piece ever since."

Mr. Wells closed the book of music, rose from the piano, and settling in an armchair, lit his pipe.

"It is a very loud piece of music. I suppose you have to keep the loud pedal down all the time," Barbara said.

"Well, quite a lot of the time. By the way, I know lots of people call that right-hand pedal the loud pedal, but it is the wrong name for it. It is really the sustaining pedal. It can help you make the music louder, and the soft pedal certainly makes the music sound softer. When you put down the right-hand pedal with your foot all the felt dampers are lifted off the strings, and they carry on vibrating for quite a long time—until you take your foot off the pedal.

"The Music Master" by Steen. In the National Gallery, London.

Maurice Ravel, a French composer, whose works include well-known pieces for the piano.

It is because the sound carries on that it is called the sustaining pedal."

"You play a lot of music by Chopin, Mr. Wells. Is he the greatest writer of piano music?"

"Well, lots of people think so. He didn't write much besides piano music. You know his waltzes, mazurkas, polonaises, preludes, studies and so on—all wonderful music for piano. But, of course, there have been other great composers for the piano—Beethoven, Brahms, Schumann, Rachmaninov, and Debussy, for instance."

"How about Bach? You often play his music."

Mr. Wells smiled. "Yes, the odd thing is, Barbara, that Bach never wrote any of his music for the piano at all. When Bach died in 1750 the piano was still imperfect and hadn't come into favour; but it came in shortly afterwards, and Mozart played a lot on the early pianos.

When you strike a key on the piano the hammer swings forward and hits a group of metal strings, causing them to vibrate, thus producing the note you hear.

Mozart at the age of seven playing music he has composed himself.

233

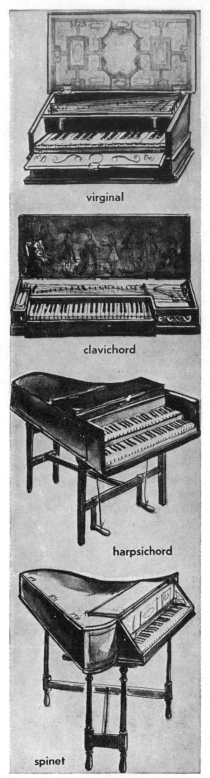

virginal

clavichord

harpsichord

spinet

Some early keyboard instruments.

They were square-shaped things then, smaller and with a much softer tone than the piano we have today. By Beethoven's time, early in the eighteen hundreds, the piano had really come to stay."

"What did they play before they had pianos then?"

"The most popular instruments were the harpsichord and the clavichord."

"I've heard of those, but I've never understood what they were."

"Well if you're interested, I've got some pictures here."

Mr. Wells reached for a book.

"Now then, this is a harpsichord. The main thing is that the strings were plucked. The plucking was done by quills—you know, from birds' feathers, or by little points of leather. These stuck out from pieces of wood called jacks, and when you pressed down a note on the keyboard the jack moved up past the string, plucking it with the quill. You can well imagine how it differed from the sound of a piano."

"More like a harp, I suppose."

"In a way, though the fact that you pluck a harp with your fingers makes a lot of difference to the sound as well. The main trouble with the harpsichord was that it didn't matter how hard or how soft you hit the key, it didn't make any noticeable difference to the loudness or softness of the sound. So they had two keyboards, sometimes more, and various gadgets working different quills and jacks to get their effects."

Billy hadn't said a word all this time, but with an air of great knowledge he suddenly asked, "What about the virginal that the first Queen Elizabeth used to play?"

"Well, the virginal, and another instrument called the spinet, were like the harpsichord, and they worked in the same way, but they were smaller and different shapes. Here you are, here are pictures of them. The strings were plucked

234

Part of a famous picture in the Louvre, called "The Music Lesson." It was painted by the Frenchman Fragonard in the 18th century.

in the spinet, virginal, and harpsichord, but the harpsichord was the most important of these instruments."

"You said something about a clavi- something-or-other just now."

"The clavichord ! Yes, now that was different again. The clavichord didn't pluck the strings, it hit them."

"Like the piano."

"No. In the piano the strings are tuned to different notes, and when the hammers hit the string they sound. But the clavichord didn't have hammers, it had pieces of metal called tangents which came up from below to press against the string. The tangent not only set the string vibrating, but also found the note wanted in the same way that a violinist finds the right note with his finger. The tangent divided the string into two parts, one part of which was permanently damped so that it would not

ANSWER THIS

Why did Bach, one of the greatest musicians of all time, never compose anything for the piano?

Edvard Grieg, 1843-1907, Norway's great composer.

235

sound, and leaving the other part free to vibrate. As the tangent pressed against the string you could keep the note going for quite a while by moving the key up and down slightly with your finger."

"Does anyone ever play a clavichord or a harpsichord today?"

"Yes, you will sometimes hear these old instruments; they are still being made; but the music of composers like Bach and Scarlatti is usually played on the piano these days. By the way, you may not have realized that the piano, or the pianoforte as it should be properly called, has its name because it could play loud and soft. Piano means soft, and forte means loud. It is Italian."

"Who was the finest pianist of all time?"

"I wouldn't like to give a definite answer to that, there have been so many great pianists: Paderewski (who was also Prime Minister of Poland for several years), Rachmaninov, Horowitz, Rubinstein and lots of others. But I

Ignace Jan Paderewski, the great Polish pianist, was also Prime Minister of his country.

The brilliant Hungarian composer and pianist, Franz Liszt, entertaining friends round the piano, during a social evening.

236

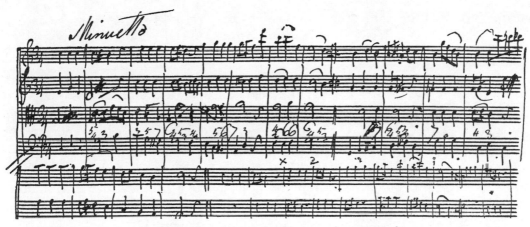

Part of the manuscript of a minuet by Mozart, showing a few corrections.

think the most celebrated was Liszt—a truly great pianist, and of course a great composer as well. Liszt was Hungarian, and he lived from 1811 to 1886, just at the time when the piano had become fairly established. He was the first great virtuoso of the piano. He was strikingly handsome to look at, and he played with such tremendous brilliance that audiences throughout Europe went mad about him. He was treated as the most popular film stars are today, and he had a similar sort of glamour. One has only to try to play some of his more difficult piano music to realize what a player he must have been."

"Did Liszt know Chopin?"

"Oh yes, they were great friends. Chopin himself was a fine pianist, but he once wrote to a friend, 'I wish I could steal from Liszt the way in which he plays my own studies!' You remember it was one of Chopin's studies I played just now—the *Revolutionary Study*."

"Play it again, Mr. Wells."

"All right. It's hard work, particularly on the left hand, but I'll play it again especially for you two. But remember I am no great player. Some day you must hear it played properly."

Mr. Wells put down his pipe. In a moment the felt hammers of the piano were hitting the strings hard, and the whole room seemed to vibrate to Chopin's stormy music.

The violinist Paganini, who inspired Liszt on the piano.

237

SONATAS AND SYMPHONIES

The great Russian composer Tchaikovsky played a major part in introducing the music of his country to the world.

ANSWER THIS

What is the difference between a symphony and a sonata?

Colin Davis conducting a symphony at a London Promenade Concert.

WHEN tea was over the children helped their mother to clear the table and to do the washing up. Afterwards they joined Mr. Wells in the sitting-room.

"You know you were telling us about symphonies having a minuet in them; I don't think I know what a symphony is. Could you play me one on the piano?"

"Well, I suppose I could, but it wouldn't be right. You see symphonies are written for orchestras to play. The same sort of thing written for the piano is called a sonata. Sometimes a sonata is for two instruments, such as violin and piano."

"I see, it is called a sonata if it is for one instrument or two, and a symphony if it is for an orchestra. But I still don't know what either of them is."

"A symphony is made up of four separate pieces of music : we call these 'movements.' So a symphony has four movements, and these are often arranged as follows :—

"The first movement is quick and fairly complicated. The second movement is slow, and much easier to listen to, a definite contrast to the first movement. The third movement is a minuet, and often quite gay; again this gives contrast to the movement before. Then to finish with, the last movement is fast and lively, something bright to round off with. That's the sort of symphony Mozart wrote."

"Did Mozart invent the symphony?"

"No. It is difficult to say who did, but Haydn is often called the 'Father of the Symphony' because he firmly established that four movement form I have just described. Haydn and Mozart lived at the same time in the 18th century. Towards the end of that century came

Shostakovich, modern Russian composer of symphonies.

Beethoven, who died in 1827, and he made one important change. The minuet was too slow for Beethoven; he wanted something much more lively, so he speeded up the minuet to make a scherzo. 'Scherzo' means 'joke,' but don't expect all scherzos to be full of good humour. A fast rhythm of three beats in a bar can sound dramatic, and some scherzos are not at all light-hearted, though according to the title they ought to be. So in Beethoven's time the accepted form of the symphony became—quick movement slow movement, scherzo, and another quick movement to end."

"How many symphonies did Beethoven write?"

"Nine, and they are amongst the greatest music of all time. Mozart wrote over forty, and some of them are played very often. You ought to hear Mozart's *Jupiter Symphony* some time; it is the last one he wrote, and perhaps his best. Haydn wrote over a hundred symphonies, but the best ones are the twelve that he wrote specially to be performed in London. You could certainly enjoy Haydn's *Surprise Symphony*, and his *Clock Symphony*."

"Have there been many other writers of symphonies since?"

"Oh yes, lots. Schubert composed nine. Brahms four, and Tchaikovsky six, for instance. There is some wonderful music in them too. The Tchaikovsky *Sixth Symphony*, for instance, has an exciting march instead of a scherzo."

"A march instead of a scherzo? Then composers change the movements if they want to."

"Yes, and when you come to some modern composers you will find they sometimes make quite big changes. For instance, Finland's great composer Sibelius has written one of his symphonies all in one movement. It all goes straight through without any stop, through slow music, quick music, and many different moods all in one movement."

DID YOU KNOW THIS?

Haydn was fond of musical jokes and his *Toy Symphony* has drums, whistles, bells, and other children's toys accompanying the melody.

A string quartet made up of (left to right) first violin, second violin, viola and cello.

Prokofiev, composer of the popular *Peter and the Wolf*, a poem set to descriptive music.

"Have sonatas gone through the same kind of changes?"

"Yes, the sonata and the symphony have developed together very much in the same way. Haydn and Mozart wrote lots of sonatas. Beethoven wrote thirty-two for the piano—you've heard me play Beethoven's *Moonlight Sonata*. Then there are sonatas by Brahms, Schumann, Chopin, and many others."

"If a symphony is for orchestra, and a sonata the same thing for piano, or for two instruments, what do you call it when it is for three instruments?"

"That's called a trio. The same thing for four instruments is a quartet, and five instruments make it a quintet."

"It's a bit complicated."

"I know it seems complicated, but remember that the important thing is to enjoy the music

240

itself, to sit back and enjoy the tunes, and the different ways the tunes are dressed up and changed by the composer. You will sometimes have to listen to a symphony several times before you really begin to understand it, but believe me it is well worth it.

"Don't be put off by the words symphony, sonata, trio, quartet, or quintet. Your knowledge of what these words mean will help, but listen to it all as music, and the more experienced you become as a listener, the more you will enjoy the music of the great composers."

Tito Gobbi, the famous operatic tenor, as Falstaff in the opera of that name.

(49)

THE STORY OF OPERA

IT was getting on for eleven o'clock at night. The front doors of the imposing opera house were a blaze of light as the audience streamed out over the red plush carpet into the street. Men in smart uniforms were popping backwards and forwards to call taxis and open car doors. There was a general hubbub of conversation and the pavement was becoming very congested with people in smart evening dress. It was from this crush of people that Billy made his way to the opposite side of the road, followed closely by Barbara. A short while after they were joined by their parents and Mr. Wells.

"I'd like to have some coffee before we start off home," said Mr. Brown. "Let's go to a restaurant."

They quickly found their way to the restaurant, and to a comfortable corner table. Some food was ordered.

"And now, Billy, what did you think of your first opera?"

"It took me a long time to get used to the fact that they were singing instead of speaking."

Joan Sutherland in Donizetti's opera, *The Daughter of the Regiment*.

241

Mr. Wells turned to Billy's sister.

"How about you, Barbara?"

"I loved it, but I did feel so sorry for Madam Butterfly. She was such a nice person—too good to die so unhappily! Do all operas have sad endings like that?"

"Oh no!" laughed Mr. Wells. "*Madam Butterfly* is a dramatic opera, like most of Puccini's operas, but there are some very funny operas, such as Rossini's *The Barber of Seville* and Verdi's *Falstaff*. Puccini's operas have a lot of fun in them sometimes. But coming back to your point about their singing instead of speaking, Billy: you've seen a lot of films haven't you?"

"I saw a jolly good one last week with Elvis Presley in it."

"I saw that too. You remember when he was strolling through the park he started singing, and with an orchestra, although there couldn't have been an orchestra for miles! In fact, he sang a lot at various times, and always with an invisible orchestra. Of course, that sort of thing is not true to life, but that doesn't spoil our enjoyment of it. The same applies to opera, only more so. An opera is a play set to music. Lots of people like music. Lots of people like music and singing, and opera gives them plenty of both."

"I wouldn't say that I've seen a great many operas," said Mr. Brown, "but there have been some I remember that were more like plays with songs added—often more speaking than singing, like the Gilbert and Sullivan operas for instance, *The Mikado*, *The Yeomen of the Guard*, and *The Pirates of Penzance*. Sullivan wrote the music, you know—first-rate tunes, too, and Gilbert wrote all the words, which are very funny."

"Of course, the Gilbert and Sullivan operas are enormous fun, Mr. Brown, but they are really operettas. Operettas are light operas, or

Rossini's *Barber of Seville* is about Figaro, a barber and the town's

Bizet's *Carmen* is about a Spanish gipsy girl loved by a soldier

busybody, who assists a count to court his lady-love.

whom she rejects as she loves a bullfighter.

comic operas, and they always have spoken words in between songs. Grand opera is sung right the way through."

"How did all this business of singing a play instead of speaking it start?"

"It started about the year 1600, and in Italy. Some Italian noblemen decided to revive the ancient drama of the Greeks. They were not absolutely sure how the Greeks performed their plays, but they thought they should be sung throughout in recitative. Recitative is a mixture of speech and song with the voice rising and falling almost as in natural speech. There are no real tunes in recitative, and I don't think there was much in the way of tunes at all in those early operas. We should certainly find them pretty dull now.

"But that was the beginning, and before long operas began to flourish so strongly in Italy that other countries began to take an interest as well. Alessandro Scarlatti was the first important opera composer in Italy, but you will hardly ever hear of his operas being performed now. Handel wrote a lot of operas in the Italian style. He was a German composer, but he became a naturalized Englishman, and most of his operas were performed in London. Gluck was another important German opera composer, and his *Orpheus* is a fine work. But after these came Mozart who only lived thirty-five years, and died in 1791 having written music of all kinds in vast quantities, including countless masterpieces. Among these were some of the greatest operas of all time. *The Marriage of Figaro*, *Don Giovanni* and *The Magic Flute* are always being performed somewhere."

"I know the overtures for all those—they are often played at concerts. What are the operas like?"

"Full of wonderful music. We must come and see them some time. *The Magic Flute* has spoken words between songs and choruses, but the

243

other two use recitative instead of spoken words, which was the usual way operas were written in the 18th century."

"You said it all began in Italy, and other countries took up the idea. Did Italy continue to develop opera?"

"Yes indeed! Italy has produced many fine operatic composers, like Bellini, Donizetti, and Rossini, but the greatest of them all was Verdi. Verdi lived in the last century, and died in 1901. He wrote a great many operas. You must have heard of *Rigoletto*, *La Traviata*, *Aïda*, *Otello*, and *Falstaff* for instance. They are always being performed all over the world. Verdi really knew how to write music to suit Italian voices, and the voice of a good Italian singer is one of the loveliest sounds you can hope to hear."

"Our music master at school says that Wagner was the greatest composer of opera."

"Well, Wagner was certainly the greatest of German opera composers. He lived at the same time as Verdi; oddly enough they were born in the same year, 1813. I think it is a waste of time trying to say who was best; they were very

Scenes from two operas by the great Italian composer Verdi. Above is a scene from *La Traviata*, set in the high society of his day. It was first performed in 1853.

different and both great geniuses. There is no doubt that Mozart, Verdi, and Wagner stand head and shoulders above most others in the field of opera."

"In what way was Wagner different from Verdi?"

"Well, when you go to see and hear an opera by Verdi, the voice is the most important thing, and often the accompaniment is very simple, and the orchestra plays fairly quietly to let the voices come through easily. But in Wagner's operas the orchestra is always an enormous one, and it often plays so loudly that the voices almost get drowned. As a matter of fact Wagner had to train special singers for his music because it needed such loud singing, and because his operas are very long and make big demands on the sheer strength of a singer to keep going through it all. Singing in Italian operas, even the grand operas, is a different thing from singing in the massive operas of Wagner. Wagner built his own opera house towards the end of his life, at Bayreuth. It is still run by his descendants, and people gather from all over

The scene for Verdi's magnificent opera *Aïda* is set in Egypt. Below the Egyptian general Radames is returning in triumph after defeating the Ethiopians in battle.

The bird-catcher Papageno, as he appears in Mozart's opera *The Magic Flute*. This is supposed to have been Mozart's favourite.

Puccini, the Italian composer of many famous operas.

the world to attend the festivals of Wagner's operas held there every year."

"Hasn't one of Wagner's operas got something to do with a swan?"

"Yes, that's *Lohengrin*. Lohengrin is a knight, and he makes his first entrance in a boat which is pulled along by a swan. I think you would like *The Mastersingers*, which is Wagner's only comic opera. Then there's *The Flying Dutchman*, *Tristan and Isolde*, and *Parsifal*. You may have heard of *The Ring*, which is really four operas in one, and which takes four nights to perform."

"What! Four nights for one opera!"

"Like most of Wagner's operas it is based on old German legends. Wagner always wrote the words as well as the music for his operas."

"You've been talking about Mozart, Verdi, and Wagner, but—" Barbara opened her programme, "—the opera we saw tonight, *Madam Butterfly*, is a famous opera, and it's by Puccini."

"Yes, Puccini was the last of the really important Italian opera composers. He died in 1924. There are still a great many people living who remember Puccini well. His operas are immensely popular all over the world—*La Bohème*, *Madam Butterfly*, and *Tosca* in particular are great favourites with audiences everywhere."

"It says in this programme 'Music by Giacomo Puccini, libretto by Giacosa and Illica.' What's a libretto?"

"That's the book of words. Wagner wrote his own librettos for instance. Puccini had two people to write the libretto for *Madam Butterfly*, and it was based on someone else's play as well. By the way, you noticed the way all the music went straight through once it started, the songs and so on being all joined together with lots of recitative music so that you hardly noticed the change from one to another. Most operas have been written like that since Wagner's time."

ount Almaviva discovering Cherubino, his page:
The Marriage of Figaro by Mozart

The story of Don José's love for Carmen:
Carmen by Bizet

Eva crowning Walther:
he Mastersingers by Wagner

"To Let the Punishment Fit the Crime":
The Mikado by Gilbert and Sullivan

COLOURFUL SCENES FROM WELL-KNOWN OPERAS

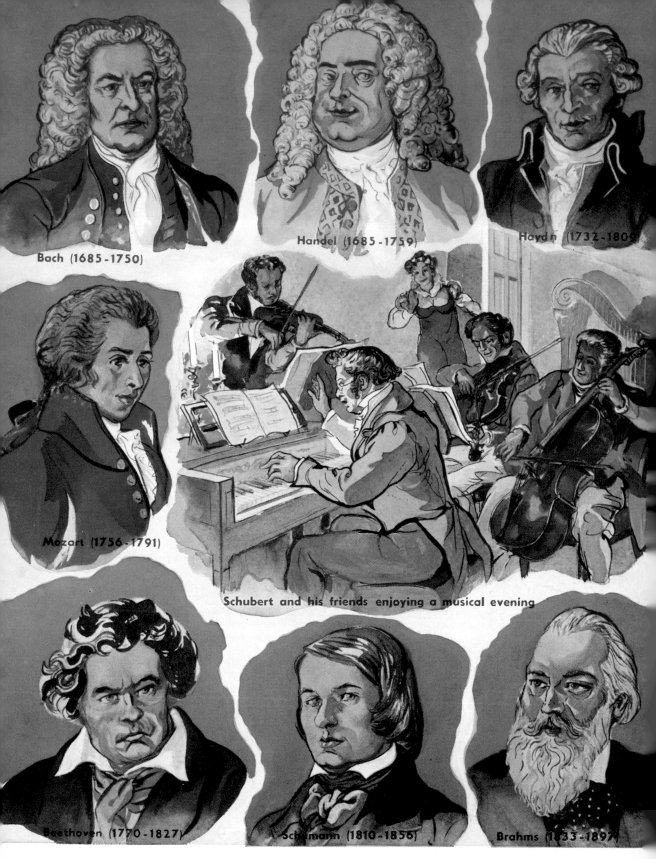

Bach (1685-1750)

Handel (1685-1759)

Haydn (1732-1809)

Mozart (1756-1791)

Schubert and his friends enjoying a musical evening

Beethoven (1770-1827)

Schumann (1810-1856)

Brahms (1833-1897)

SOME OF THE WORLD'S GREATEST COMPOSERS

50

ENGLISH MUSIC

"You remember that long talk we had the other night after the opera, Mr. Wells?"

"Yes, Barbara."

"I've been thinking about what you said. You talked about Italian opera, and German opera. . . ."

"And if I'd had time I would have talked about Russian opera, and French opera, and. . . ."

"But what about English opera? You never said a word about English composers at all."

"That's not quite true. You remember your father was talking about Gilbert and Sullivan. They're English all right."

"Yes, but all the really great composers seem to be foreigners—you know, Wagner and Verdi, Mozart, Bach and Beethoven—none of them is English."

"Well, let's get the opera question sorted out first. England has never developed opera like countries on the continent have. Every town of any size in Italy for instance has its own opera house, and opera is part of Italian life, but not in England. In London there are two opera houses, Covent Garden and the Coliseum; and there's Glyndbourne opera house tucked away in Sussex, and running for only a small part of the year. No other city or town in the British Isles has an opera house of its own. Consequently British composers haven't troubled to write operas to the same extent that the Germans and Italians have. But since the war things have begun to change. You've heard of Benjamin Britten, haven't you? Well, since the war his operas such as *Peter Grimes* and *Albert Herring* have had great success, and have been performed a lot here and abroad."

"How about other composers? Are there some really important composers in England?"

A cartoonist's impression of Gilbert (upside down) and Sullivan (on the left). During their long and successful partnership they were never once photographed together.

Part of the manuscript of Dr. Arne's arrangement of the British National Anthem.

An early English concert party from a print of that time.

The English composer Ralph Vaughan Williams is perhaps best known for his symphonies, which often echo folk-songs.

"Yes, indeed. It was not always so, but there was a time known as the Golden Age of English Music, which was when the first Queen Elizabeth was on the throne, when Shakespeare was alive. That was also about the time when opera was beginning in Italy. There were fine composers then. Madrigals were a favourite form of composition. Madrigals are part-songs, and the singing of madrigals was a popular pastime amongst educated people in Elizabethan days."

"Wasn't Purcell alive then?"

"No, Purcell came just after. Incidentally he composed the first English opera of importance, *Dido and Aeneas*. Purcell is a most important composer, but for a long time we seemed to be dominated by foreign composers. Handel, for instance, lived in England and became a naturalized Englishman. Then Mendelssohn, another German composer, seemed the most important musician to English audiences during the time of Queen Victoria."

"But we have got a lot of composers of our own again now, haven't we?"

"Yes, and the interesting thing is that it is during the reign of the second Queen Elizabeth. We might easily call this the Second Golden Age of Elizabethan music. The tide turned about the beginning of this century when Edward Elgar produced a series of genuine masterpieces. You must hear his *Enigma Variations* for orchestra some time, in which he gives musical pictures of several of his friends; and one of his choral works, *The Dream of Gerontius*. Of course, you know *Land of Hope and Glory*—that is a tune Elgar originally wrote for one of his marches.

"Other composers appeared at the same time as Elgar. Frederick Delius, for example, who composed rather dreamy music with most lovely harmonies : pieces like *Summer Night on the River*, and *On Hearing the First Cuckoo*

Gustav Holst is another important English composer. The cartoonist here has caught him conducting one of his own works.

ANSWER THIS

Who wrote the following pieces of music, and what are they:
(a) *Peter Grimes*.
(b) *Dido and Aeneas*.
(c) *The Wasps*.

A scene from Benjamin Britten's opera, *Peter Grimes*. This work established the composer's reputation, both in Britain and abroad.

in Spring. Gustav Holst is another famous composer. He sounds foreign doesn't he? His ancestors came from Sweden, but they had been settled in England for a long time. Holst wrote *The Planets*. You remember we heard this suite on the radio not long ago, played by the B.B.C. Symphony Orchestra. There was Mars, the bringer of war; Jupiter, the bringer of jollity; Venus, the bringer of peace, and so on."

"But there have been other composers since, haven't there?"

"Indeed there have! So many have there been that one can hardly believe it. I think the greatest of them all is Vaughan Williams. You know some of his hymns too, I expect, particularly *For All the Saints*. But he wrote some tremendous symphonies, choral works, and all sorts of other things. Didn't we hear his overture *The Wasps* together? Vaughan Williams is a really great composer. Then there's John Ireland. I've played some of his piano pieces, and I think you know his song *Sea Fever*. Sir Arthur Bliss is important. He's Master of the Queen's Music. Among the outstanding English composers there are Sir William Walton and Sir Michael Tippett and a number of others we have not time to mention. In fact, this really is a second Golden Age of music."

51

MUSIC FOR DANCING

IT was Thursday evening. Mr. Brown had not returned home yet and the others were waiting for their evening meal. The children were bored and Bill turned on the television. The sound of a "pop" group roared from the loudspeaker as the picture appeared on the screen. It was a loud piece of music and each member of the group was also singing at the top of his voice.

"What a noise," said Mother. "For goodness' sake turn the sound down."

"We like it," said Barbara. "Don't we, Bill?"

"Yes," said her brother, "this is better than a lot of classical music."

"Why, it hasn't even got a tune," said their Mother, who always like what she called "a good tune."

"But it's got a good beat," explained Barbara, "and that's what makes it great for dancing."

Here are some newcomers to high society dancing at a ball.

The Beatles, most famous "pop" group of all, as they were in 1963 when they started.

"When I was a girl," persisted their mother, "we had good dance tunes played by good dance bands—tunes that you could sing as well as dance to. In those days, big dance bands were all the rage and had been for many years. They appeared on the stage, on the radio, in dance halls; and everywhere they appeared people clapped and clapped and wanted more. The tunes that they made popular lasted for ever so long, and even today you can still hear them played—'standards' you call them."

Mother paused for breath, so anxious was she to tell them about the dance music that had caught her fancy when she was a girl.

"They are all right," grudgingly admitted Barbara, "but our 'pop' music is for the young people of today. They like plenty of noise as well as rhythm, something they can dance to, and they don't care if the tunes don't last very long. There are always plenty more waiting to be tried out. I'd like new tunes every week."

"Some of them are all right," said Mrs. Brown, anxious to be fair, "especially those that make good songs and are sung by good singers. There are some fabulous new songs and I'm sure that some of these will last for a very long time."

"All these 'pop' groups seem to play the guitar," observed Billy. "Was it the same when you were a girl?"

"Well, no," replied their Mother. "The saxophone was still a popular instrument, for it made plenty of sound and was easy to learn. Small groups of part-time musicians who played for club dances were often no more than a pianist, drummer and saxophone-player, but they could fill a hall with their music. The big bands had all kinds of instruments, rather like an orchestra. In fact, we called them dance bands or dance orchestras and both names seemed to fit. They had trumpets and trombones, a double bass, sometimes violins, a piano and

Two dance champions. Competition dancing has become a great attraction for both dancers and television viewers.

A dance orchestra plays to a crowded floor of dance enthusiasts.

253

At a discotheque the music comes from gramophone records, or discs.

Elvis Presley, the American performer who has long been on the "pop" scene.

cymbals, the clarinet, and so on."

"We have drums today in the groups," exclaimed Billy.

"And sometimes an electric organ," added Barbara. "And sometimes there's a trumpet. And the guitars are electric, too, for they have wires fitted to them to take the sound through an amplifier."

"Years ago we had a lot of jazz, which was terribly exciting," said Mrs. Brown, "and there were other kinds of dance music, like swing, skiffle, and rock and roll, each with its own exciting rhythm. All these were wonderful to dance to. And they were in addition to the foxtrot, waltz and quickstep. You can still see what it was like in the ballroom programmes on television."

"We still have jazz," said Barbara, "all kinds of it, like progressive jazz and traditional jazz. It's now a part of music, like the symphonies. And there are other kinds of new music like the new 'folk songs' as well as Country and Western."

254

52

HOW SHOULD WE LISTEN TO MUSIC?

It was Barbara's birthday, and her eyes lit up with joy when she saw all the presents waiting for her in the morning. Among them was a gramophone record, and she knew without looking that this was a present from Mr. Wells. However, the day still had to be spent at school, so it wasn't until the evening that she had time to spend with her new possessions, and by then Mr. Wells had come round to wish her many happy returns in person.

"I thought you would like that piano piece by Debussy, Barbara. You don't know much of his music yet do you?"

"No. I know he is a French composer, and that is about all. The name of this piece is in French too, but I cannot pronounce it."

"'La Cathédrale Engloutie,'" said Bill in a rather superior voice.

"In English we call it 'The Submerged Cathedral.' The story behind it is that there is a cathedral under the sea, just off the coast of France, and when the tide is low the villagers can see the spire; sometimes they hear the tolling of bells, and the organ playing. That's the legend and Debussy describes it cleverly in music."

"Well, I haven't played the record yet, so let us put it on now."

The three of them sat down and listened to the solemn opening chords suggesting the depths of the sea. There was no mistaking the mighty tones of the organ when they came, nor the tolling of the bells.

"I do like that," said Bill when it was finished.

"There is not really much tune in it," said Barbara. "It's all sound effects. It does sound like a cathedral under the sea, though."

Father and daughter take part in bell-ringing, such as may have inspired parts of Debussy's *La Cathédrale Engloutie.*

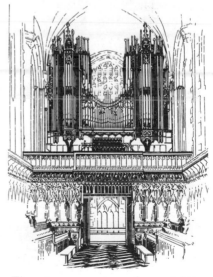

The pipe organ is perhaps rightly called "the king of musical instruments." Here is a beautiful example from New College, Oxford.

"Well, I think you are both quite clever young people, because you seem to have listened to it the right way. When Debussy's music was first performed there were many people who could not understand what he was after at all, it was so unlike any they had heard before."

"I have never really thought about listening to music in different ways. I thought one just listened for a good tune and that was that."

"With a lot of music that is enough, Barbara, but the music of Debussy would not mean much to you if you were only listening for tunes. He is much more interested in the sound of chords, and the effects he can make with them. Some day you must get to know his orchestral pieces, such as *The Afternoon of a Faun*, and *The Sea;* and some more of his piano pieces, such as *Moonlight*, and *Reflections in the Water*. The titles pretty well tell you what to expect. Let us listen to the piano piece on the other side of that record. It is another Debussy piece, *Gardens in the Rain*."

They listened to Debussy's music with its impression of rain pattering down on deserted gardens.

"Is there any name for that sort of music?"

"Yes, it is called 'impressionism,' and Debussy is the leading 'impressionist' composer."

"It is certainly very different from the music of Mozart, but Mozart lived a long time before Debussy, didn't he."

"Oh yes! Let me see; Mozart lived from 1756 to 1791 and Debussy from 1862 to 1918. A lot happened to music between those dates. Before Mozart and Haydn there had been Bach and Handel, and all those four were what we call classical composers. The ordinary person often uses the word 'classical' to describe any music that isn't dance music or popular music of some kind; but musicians, and people who are interested in music, use the word classical only for this earlier group of composers. The classical

Claude Debussy photographed in his study. Before he died in 1918 this French composer had introduced a form of "impressionism" into music which has influenced later composers to this day.

Franz Hals's "Singing Boys" are obviously deeply interested in their "classical" music. The picture is in the Kassel Art Gallery, in Germany.

256

composers were very interested in the shape or pattern of their music.

"Then came what we call the romantic period, when composers set out to express their feelings and their emotions more strongly in music. Liszt was a romantic composer, and he couldn't get on very well with the set form of the symphony, so he invented the symphonic poem. The symphonic poem is an orchestral work which sets out to tell a story, and the music just follows the course of that story as it happens. I think you know *The Sorcerer's Apprentice* by Dukas. It tells the story of a magician's apprentice who tries to work some magic while his master is away, with disastrous results—great fun it is too.

"But you must never forget that Bach, Mozart and Beethoven have written music which is never likely to be surpassed for sheer beauty, and for expressing noble thoughts."

"That's another new idea to me too—expressing thoughts in music."

ANSWER THIS

Name two of Debussy's descriptive pieces.

This is how Walt Disney in his film *Fantasia* drew the sorcerer's apprentice putting the bewitched broom to work.

"Well, why does some music make you feel gay, and other music make you feel sad? Because that is the thought behind the music, and the more experienced you become as a listener the more thoughts you get from the music.

"But to understand music properly you have to practise listening just as you have to practise anything else worth doing, and the best way to practise is to listen to as much music as you possibly can. Don't be put off if you don't like the piece the first time—perhaps you will like it much more on a second or third hearing. Get to know some pieces very well. Remember, there are lots of exciting experiences waiting for you in music and you may find that careful listening will open up a new world for you."

Gramophones like this, with the early type of record, distorted sound, but today's records and machines make listening a pleasure.

(53)

A MUSIC PARTY

There have been very many famous young musicians in the past, playing on all kinds of instruments. Here is Master Viotti Collins, as he appeared at the age of seven, showing his skill on the violin.

MR. WELLS was thoroughly enjoying himself. There were two things in life that he particularly liked; one was being with children, and the other was having anything to do with music. And now, here was his sitting-room full of boys and girls, and some of them had brought musical instruments with them. Billy and Barbara had just arrived.

"Barbara, you'll find a seat over there. Bill, you'll have to squeeze in the corner by the piano. Well, I think you've all been introduced to each other by now, and some of you are old friends anyway. Most of you know why I asked you to come here this afternoon. All of you are interested in music, I know."

They were all listening to Mr. Wells intently.

"We're going to have some music and fun together, but I've got something important to discuss with you later on. . . ."

"Something to do with chocolate cake?"

Everyone laughed because they had all been to tea with Mr. Wells at various times, and they knew how fond he was of the special cake that always appeared on such occasions. Mr. Wells tried to look very indignant, and he turned to the girl who had spoken. She was sitting next to Barbara.

"Marion, you know I never discuss chocolate cake; I only eat it; but for being so saucy you can be the first one to play."

There was certainly no difficulty in getting Marion to play. She was a fair, rather tall and good-looking girl, and when she stood up Barbara noticed for the first time that she had been sitting on her piano accordion case which was standing on its end. She took the large instrument out of its case, and Barbara helped her to strap it across her shoulders. Without any more ado she struck up a popular tune, full of life and gaiety.

Marion was full of confidence, and her right hand moved easily over the keyboard at one side, playing the melody, while her left hand was busy on all the buttons that provide the chords and

The piano accordion is a popular musical instrument today, both for the soloist and for the dance band player.

DID YOU KNOW THIS?

Although the piano accordion has only been in use for just over a century, it is now one of the most popular musical instruments in the world.

harmonies. The instrument was kept on the move, opening and closing, so that the bellows in the middle kept plenty of air pumping through for a good full tone. There was a big round of applause when she finished with quite a professional flourish.

"Absolutely marvellous!" said Mr. Wells. "My goodness, you *have* got all those buttons and things well under control now. How long have you been playing?"

"Just over four years."

Marion had unstrapped the instrument, and was resting it on the ground.

"Well, thanks for a wonderful start to our grand concert. You know that your piano accordion makes its music by blowing metal reeds to make them vibrate; but you have to have those big bellows built in to do the job

An accordion for beginners.

because such a lot of air is needed. Alan's instrument is just the same, with metal reeds, but you have to do your own blowing, don't you, Alan?"

A ginger-haired boy with freckles stood up, and from his pocket he pulled a mouth-organ. Like most players who take this instrument seriously he preferred to call it a harmonica.

"I've bought a new instrument since I saw you last, Mr. Wells. You know I had just an ordinary suck-and-blow harmonica. I have a chromatic harmonica now."

Alan proudly showed his shining new instrument.

"I say, that's a smart piece of work! You still have to suck and blow of course."

"Oh yes! But you see this button at the side. It works a slide to put all the notes up half a tone, so that I can play any tune you like on this instrument, or at least, I will be able to once I've mastered it properly. And I can play trills and turns, and I can get all sorts of fine effects I couldn't get on my old one."

"How exciting! Are you finding it difficult to play?"

"I am, but I'm having some lessons now from a man who is an expert. He's teaching me how to use my tongue so that I can close some of the holes to get single notes when I want them, instead of the usual chords you get by blowing into several holes at once. And he's teaching me to get different kinds of tone by shaping the hands round the instrument and so on."

"It sounds most impressive. Well, let's hear what you can do with your new chromatic harmonica, Alan."

"I'll have a try at *The Londonderry Air*. But I won't promise it will be at all perfect. Remember, I'm still getting used to it."

Alan cupped his hands round the harmonica and started playing. He did make some pretty

Larry Adler, the great American harmonica player, has probably done more than any other single person to exploit this instrument's musical possibilities. Vaughan Williams was so impressed that he wrote a *Romance* for the harmonica and dedicated it to Larry Adler.

You do not have to be a great musician to enjoy playing the harmonica for you will soon learn to produce simple tunes.

260

obvious mistakes, but nevertheless they were all very impressed. Most of them had played a mouth-organ at some time or other, but none of them had realized that it could be made to sound as interesting as this.

When they had finished clapping Alan's performance, Mr. Wells called on a brother and sister to play for them.

"Now, Sheila here plays the recorder. You probably know that the recorder was a very popular instrument in Elizabethan times. As we are now in the reign of Queen Elizabeth the Second, it's very appropriate that this instrument should have come back into favour again during the past few years. What kind of a recorder is it you play, Sheila?"

"This is called a descant recorder, which is the most popular kind. You can buy other sizes. There's a treble, and a tenor, and so on. They play lower notes, and you can have quite a good recorder band with all the various sizes. This one is made of wood, which is best, but you can get very cheap ones made in plastic. I learnt to play on a plastic recorder."

"You just blow into the mouthpiece at the top, and finger the holes."

"That's right. It's very simple really."

All this time Sheila's brother, Christopher, had been standing by, holding what looked like a very large black egg with holes in it.

"Now Christopher, tell us something about your instrument."

"Well, this is an ocarina. This one was made in Austria, where they were invented, I believe. It's made of terra-cotta, which is a sort of clay, baked very hard. I just blow into this mouthpiece that sticks out, finger the holes for the notes, and out comes the music. You really couldn't have anything much more simple!"

"Thanks, Christopher. And now these two are going to play you a duet which I have practised with them. Here are three Scottish tunes, 'Loch

This is the sort of harmonica that is often used by professional players. It has 12 holes with 48 reeds.

The recorder, almost forgotten for hundreds of years, is today the most popular of all musical instruments in schools.

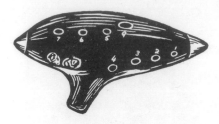

The ocarina's soft, pleasant sound is limited in range, so it is usually made in several sizes to give a variety of pitch, so that some play high and others low.

Lomond,' and a couple of others that I expect you will recognize."

Although the recorder and the ocarina are not usually associated together, they did sound very pleasant. They both had a quiet, sweet tone, so that they blended well, but there was also a subtle difference between them that was fascinating to listen to. Mr. Wells accompanied them at the piano, and at the end all three of them took deep bows together as though they were appearing before an enormous audience at some famous concert hall.

"Now Andrew, have you got your guitar, handy?"

"I've left it out in the hall, Mr. Wells. I won't be a minute."

Andrew was a fifth form boy at a big local school, and he was quite well known for his playing of the guitar. He brought it in, and asked for an E on the piano. He then quickly tuned the six strings, and a beautiful sonorous tone filled the room as he tried out various chords to see that his tuning was all right.

"Let me see, this is a real Spanish guitar, isn't it?"

"Yes—flat at the back; six strings which I pick with my right hand. My left hand finds the notes on the finger-board—that's the long neck. You can see the strips of metal all the way up the finger-board; they are called the frets, and are what I press my fingers against to find the right notes."

"I know you play lots of solos, Andrew, but what about singing us one of your songs to your own accompaniment?"

"Yes, all right then. Here's a humorous sea-song called 'Hullabaloo, Balay.' "

Andrew had appeared at many concerts, and was obviously at his ease. There was a twinkle in his eye as he sang, and as he plucked and strummed the strings of his guitar, sometimes letting the chords ring out, sometimes making

Learning to play the guitar has become popular among young people, like learning to play the piano before the War.

them short and sharp, or just playing quiet single notes according to the passing mood of the song.

There was a burst of applause when he finished.

Mr. Wells rose from the piano stool where he had been sitting to listen with the rest.

"Thank you very much, Andrew. We must hear some more from you later, and that goes for all of you; but now I am going to come to the important point. Here we are having a good time together, and I think some of you are making friends you wouldn't have made otherwise. Well, what about doing this regularly? What about forming a Music Club? I expect you know others interested in music who might like to join as well."

"That's a good idea," said Bill, "so long as you don't expect chaps like me to do anything."

"Ah! But I would expect you chaps to do something. We would need a secretary, for instance, to send notices of the meetings, and to make out the programmes, and so on."

"Barbara's the one for that," said Bill. "She was saying only the other day that she'd like to learn shorthand and typing so that she could become a secretary for someone."

"All right, we could settle things like that later. But more important still, some of you listeners could learn to play an instrument. You have seen that the recorder and the ocarina are easy enough to play. You can play tunes on them within a few minutes! Of course it would take quite a time to play as well as Sheila or Christopher. But why not? The instruments are cheap enough! And if Alan can play the harmonica so well, why not you?

"It's a big thing taking up the piano accordion, or Spanish guitar of course. The instruments are quite expensive, and they take quite a time to learn properly, but then you can see from

This is a concert-model Spanish guitar, hand-made, and fitted with nylon strings.

DO THIS
Name three different types of recorder.

263

Recorder and violin blend pleasantly together as these young people are ready to prove, and there are many simple duets which can be easily played on these two instruments.

Marion and Andrew just how worthwhile it is. Anyway, these are not the only instruments in the world, as you know. Someone might want to play the bagpipe for instance, in which case I'd put on a kilt and do a Highland fling for you. But I think every member of the club ought to play something. What do you think?"

The boys and girls obviously approved because they all started talking at once. But there was no doubt about their general enthusiasm.

"Well, we don't have to be in a hurry about this. We've got plenty of time to talk it over. I've got lots of ideas—giving some concerts for charity for instance, and perhaps making up some kind of small orchestra as well. But we can go into all that over tea. Let's go into the dining-room. You can leave your instruments here. I believe, by the way, that there's some chocolate cake for everybody."

After music, the performers get their reward.

264

Ballet and Dancing

PEOPLE have always danced to express their feelings of joy or sorrow, and the different races of the world have their own special dances which reflect something of their racial characters. From these beginnings the great art of ballet has grown—at its best a perfect combination of music and movement.

(54)

HOW THE BALLET BEGAN

"I CAN hardly believe it's true!" Barbara exclaimed to Bill as they hurried to the bus stop to meet their cousin, Georgina. "We are actually on our way to our first ballet!"

But it was true, and there was Georgina, slim and smiling, waiting for them with a box of chocolates tucked under her arm! Their cousin was taking them both to see *Swan Lake* as a Christmas treat, and she was just the person to go with, for she was a dancing teacher.

"Would there be time, do you think," Barbara asked when they were seated in the bus, "to tell us something about ballet?"

"Well, I expect you know that ballet is a sort of play in which the story is told with dancing and music instead of words, and it all began at the Court of the Kings of France about three hundred years ago. You see, Louis XIV was a very fine dancer, and he and his courtiers liked to make up these entertainments which they called ballets, in which they all took part."

"Did they do all the ballet steps?" inquired Barbara, who had seen ballet dancers on television and rather liked the idea of everyone at the Court spinning rapidly round and round or skipping about on their toes.

Louis XIV, the French king who founded the first ballet school, was himself a very fine dancer. Here he is dancing a minuet with one of the ladies of his court.

DID YOU KNOW THIS?

When *Swan Lake* was first performed, in 1877, the audiences did not care for it at all, and Tchaikovsky died just before the successful new production in 1895.

The lords and ladies of Louis XIV's court taking part in a ballet.

"Oh dear, no!" laughed Georgina. "Their dances, such as the Minuet and Gavotte, were pretty slow on the whole, and the ladies wore heavy dresses that swept the ground. The real ballet steps came later when, because these entertainments had grown so popular, King Louis decided, in 1661, to found a school where people could be trained as expert and professional dancers. He called it The Royal Academy of the Dance, and it is still the most famous ballet school in France. Here the king's dancing master laid down the rules on which classical ballet is based, and teachers from the school travelled all over Europe—to Italy, Denmark, and Russia—spreading the art of ballet.

"Is that why ballet words are always in French?" Barbara asked.

"Yes, just as musical terms are in Italian. And this made them understandable in all countries. You can imagine that once people started to get down to serious study all kinds of

La Camargo shortened her skirt and wore heelless shoes so that she could dance difficult steps like the *entrechat* shown here.

266

new and difficult steps and dances were soon invented, but they were almost entirely for men."

Bill looked surprised at this. "Why, I thought dancing was really for women and rather feeble for men," he said.

"There's nothing feeble about the strenuous life of a dancer," replied Georgina. "You've got to be really tough if you want to get anywhere. But in Louis XIV's time women were still hampered by their dresses, and so men were given all the most interesting and difficult steps until La Camargo, the first great ballerina to come from the school, did what was considered a most daring thing. She was very gay and lively and, because she wanted to do all these interesting steps, she shortened her skirt by several inches, causing quite a scandal. She also refused to wear heels on her dancing shoes, and became the first woman to do an *entrechat*."

"What's that?" asked Barbara.

"It's the step in which you jump in the air and criss-cross your feet quickly several times before you come down. You will see the Prince do it in the Ballroom Scene of *Swan Lake* this afternoon, so watch carefully," Georgina told her. "But though Camargo's new ideas were soon copied," she continued, "men were still more important until, in the 19th century, a wonderful new dancer appeared—Marie Taglioni, the great Swedish-Italian ballerina. She was very light and fragile, and to stress this and gain more freedom she discarded the heavy, elaborate costume and wore the first all-white gauzy ballet dress. Most exciting of all, she was one of the first dancers to go on the tips of her toes—the *pointes*, as they are called."

"I expect that caused another sensation!" Barbara remarked.

"So much so that people went quite mad about Taglioni and flocked to see her wherever she went. Now everyone only wanted to see

Marie Taglioni, a famous ballerina of the romantic age, wore the first all-white gauzy ballet dress and danced on the tips of her toes.

Ballet declined in the romantic age because the male dancers did nothing more than form a background to nymphs and fairies.

267

A male dancer performing a vigorous springing step—an example of *élévation*, that is, dancing in the air.

A ballerina in the short ballet skirt, known as the "tutu", performing a *fouetté*—a step in which the dancer spins round.

nymphs and fairies floating about the stage; the man's vigorous style went quite out of favour, and soon his only job was to partner the ballerina. Even that rôle was often taken by a woman dressed as a man."

"I think that sounds awful," said Barbara emphatically. "It must have made ballet so dull—just like always having a girl for a partner at a dance!"

"That is just what it was," replied Georgina, "and eventually ballet became dull and fell into decline. Fortunately this did not happen in Russia where, under the patronage of the Tsars, it had grown and flourished. For the Russians have a natural gift for ballet, and always took the best from any new development in the art."

"What were the Russian ballets like?" asked Barbara.

"They were long and splendid, like the famous *Sleeping Beauty* and *Swan Lake*, and Tchaikovsky was composing his finest music for them. The dancers, both male and female, were without equal in the world. It was now, towards the end of the century, that the short ballet skirt first appeared, enabling its wearer to perform all the very difficult steps the Russian audience loved. Everyone was very excited, for instance, when a ballerina first did the 32 *fouettés* in *Swan Lake*—that's the step where the dancer goes round and round in one place rather like a top. The whole action was held up while rival ballerinas tried to out-do each other, and you could hear the audience anxiously counting the number of revolutions made by a favourite dancer, before bursting into applause."

Both children laughed at this and Barbara wanted to know if that would happen at the performance they were going to see.

Georgina smiled. "The ballerina will certainly do the 32 *fouettés*," she said, "but without any fuss, because that would spoil the

Serge Diaghilev, the Russian who created modern ballet.

flow of the story. It was a Russian called Serge Diaghilev who, by deciding that music, scenery, and dancing must really fit the story, gave us ballet as we know it today. He formed a wonderful company which he took to Paris in 1909, making a tremendous sensation. Nothing like it had been seen before; interest in ballet revived everywhere, and Russian ballet came to mean all that was new and exciting, all that was beautiful and harmonious in the dance.

"Later on a young Irish girl who had taken the stage name of Ninette de Valois joined the company. She watched and learnt from Diaghilev, for she had one great ambition, and that was to create an English national ballet. This was not easy, because the English loved watching ballet but thought only Russians were any good at it. She eventually started a school, and in 1927 managed to get Lilian Baylis, who ran Sadler's Wells Theatre in London, to believe in her and to give her the opportunity of putting on pupils from her school in small ballets from time to time. But goodness me!" exclaimed Georgina, "here is the stop for our theatre!"

Neither of the children had been in such a large theatre before, and thought it was very imposing with its sweeping circles, its boxes, rosy lights, and great crimson curtains; it was also friendly and welcoming, filled with an air of enjoyment and pleasures to come.

As they watched the house filling, Barbara gave a sigh of pleasure, and then asked, "Is there time to finish the story, please?"

"Well, de Valois and her pupils were so good that people had to agree that the English made excellent dancers. Her company grew, moved to Covent Garden Opera House, became world-famous, and was renamed the Royal Ballet."

At this moment the lights slowly dimmed, and a hush descended on the audience as the first notes of Tchaikovsky's lovely ballet music floated on the air.

Bill and Barbara with their cousin Georgina watch *Swan Lake*.

ANSWER THIS

Why is it that the terms used in ballet are always in French?

269

55

HOW A BALLET IS MADE

Odette, the Swan Princess dancing with the Prince in *Swan Lake*. This is a classical ballet and contrasts strongly with *The Three-Cornered Hat*, a ballet based on Spanish folk dances and arranged by Leonide Massine, the great Russian ballet dancer. Below he is seen with Margot Fonteyn in an early performance of this popular and colourful ballet.

THE curtain rose on the wonderful ballet of *Swan Lake*, and the children sat entranced as the story unfolded of the Prince who goes hunting and falls in love with a beautiful Princess by an enchanted lake. She and her maidens are under the spell of a wicked Wizard who has turned them into swans, except during the hours of night, when they regain their human forms. Only true love can free them, and the Prince promises to marry the Princess, vowing eternal faithfulness. At a magnificent ball the next evening, the Wizard and his daughter, Odile, appear at the castle. He casts a spell on the Prince, making him believe Odile is the Swan Princess and causing him to break his vow. But after some exciting happenings the Wizard is defeated and the Prince and Princess live happily ever after.

During an interval Bill and Barbara went upstairs with their cousin to a large room behind the Grand Tier. Here everyone was having tea and they found a small table reserved for them—Georgina was doing things in style !

"I think the ballerina is absolutely marvellous !" sighed Barbara rapturously, as she sipped her tea. "She makes it all seem so easy—but I don't expect it is !"

"Her part is one of the most difficult in classical ballet," Georgina told her. "You would be jolly lucky if you could do it well after nine years of hard training. One famous ballerina, Beryl Grey, did it on her 15th birthday—but that was exceptional. Every dancer hopes to dance the lead as the Princess or Odile in *Swan Lake* one day, for not until she has proved herself in great classical ballets can a dancer become a ballerina. But of course, not many dancers achieve this ambition.

Here is the *corps de ballet* of the Royal Ballet Company. They dance together to create patterns of moving grace and beauty.

"When you see someone dance as the Swan Princess you are seeing something that has been handed down by a·succession of great ballerinas who have passed the rôle on with love and care, one to the other. This is an example of tradition in ballet, because all rôles and ballets have been passed on mainly by memory."

This was a great surprise to Barbara. "Surely," she asked, "it can all be written down, like music or shorthand?"

"People have tried to find some system like that, but it is difficult, as you may imagine, to set down every little movement of a large ballet, and only recently has one been invented that is satisfactory."

"Then," remarked Bill, as he carefully selected a cream bun, "all the steps are decided on from the beginning, and you don't just

DID YOU KNOW THIS?

Among the many great dancers who have danced the leading role in *Swan Lake* was Anna Pavlova. She toured everywhere with her company and helped to make the world ballet-conscious. She was the greatest ballerina of her age and will always be remembered for her performance in *The Dying Swan*, a solo dance arranged for her by Fokine to music by Saint-Saëns.

Niels Kehlet dancing the part of Harlequin in Fokine's *Le Carnaval*.

This is an incident in a ballet called *Light Trap*, where a convict catches a butterfly.

twiddle your legs to the music and make it up as you go along?"

"Oh dear, no! The choreographer—that is the man who invents the dance movements—tells the dancers exactly what they must do. Some choreographers have everything cut and dried when they come to a rehearsal, and the dancers have to fit themselves to their ideas; others like to build up as they go along—to watch how the dancers respond and to get ideas from that. In either case it is a long and complicated business, and takes many days and weeks of hard work when a large company is concerned and soloists and *corps de ballet* all have to learn their parts and fit in with each other."

Bill began to see that it was not quite so simple as he had imagined, and asked whether the choreographer had to think about the music and scenery too.

"Yes, indeed, and both can make or mar a ballet. They must be chosen to fit the type of ballet he is creating."

"Are there many different kinds of ballet?" Bill then asked.

"More than I can tell you about now, but they include the fairy-tale ballets, such as *The Sleeping Beauty* and *The Firebird*, amusing ones like *La Boutique Fantasque*, in which the dolls in a toyshop become alive when the shop is closed for the night, and sad ones like *Giselle*. They may be charming period pieces, such as *Les Sylphides*, or centred on a modern theme, like *Miracle in the Gorbals*. Some have no story at all and give pleasure simply by the beauty of the dancing: *Symphonic Variations* is a good example of this. But all are harmonies of colour, movement, and music. In this next act notice how beautifully the music and the steps go together and what a wonderful setting the scenery makes for both. But there goes the warning bell. We must go back to our seats, because the curtain will be going up very soon!"

272

PAS DE QUATRE IS A BALLET IN WHICH THE STORY ELEMENT IS SLIGHT, BUT WHICH CHARMS US WITH ITS DELIGHTFUL PATTERNS AND ATMOSPHERE

THE ROYAL BALLET COMPANY IN THE WEDDING SCENE FROM COPPÉLIA

Red Indian tribal dance

Spanish folk dance

American square dance

Argentine tango

Zulu war dance

NATIONAL DANCES REFLECT SOMETHING OF THE CHARACTER OF A PEOPLE, AS

Tyrolean dance

Cossack dance

Japanese dance

Indian nautch dance

Balinese temple dance

THESE PICTURES OF DANCES FROM MANY DIFFERENT LANDS CLEARLY SHOW

lights

scenery

rehearsal pianist

stage manager

director

premier danseur

soloists

prima ballerina

choreographer

members of the corps de ballet

A BALLET REHEARSAL—THE CHOREOGRAPHER EXPLAINS THE STEPS

56

THE MAKING OF A DANCER

This picture shows the basic arm positions used in ballet.

"Do you have to be awfully clever to become a ballet dancer?" Barbara asked her cousin at the end of a wonderful afternoon.

"You needn't be exceptionally clever," Georgina told her, "but you must be quick and intelligent; and you must want to dance so much that you are prepared to stick the long training. I am seeing a famous ballerina after she has had a lesson on Monday. Would you like to come with me and see and hear something about how a dancer is made?"

Barbara was very thrilled at this suggestion, but surprised to hear of a ballerina still going to ballet classes.

"A dancer never stops learning and trying to perfect her art," Georgina explained, "and the greater the artist, the more she realizes how much there is to learn. Every morning she will go for an hour to one of the classes given for her company or to a private lesson from a

Learning to be a ballet dancer requires long and hard training, but to become a ballerina must be the dream of many a girl.

All movements in ballet start and finish with these five basic positions of the feet.

277

A mixed class of ballet students performing exercises at the *barre*.

This picture shows a girl student performing an *arabesque*.

DID YOU KNOW THIS?

The five basic positions of the feet shown on page 277 were used in a modified form as early as the beginning of the 18th century.

special teacher. Sometimes she goes to both, besides having her daily practice at home. And this she will do every day of her dancing life. So you see, Bill," continued Georgina, with a twinkle in her eye, "the 'twiddling,' as you called it, is quite hard work. But what about joining us and seeing for yourself?"

When they arrived at the ballet studio on Monday morning, they found a class was just about to begin. Georgina introduced her two young cousins to the teacher, who invited them to watch her pupils while the ballerina was changing after her lesson.

The room was large, with wide mirrors that went right down to the floor, and a wooden hand-rail, known as a *barre*, ran along the walls. Here a mixed class of advanced students stood, poised and erect, along the sides of the room, lightly grasping the *barre* with one hand. To the accompaniment of a piano they performed various exercises, while the teacher moved up and down the line, correcting faults : fingers held too stiffly, a bent elbow, a head poked forward—nothing escaped her watchful but kindly eye, and the class progressed in an atmosphere of quiet concentration. But this

278

changed when they left the side and came into the middle of the room to practise all kinds of things, including *arabesques*, *pirouettes*, and steps of partnering. Bill and Barbara were amused to see that even the most assured ones staggered and fell about.

Georgina pointed out that usually boys and girls had separate classes, because though they went through the same exercises, there was a lot of difference in the way they performed the actual steps and movements, especially as they progressed. The girls were more supple and graceful, their steps quicker and lighter, and they turned a *pirouette* in a different way. The boys did more jumping and covered more ground. They never went on their *pointes* and their dances were more athletic and exciting. As this was a class for partnering as well, the dancers were also learning to work smoothly together.

At this moment the ballerina appeared, elegant and smiling. She was so friendly that Barbara soon forgot her shyness when the ballerina asked her if she would like to be a dancer. Barbara had to admit that after seeing *Swan Lake* she had been full of the idea.

"Lots of people feel like that after their first ballet—but it usually wears off!" the ballerina told her. "You are just about the right age, though, to start learning, for it is unwise to begin serious training before nine years of age."

"Did you find it very hard?" asked Barbara.

"Yes, it was hard," the ballerina replied, "but I did not mind. I started with one class a week, but this gradually increased to eight, and it all had to be fitted in with school lessons. Before long I had little time for anything else. When other children were playing games, going to parties, meeting friends, I had to go to class, prepare for an examination or rehearse for a display, while my mother insisted that I never missed my daily practice before and after school. But I never felt that there was any real hardship

Here is a male dancer performing a *pirouette*, which is a complete turn of the body made on one leg.

Boy and girl students learning to work together so that their performance will look easy and beautiful on the stage.

279

Margot Fonteyn, one of the greatest of ballerinas.

in this. I enjoyed it all, for I loved my teachers, and ballet school was such fun. The harder I worked, the better I became, and it was very exciting to find I was mastering steps I saw performed on the stage."

"You went to the Royal Ballet School, didn't you?" asked Georgina.

"Yes, I managed to win a scholarship to it. I was also fortunate in that I was able to join the Royal Ballet Company much sooner than is usual, and less than a year later had the chance to dance in *Swan Lake*. Most students must count themselves lucky if, at the end of eight or nine years, they manage to find a place in the *corps de ballet*, and even more so if they eventually become soloists or leading dancers, for places at the top are very few indeed.

"But there is a brighter side," the ballerina continued, smiling at Barbara's rather downcast expression. "You may have to work hard and unceasingly, but your life will always be full of colour and variety and never dull or monotonous. You will travel and meet all kinds of interesting people; you will know the joy of movement, of comradeship, and the great satisfaction of working with others in the creation of something of beauty. Above all, you will know the delight of bringing pleasure and happiness to many people."

A little later, when the children and their cousin had come out once again into the wintry sunshine, Georgina asked, "Now that you have seen a little of both sides of the curtain, what do you think of it?"

"I think it looks jolly hard work," Billy replied emphatically.

Barbara did not answer at once, for she was remembering the radiant personality of the ballerina she had just met, and the enchantment of the world beyond the footlights.

Then she sighed deeply, and said, "*I* think it's worth it!"

DID YOU KNOW THIS?

One of the greatest dancers and teachers in the history of ballet was Enrico Cecchetti, born in 1850. His teaching method has spread all over the world.

280

57

DANCING ROUND THE WORLD

WHEN Georgina came to see them again, the children eagerly discussed the ballet with her.

On the whole Barbara had been most thrilled by the ballerina's solos, while Bill had been impressed by the spirited dances in the Ballroom scene—the Hungarian Czárdás, the Polonaise from Poland, the Italian and Spanish dances.

"Those are what are known as character dances," Georgina told him, "and they are called that because they have a special style or character of their own. They are not based on the classical ballet steps but taken from folk dances—the oldest dances of all."

"We saw a folk dance in Cornwall last year during the holidays," Barbara broke in. "It was great fun because it was out-of-doors and there was a man dressed up pretending to be a horse, who went capering about. Anyone could join in

The Hobby Horse and his "Teazer" dancing through the streets of the town during the annual festival at Padstow in Cornwall.

The Hungarian Czárdás danced in the Ballroom scene of *Swan Lake* is an example of how folk dances are adapted for ballet.

The Westminster Morris Men performing one of their ancient dances, which date back to the reign of King Edward III.

From Yugoslavia, a country with a warlike tradition, comes this exciting sword dance.

and go dancing after him—all around the town and even in and out the houses !"

"That was the Padstow Hobby Horse dance," Georgina said, "and it will show you just how old folk dancing is, for that one dates from pagan times. Primitive peoples thought that if when they danced they imitated animals, or went through the actions of their work—as in Morris Dances when they pretend to plant beans and gather peas—they would please the gods and so be rewarded with more horses and cattle, or a good harvest."

"But why should Christian people still do those sorts of dances?" asked Barbara.

"Well, you see, when the old pagan beliefs died out people still went on performing the dances for pleasure, and forgot their original purpose. Of course, these simple dances have changed a great deal with the passing of time, often becoming very beautiful and needing much skill in performance. Others are just jolly affairs with everyone joining hands in a ring or interweaving, skipping and making up steps as they go along. But traces of the old beliefs are still there and on special occasions, such as weddings or birthdays, these dances are supposed to bring luck. You can still see dancers representing seals, bears, or hares in Finland, and in the countries of the great forests there are wood-cutting dances. In Italy and Portugal dances may illustrate the gathering of grapes or the making of wine, because these things are so important to the livelihood of the people in those countries. Some of these dances have now become children's games, and in the South of France the children dance in a ring, pretending to sow, reap, and thresh the corn, as their ancestors did long before Christ was born."

Bill wanted to know if there was any meaning behind the Highland Fling of Scotland.

"That's an interesting question," Georgina said, "because you have hit on another kind of

Italian dancers from Naples taking part in an international folk-dance gathering in London.

national dance, one that comes from a country noted for its warlike history. The Highland Fling is sometimes said to be a dance of victory after battle, although we cannot be sure of its origin. But you may have seen pictures of soldiers of Highland regiments dancing between swords laid crossways on the ground, and it seems certain enough that this is a war dance from Scotland's past. In Yugoslavia, another country with a warlike tradition, they have a dance in which the men leap and twist in a circle, sweeping their swords through the air with what they call a "whiffling" sound. You see, folk dances always reflect the character of a people, and I think the proud and fiery dances of Spain and the rather staid but cheerful ones of the Dutch are good illustrations of this."

"I saw some Indian dancing in a newsreel not long ago," Barbara said, "but it was very strange. The dancers stood in the same place most of the time and only moved their hands and arms. I didn't understand it at all."

Dancers from Brittany, France.

DO THIS

Turn to page 285 and you will see a coloured picture of a Highland dance. More folk dances are shown in colour on pages 274-275.

283

The waltz reached the height of its glory in the gay Vienna of Johann Strauss and his son of the same name, and the old-fashioned waltz, from which the modern waltz was developed, is still called the Viennese waltz.

Two dancers performing the cha-cha, a dance that began in Latin America.

"No, unless one knows the meaning of the movements, Indian dancing is not easy to understand," Georgina agreed, "and it is the same with the dances of Japan and China. But even the smallest gesture has some meaning, and although much of it is religious, charming stories of birds, bees and flowers are told with beautiful movements of the hands and arms. These are very different from the wild dances of less advanced peoples, such as the Zulus of South Africa or some South Sea Islanders. As in the early dances of the white man, they are trying to please their gods or rouse their own fighting instincts; but all are linked, throughout the world, by man's desire to express himself in movement."

"Where can one see these folk dances?" asked Bill.

"The best place in the British Isles is at the International Eisteddfod at Llangollen in Wales, where dancers come from all over the world in their gay national costumes and dance to the accompaniment of pipes, guitars, accordions, and other musical instruments; and you will see them if you go abroad—away from the large towns. In Britain you do not often see folk dancing. With the increasing attractions of town life and modern forms of entertainment folk dancing tends to die out. You see, folk dancing seems to need the open air or the farmer's barn that is cleared after the day's work for an evening's merrymaking."

"I suppose then," Barbara said, "the people in towns started ballroom dances?"

"Yes, but they were taken from folk dances and toned down to suit a more formal way of life. Even today waltzes, quicksteps, rumbas, tangos, and foxtrots of the modern ballroom, as well as the lancers and polkas of old-time dance sessions, come from the folk dances of Europe, Africa and America. So you see, all over the world people love to dance."

DANCERS AND PIPER AT A HIGHLAND GATHERING

SOME HOBBIES: COOKING, SCRAPBOOK, PHOTOGRAPHY, TOY THEATRE

Hobbies

Hobbies are the things we do in our spare time. Every one should have some special interest, and the hobby that you start as a child may continue to give you fun and pleasure for the rest of your life.

(58)

THE HOBBY CLUB

One day Billy came home full of excitement. "They're starting a Hobby Club at school," he said. "The first meeting is next Thursday evening. Let's go."

On Thursday Billy and Barbara both went out to the Hobby Club after tea, and they found 30 or 40 other children already in the hall, some of them clutching albums or models in their hands. Presently Mr. Woodford, the master who was organizing the club, stood up and said, "I'm going to ask each boy and girl to give us a little talk about his or her favourite hobby; then we'll sort ourselves out into groups which have the same interests. Now who's going to start? First I'll ask any one who collects any-thing at all to tell us about it. Well now, what about you, Donald?"

(59)

STAMP-COLLECTING

At that, a boy came to the table with a thick red album under his arm, and said, "I collect stamps. I began by asking for any foreign stamps that came on letters at home. I carefully soaked the stamps off the paper in a little warm water, and then I arranged them by countries. As you may guess, I soon found that I had more

An album for stamps.

A stamp with the gummed hinge fixed to it. After the loose part of the hinge has been slightly moistened with the tongue, it is ready for mounting in the album.

than one stamp of the same kind from countries like France and Switzerland, but I put aside one example of each kind of stamp for my own collection in a special tin, and the rest I put together for 'swops.' This is the time to buy a stamp album, with a different page for each country; and then you stick the stamps from your collection in it, each one on the right page, using special sticky mounts or 'hinges.' You should never just stick the stamp in the book by its own gum, as this makes it impossible to change it afterwards.

"Now that I was getting interested, Dad asked a friend of his who works in an office to look out for stamps for me, and he used to send me stamps from all sorts of countries that I'd hardly heard of; some of them had lovely pictures on them. And as they came I mounted them on the right pages of my album. Soon I had stamps of some kind for over 20 different countries, and whenever I got a new country I used to look it up in the atlas, and find out where it was.

"By this time I wanted to spend some of my pocket money in making the collection better, and I used to go into a stamp shop. The man there told me the best thing to do was to buy a big envelope of assorted stamps for about £1. There were hundreds of stamps in it, and it took me some time to get them all sorted out when I got home; of course, I found that I already had some of them, so these went into the tin of 'swops,' but with the rest I nearly filled up some of my pages, and got examples of eight more countries.

"As my album was nearly full I asked for a bigger album for my birthday, and here it is with hard covers and lots of information in it so that you can tell what countries stamps come from—for they sometimes have their names written in languages and even letters that you can't understand. When I transferred the

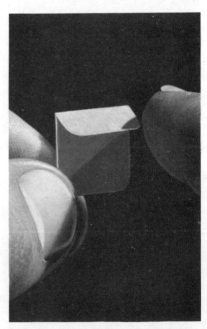

The gummed hinge folded before moistening. The shorter part is fixed to the stamp, the longer to the album.

288

collection from my first small album into this I was jolly glad that I had stuck the stamps in with proper mounts.

"I still sometimes get stamps that I haven't got, on letters that come through the post, but I'm trying to get at least one stamp for every country that's in my album, and by going to the stamp shop I'm gradually filling in the gaps. Meanwhile I've hundreds of 'swops' here which I'd be glad to exchange."

"Have you any valuable stamps?" someone asked. "I've heard of stamps worth thousands of pounds."

"Not likely," answered Donald. "All the stamps I've collected so far are modern ones. But the great thing about stamp collecting, or philately as it is called, is that one need never stop. If you have a little money to spend you can begin buying old stamps, and those are the ones that are worth the money. If you are

Placing the stamp in the album. Be careful not to moisten the actual gum of the stamp, but only the gum of the hinge.

handling old and rare stamps you should never even pick them up in your fingers, but use a pair of tweezers so as not to damage them. Even a modern stamp may be quite valuable if there has been a mistake in its printing, like printing the picture upside down. And there are lots of little things to look for, like the watermark on the paper and the perforations round the edges. There are so many stamps in the world that one man couldn't possibly collect them all, and big collectors usually do no more than try to get together all the stamps of one country, so as to make that collection absolutely complete. But some early stamps are so rare that only one copy is known to have survived, and for many others you may search for years before finding one for sale.

"If you are really interested there are special stamp magazines and societies that you can join, and you are always learning something new about rare stamps, and forgeries and bogus issues and so on."

Do not handle the stamps with your fingers. Use a special pair of tweezers with which to pick them up.

MATCHBOX LABELS

Peeling a matchbox cover off its box in warm water.

THE next boy who came to the table was also carrying an album and he said, "I collect matchbox labels. These are very like stamps in many ways; you can get a good number without having to pay anything at all, for instance; all you have to do is to collect empty matchboxes from your friends, and soak the labels off by leaving them in warm water. When the paper covers have floated off the thin wooden boxes you should wipe any surplus gum off the paper with cotton-wool, and then dry them between sheets of clean blotting paper, with a book on top to stop them curling up. They are then ready to be mounted in an album with 'hinges,' just like stamps.

"When you have got examples of all the different kinds of matchboxes that are sold in your district it is time to try to get some old or foreign ones. My elder brother is in the Merchant Navy, and he brings home empty boxes from all the countries he visits, and I've got lots of splendid labels in that way. The designs on the modern English boxes are not very interesting, but you'd be surprised at the lovely pictures on some foreign boxes; some of the boxes from India and the East have pictures of oriental gods on them, and there are lots of scenes from history, portraits of famous men, sports and animals and so on. The pictures on matchbox labels are bigger and brighter, and, I think, more interesting than those on stamps.

"Labels have been stuck on matchboxes ever since matches were invented, over a hundred years ago, and the earliest labels are even older than the first stamps. You can buy old labels just like old stamps from special shops, but there aren't as many matchbox dealers as there are stamp dealers, because there aren't so many

Some popular designs.

label collectors or 'phillumenists' as they are called. This is a good thing in some ways, as old labels are cheaper than stamps; you may still have to pay 20 to 30 pence for an early rare label but even the rarest ones don't cost more than a pound or so, and you can buy any number of foreign labels for a penny each, or less.

"In Great Britain there is even a British Matchbox Label and Booklet Society, with a special section for juniors. It issues a magazine and lists of 'swops'. In this way you can exchange your duplicates with other collectors and build up a very interesting collection. My dad says that he wouldn't be surprised if matchbox labels didn't soon become almost as valuable as stamps, as more and more people start collecting them."

An early English box of matches, with two kinds of "fusees."

Cheese labels from Holland, Denmark and Switzerland.

(61)

CHEESE LABELS

"I COLLECT something just like that," said a girl, jumping up; "I collect the labels on cheese packets. Do you know that there are about 100 different kinds of English cheese labels to be had, and over 500 different Swiss ones? You can get labels from Dutch, Danish, German and Italian cheeses too. My mum buys every new kind she sees so that I can add its label to my collection. I've heard that there's even a shop where you can buy the labels, too, for a few pence each.

"I keep my collection in an album, just like your matchbox labels, and there's a name for a cheese label collector, too," she added proudly, "he's called a 'fromologist'."

"Well, I only hope your family likes cheese," said Mr. Woodford, laughing. "There's no end to the things you can collect—cigarette cards and autographs and books and so on. But I'd like to hear a bit more about how some of you arrange your collections."

291

A BOX OF POSTCARDS

At that a girl came up to the table, holding a long narrow box under her arm. "I have made a collection of postcards of views of foreign countries," she said. "It started when my sister went on a holiday to Switzerland, and sent me a card from every place she visited; I kept these, and then gradually added cards from other countries that were sent to me by relations and friends. My brother made this wooden box to keep them in; luckily almost all postcards are the same size, so they can all be kept neatly in the same size box. I arrange them by countries, in alphabetical order, and within each country by the names of the town, or mountain or whatever is on the picture, also in alphabetical order.

"I also keep a special atlas with my postcards, and whenever I get a card of any place I underline the name of that place on the map in my atlas. If you look at the map of Italy, for instance, you will see that Rome, Florence, Naples and Capri are underlined; and if you look in the box you will find views of all these places on my cards.

"One day I hope I'll go abroad and see some of these places for myself; meanwhile I'm

Postcards from Italy. Views of Pisa (at the top), Rome, and Venice (at the bottom).

How to arrange a postcard collection.

learning lots of geography, which is very useful. And if any of you go abroad for your holidays, please remember to send me a card from where you're staying; it won't be thrown away, I promise you."

(63)

KEEPING A SCRAPBOOK

"I FIND it very interesting to make up scrapbooks," said the next boy; and he put three big albums down on the table. "This one is for the serial from the magazine I read; I cut it out each week and stick it in. The serials sometimes go on for so long that you forget how they started, and it's jolly useful to be able to turn up the first numbers and read them through again.

"Then this is my holiday scrapbook. I stick in photographs that we took on our holidays, and postcards of the places we visited; I draw a map of the country we explored; I stick in bus tickets of the excursions we went on, and anything else I can think of. It's nice to look back through these pages in the winter and to remember the good times we had.

"And the third scrapbook is just odds and ends; any interesting picture that I see in a magazine at home I cut out, when Mum and Dad have finished with it, and stick in this volume. I find that I've got some pictures of ships, some of aeroplanes, some of horses, some of wild animals, and so on, so I'm numbering the pages and making an index at the back of the book. I can then quickly turn up all the pictures of aeroplanes for instance, if I want to look at them all together.

"Sometimes albums get too fat when something is stuck on to every page, and it's a good idea to cut a couple of pages out of the book every so often, so as to make it easier to handle and keep on the bookshelf."

Some of the things you can put in a scrapbook to remind you of a happy holiday.

293

A model tank engine, for short journeys.

A mineral wagon for goods trains.

Two "home" signals controlling a double line railroad. In some models these can be electrically worked from a distance.

MODEL RAILWAYS

"I'M afraid I can't bring my hobby with me to show you," said the boy who spoke next, because it takes up the whole floor of a room at home. It's a model railway.

"You can start with clockwork trains, but sooner or later any one who gets at all interested wants to have an electric set. With an electric control you can make your train start, stop, go slow, and go backwards all by moving one lever in the corner of the room. There's no end to what you can make it do.

"To start with, of course, you must have a track. Usually trains will only run on the type of track they are made for; so it's worth considering carefully what system you're going to have before you begin to buy anything. There are several different types : one kind runs on two rails; two other kinds have a special rail in the middle; but the wiring of these two is different, so that while only one train can run at a time on one kind of track, the other can take two. You can see and compare all these different systems at a good model railway shop.

"As well as choosing the make you must also decide the scale you want. The various sizes are given numbers: ooo (or N) gauge is the smallest, to a scale of two millimetres to a foot; oo gauge, at four millimetres to a foot, is by far the most popular nowadays and is the best for the ordinary home; gauge o is twice as large, and is used for some of the clockwork systems; and gauge 1 is larger still and is the thing for expert scale modellers and out of door model railways.

"Laying out a track is the most interesting part of the hobby. You can arrange stations, sidings, points, bridges, signals, turn-tables, engine sheds, tunnels, level crossings, and lots

France

Mozambique

U.S.S.R.

Ethiopia

France

Japan

Greece

U.S.S.R.

Yugoslavia

Iceland

French Cameroons.

Liberia

French Equatorial Africa

Hungary

Belgium

Spain

Belgium

Liberia

Uganda

Belgian Congo

Hungary

Barbados

Germany

INTERESTING POSTAGE STAMPS OF MANY COUNTRIES AND PERIODS

Yugoslavia

India

Austria

Belgium

BRYANT & MAY, LONDON

ALPINE VESUVIAN

Great Britain, 1871

India

Venezuela

Yugoslavia

Sweden

India

Sweden

COLOURFUL MATCHBOX LABELS OF THE PAST AND PRESENT

CHEESE LABELS FROM THE DAIRY COUNTRIES OF EUROPE

AN ELECTRIC MODEL RAILWAY TRACK SYSTEM

of other things, to your own plan. You can make scenery along the side of the track, and rivers for it to cross, and villages at the stations.

"Then comes what's called the rolling stock. You can get model engines, either resembling electric or diesel-electric locomotives; or steam locos, reminding us of the steam age just passed; you can get corridor coaches and suburban coaches, and all kinds of goods wagons—coal and oil and cattle and so on.

"Now to make the railway go. Electric railways can be worked either from the mains or from batteries. If you use the mains you need a transformer to convert the high voltage that comes to the house into something lower that is quite safe if you touch it; model railways usually use 12 volts. In either case you need a controller to regulate speed and direction.

"If a carriage gets de-railed and lies across the track, or if the track is not correctly joined together, you may get a short circuit. When this happens the fuse in the transformer may blow, but your control unit will probably have an overload cut-out, which is like a knob that pops up whenever anything goes wrong. This saves the windings in the transformer from damage. If you put things straight and press it down, you will be all right again.

"I think that having a model railway is the most interesting hobby in the world, and lots of grown-up men go on making them all their lives. I think my dad plays with mine as much as I do! But there's one big snag. It is very expensive to buy all this wonderful equipment. You really need a rich uncle to pull twenty pounds out of his notecase to give you a good start! But you can sometimes buy a set second-hand, and once you've started you can add gradually as you go along; a goods wagon, a signal, or a length of rail does not cost a great deal. You can make stations and bridges and lots of things yourself.

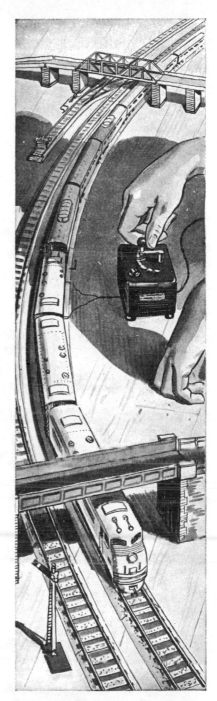

An American-style, coast-to-coast model diesel loco, with trans-continental passenger cars, vista dome and observation coaches, roars across the living-room floor at a touch on the speed control unit.

Model of an overhead electric supply locomotive, with pantographs.

Model of a diesel-electric locomotive.

A beautiful model of a famous express engine reminding us of the great days of steam.

"If you get really keen, you can lay your own railway track; grown-ups often make their own locomotives and carriages. There are magazines to read, and exhibitions to see, and clubs to join. It's a hobby that never comes to an end."

(65)

LOCOSPOTTING

"My hobby is also railways," said the next boy. "I'm a locospotter. I've always liked playing with trains and watching railways, and a year ago I started to write down in a notebook the numbers of every engine I saw. Soon my notebook was getting in a proper muddle, and I was writing the same number down twice without knowing it, so I got a jolly useful book giving the numbers of every locomotive running on the railways, and I joined the Locospotters Club. Now whenever I see a loco I put a tick against its number in the book, and find out all about it—its name, weight, size and arrangement of wheels, and so on. Only a few engines have names, but the number tells you straightaway what class of loco it belongs to, and the date when it was introduced.

"I often spend an afternoon during the holidays at a spot on an embankment near my home, where I can watch the trains go past. Sometimes I go on to the platform at the station. If you do this you should always ask the stationmaster or one of the porters where you can stand, and every member of the club has to promise to keep the club rule, not to interfere with railway working, not to trespass on railway property, and not to get in the way of the railway staff.

"Since I've joined the local branch of the Locospotters Club, I'm looking forward to going on visits to railway works and engine sheds when I'm a bit older."

A bridge is a good point from which to spot trains. You need to see the side of the locomotive too so that the wheel arrangements can be noted. The letters and figures on the front of the locomotive indicate the type of the train, its destination and the number for its journey. In addition, each locomotive has its own number. So there is quite a lot to spot about each locomotive.

BRASS-RUBBING

The girl whose turn it was to speak next put several big rolls of paper on the table in front of her. "I expect that you've all seen the brass memorials on the floors of old churches," she began. "They usually show a Knight and his wife, or perhaps a priest, and they were put there on top of their graves as tombstones. I find it very interesting to go round churches making 'rubbings' of these old brasses, and it's wonderful what good copies can be produced.

"First of all, of course, you should always ask the Vicar of the church for permission, but he will usually be only too glad to give it. Before you start you should make sure the brass is absolutely smooth and clean, and it's a good idea to have a nailbrush with which to brush the dirt out of the lines and a duster to dust the surface; then you want a big sheet of paper; the best kind is a roll of white lining or ceiling paper, fairly tough but not too thick, which is sold in lengths of 12 yards, about 30 inches wide. Start at the top of the brass, and put the end of the roll under some books or hassocks to keep it flat, or you can fix it down with adhesive tape; then gradually unroll it towards you, rubbing on the paper as you go.

"The actual rubbing is done with a lump of 'heelball' or cobbler's wax, a mixture of beeswax, tallow and lampblack. The man who mends your shoes will probably let you have some. You just rub it evenly over the whole brass, and you will find that the flat parts of the brass come out black but that where the brass has been cut into to make the picture the rubbing makes no mark and shows as white on the paper. The 'heelball' will not smudge, and you can even polish it up with a handkerchief.

"When you get home you can cut the rubbing

A 15th-century brass portrait of a knight, from a church in Norfolk. You can learn a lot about armour from studying these tombs. See, too, the curly moustaches that this old gentleman wore.

A brass-rubbing from Kent, showing a young knight and his wife, with their coat of arms. Both this rubbing and the one opposite are in the Victoria and Albert Museum.

out and mount it on a piece of thicker paper, and it makes a very unusual decoration to hang up. But as most brasses are rather large you won't be able to hang up very many of them, and most of them will have to remain rolled up. You should always remember to write on each roll the church where it was taken, the name of the person represented on it, the date it was made (if that is given), and the date when you made the rubbing.

"Funnily enough, the pictures are usually much clearer on the rubbing than they are on the actual brass. You can learn lots about history and the costumes of the middle ages from these rubbings; they began making brasses in about 1300 and they went on till about 1600, but the earliest ones are the best. Some of the figures are life size, but many are smaller, some as little as 12 inches high. Sometimes there is a brass monument to a whole family, with the father and mother at the top, and a whole line of children, shown grown up but much smaller, underneath.

Making a brass-rubbing in an old church.

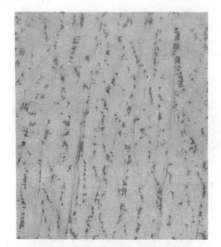

A sycamore bark-rubbing.

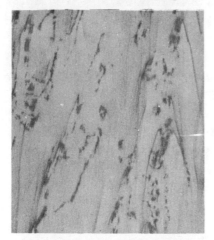

A horse-chestnut bark-rubbing.

A hawthorn bark-rubbing.

"I've not only learnt lots of history from this hobby, but I've had a chance of visiting and really examining lots of lovely old churches that I've discovered on bicycling expeditions."

(67)

BARK-RUBBING

"I TAKE rubbings just like that," said a boy in the audience, "but I'm interested in natural history, and I make rubbings of the barks of trees.

"All you have to do is to pin a piece of white cartridge paper to a tree trunk with drawing pins, and then rub it up and down, not cross-ways, with a piece of cobbler's wax. You can get lovely patterns like this, and every tree has a different kind of bark. Two of the best ones are wych elms and sweet chestnuts; a smooth tree like the beech isn't so good.

"A good size of paper to use for each rubbing is 12 inches by 18 inches, and you should, of course, always write the name of the tree on the back of the paper for a record."

Making a bark-rubbing.

"That sounds very interesting," said Mr. Woodford. "I wonder if there are any other natural history collections that any one can tell us something about."

(68)

PRESSED PLANTS

AT that a girl stood up and said, "I get a great deal of pleasure from making a collection of pressed plants. It seems such a pity that the lovely flowers we see growing in the garden and in the fields should wither away and die without leaving a trace behind, but if you press them carefully you can preserve them for a long time.

"The way to do this is to take a simple plant press with you when you go out into the country; you can buy one from a naturalist shop, or make one for yourself with a small-sized newspaper and two pieces of card, cut to the size of the page, tied with tapes. When you see a plant you would like to preserve, you should cut its stem neatly with a sharp penknife, and

Restharrow
Species.. Ononis arvensis
N.O. Leguminoseæ
Habitat.. Barren wastes.

A wild plant, one of the pea family, properly pressed and mounted, with its botanical details noted on the sheet.

Mounting a pressed plant in a loose-leaf album.

305

Another member of the pea family.

This wild plant belongs to the same family as the rose. Always press both the leaf and the flower of a plant.

place it straight away between the sheets of the plant press, making sure it is fairly dry first. When you get home you can place the plant between fresh sheets of newspaper or blotting paper, and press it for a week or so under the weight of several books; if the plant is juicy and the paper gets damp you should change it for fresh sheets. The plant should be arranged in the press in a good position, to show as much as possible how it grows; you might press two examples of the same plant side by side, one with the petals of the flower closed and the other open to show the stamens. Only light pressure should be applied for the first day, but this can be increased as the plant becomes dry; small pads of folded blotting paper or cotton-wool may be placed on either side of thick stems to save them from getting too badly crushed.

"After a week or so the plant will be ready to be taken out of the press, and you can mount it in an album with strips of transparent gummed paper. Don't forget to write on the sheet below it the name of the plant—its English and botanical name if possible—and where and when you found it. An even better way of mounting is to gum the dried plant on to a piece of card, which should be covered with Cellophane and kept upright in a deep drawer or cabinet.

"When you have a collection of pressed plants like this it is easy to examine them carefully, to note all the differences between the various families, and to learn a great deal about how they grow.

"You can press seaweed, too, in just the same way. It can always be gathered on the sea shore at low tide, but the best time of all is after a storm. I have collected lots of different specimens on my seaside holidays. You'd be surprised how pretty they look; they're not really weeds at all, but the flowers of the sea."

PICKING WILD FLOWERS IN THE SPRING FOR PRESSING

THE FIRST STAGE IN MAKING LEAF SKELETONS—SOAKING IN WATER

LEAF SKELETONS

The skeleton of a magnolia leaf.

Lift the skeleton on a knife.

"I KNOW another way of preserving leaves," cried a boy. "You keep their skeletons."

"I never knew leaves had skeletons," said someone.

"Oh, yes, they have," the boy answered. "If you've ever looked at a leaf after it's fallen to the ground you can often notice how the tracery holds together after the rest has rotted away. To preserve these, put freshly picked leaves to soak in a big earthenware bowl or pail filled with rain water, and leave it in a warm sunny spot in the garden. After a month or so some of the leaves will begin to lose the green pulpy stuff that covers them. When the leaf seems ready, slip a piece of cardboard underneath it, lift it out of the pail, and wash it under a cold tap; it may need a light dab with a soft brush, or even a touch with a pin here and there in obstinate corners, to get rid of all the green. You then have a perfect leaf skeleton, but if you want to preserve it you have to treat it in a special way.

"A chemical preserving mixture can be made like this. Take about half a pound of pure chloride of lime or bleaching powder, which is bought at a hardware shop, and stir it carefully into half a gallon of cold water. Let the solution stand overnight and then pour it off into bottles, leaving the sediment behind. Fill an earthenware dish or saucer with some of the solution, and lay the leaves in it. They will be bleached white in from six to twelve hours. Then lift them out carefully, on the blade of a knife, as they will be very brittle, and rinse them with cold water. It's a good idea to float them on to cards in the water to avoid handling them with the fingers. Finally, dry them between sheets of blotting paper.

"This mixture of chloride of lime can damage

the skin or clothes, so it should be *handled with great care*. My dad always makes it up for me, and he says that children should never play about with it by themselves; he tries not to dip his hands in it at all, and always washes his hands well immediately after using it; if any is splashed on to the face, or especially the eyes, it must be washed off at once with plenty of cold water.

"The leaf skeletons look best mounted with transparent sticky paper on to sheets of black cardboard. You can write the names of the trees underneath in special white ink. It looks jolly good, and no one can guess how it's been done."

Part of the skeleton of a poplar leaf shown life-size.

(70)

LEAF PRINTS

ANOTHER girl now jumped up and said, "I've discovered that one can make prints of leaf patterns. You should paint Indian ink or thick water-colour on to a leaf with a fairly dry brush, and then place it on some paper, and press. It's useful to keep plenty of old newspaper handy to keep the table clean; and if you choose leaves with stalks to hold your hands don't get so dirty. You can 'print' either the upper or lower side of the leaf, and get different pictures from each. You can also 'print' on to cotton or

Below are some examples of leaf prints.

beech

plane

lime

310

The print of a lilac leaf.

any material like that, and by using different colours and arranging the leaves in different patterns you can decorate curtains to look very pretty.

"I keep a special album for my leaf prints, in which I mount specimens of every kind of tree I can discover. It's better to cut the best prints out of your printing paper than to try to print straight on to the pages of the album, as you sometimes make a bit of a mess the first time. I write the name of the tree under each print, and I'm always looking for new examples to add to my collection."

(71)

SPATTERWORK

The fronds of the male fern outlined by spatterwork. There are over a dozen common types of fern. You could make a collection of their fronds in this way.

"I KNOW of another way of preserving leaves—or at least the shapes of them," said a girl; "it's called 'spatterwork,' because you spatter the object with paint. Ferns show up very well like this if you arrange them in a nice pattern on to the sheet of paper, or whatever you want to decorate; you may need to press them for a few minutes to make them lie flat. Then you dip an old toothbrush lightly into some powder paint, mixed rather thickly with water, and holding it over the leaves, rub its bristles gently across an old comb with finely set teeth. This will send a spray of paint over the paper. Do this again and again until the tone is deep enough, and also try to graduate it, so that it's darker in the centre. Of course, when you're experimenting with this method you should spread plenty of newspaper over the table, and wear an old overall over your clothes, in case some of the paint flies in the wrong direction!

"If you now remove the ferns, you will find that there is a white space underneath each one, exactly reproducing their beautiful shape."

311

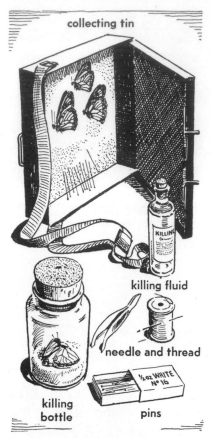

collecting tin

killing fluid

needle and thread

killing bottle

pins

Things needed for hunting butterflies.

72

COLLECTING BUTTERFLIES

"My hobby is also natural history," said the boy who stood up next, "but I have made a collection of butterflies. Catching them and mounting them is quite an art. First of all you need a butterfly net, of course, and with practice you learn how to net a butterfly not only while it's resting on a leaf but also in flight, and how a quick turn of the wrist will close the mouth of the net and stop the butterfly flying out again. When the butterfly is caught it has to be killed without damaging it in any way, and for this we use a killing bottle, which has something in it whose smell will kill the butterflies. You can buy a killing fluid, a small drop of which on some cotton wool will act very quickly, and keep this in an ordinary jam jar with a tight cork lid, or you can buy specially prepared killing bottles from a chemist or naturalist.

"Persuading the butterfly to fly into the killing jar out of the net without losing it in the process needs a bit of practice, but you soon get

How to hold a butterfly net. A long handle is seldom necessary.

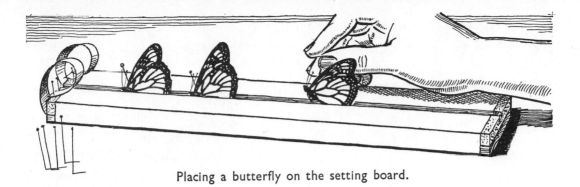

Placing a butterfly on the setting board.

the hang of it; then you put the lid on the jar, and the butterfly quickly goes to sleep and never wakes up again. It's quite painless.

"When you're sure that it's really dead you can take the butterfly out of the jar and put it in a 'collecting box' until you get home; this is an ordinary tin, with a layer of cork in the bottom; and if you keep this cork damp it will prevent the body of the butterfly stiffening after death. You should pin it to the cork with a proper black entomological pin, placed sideways through the middle of its body.

"As soon as you get home you must prepare the butterfly for display by arranging it on a setting board; this is just a piece of wood with a groove cut down the middle in which the insect's body is pinned. Its wings have probably closed together since it was caught, and you have to open them out carefully and fix them on to the wood on either side of the groove so as to display them in the best way. By gently pinching the body between your finger and thumb the wings will open enough to allow you to place a pin downwards through its thorax— the thick middle part of its body—and into the groove of the setting board. You now have to arrange the wings, and it is very important that these are well placed; the line where the upper and lower wings join should stretch straight out from the body, and at right angles with the groove. In arranging them you should never handle a butterfly with your fingers at all, but

insect forceps

setting needles

setting paper

pins

relaxing bottle and fluid

Things needed for setting butter-flies. The relaxing bottle is needed if the butterfly has become stiff.

313

Setting: stage 1.

Setting: stage 2.

Setting: stage 3.

use forceps (pair of tweezers) and a setting needle, mounted in a piece of cork. Of course, you don't fix the wings down with pins, as this would damage them, but you use tape, which you get in rolls specially made for the job. After a little practice you soon find the best way to fix the wings neatly in position.

"You should leave the butterfly on a setting board for a few weeks to allow it to become firmly 'set' in this position; if you take it off too soon the wings may close up again. The setting board should not be left about to get dusty or moth-eaten but should be kept in a warm dry place; an old meat safe is a very good place, with a few moth balls put in it. You will probably need several setting boards of different sizes, for the different sizes of butterflies you may catch.

"Then one day, at the end of the season perhaps, you may decide to mount your specimens. I asked for a special display cabinet for my birthday, and they look fine in this, but you can use a shallow drawer lined with black velvet, which shows the colours off well too. All you have to do is to unfix the setting tapes, and carefully lift the butterfly out by its pin and fix it in your mounting box. To give the finishing touch you should write the name of the butterfly on a small card—you can get a sheet with the Latin and English names printed on it ready for cutting out—and the date and place where you caught it, and pin this beneath the specimen with the same mounting pin, so that it never becomes separate. A butterfly without this information always beside it loses its real scientific interest and value.

"Of course, you can set and mount moths in just the same way, but these usually have to be caught at night. Oh, and there is one very useful thing you always ought to carry with you, and that is a needle and thread to mend your butterfly net if it gets torn while you're out."

314

73

KEEPING SILKWORMS

A silkworm moth laying its eggs.

"I COLLECT a kind of moth," said the next girl; "it's called a silkworm. We get the eggs from a silk farm, where they are bred, or from a naturalist's shop; they have been laid in the summer by silkworm moths, and they lie sleeping all through the winter until the spring; as soon as the leaves are out on the trees and bushes you can lay the eggs on a piece of paper, and in a few days out of the side of each egg a tiny worm will crawl.

"The food they like is mulberry leaves; so unless you have a mulberry tree in your garden or very near, it's not worth while trying to keep silkworms at all. You should cut up some mulberry leaves into thin strips, and put them among the worms; the worms will climb on to the leaves, which you should then pick up with a pair of tweezers and place in the rearing tray.

"The rearing trays are trays arranged one above the other in tiers. Their size depends upon how many worms you are rearing; you can calculate that 200 worms need one square yard of tray. The trays should be kept not less than 18 inches apart and made with bottoms of wooden slats, that will let plenty of air circulate. The whole thing should be kept in a light, well ventilated room, or hut, or greenhouse; it should be dry, free from draughts, and kept at a steady temperature of 70 to 75 degrees Fahrenheit.

"The creatures live as worms for only 30 to 35 days, but during this time they need constant attention if you want to get good results. They should be fed with fresh mulberry leaves, cut finely at first, every four hours; during the night they can last for six or seven hours without fresh food. You must *never* give them damp mulberry leaves, and you should remove uneaten

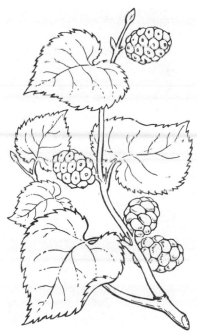

The leaves and fruit of the mulberry tree. It is from eating these leaves that the worm produces silk.

315

Rearing trays for silkworms.

Silkworms feeding.

leaves every few days. They will do very little except eat, and will grow very fast; each worm bursts out of its skin into a new one four times during its short life. In their final shape they are three or four inches long and almost white in colour.

"When the worms look like this you know that they will soon begin to spin, and you should provide some nice surroundings in which they can make their cocoons. Dry twigs or straw are very suitable. They will climb into this, rig a little 'safety net' to stop them falling out, and begin to squeeze a liquid out of a hole in their 'lips', which dries hard like a thread in the air. They carefully wrap this round themselves, in a figure eight pattern, for three days. They now look like long yellow peanuts. Inside the cocoon the worm turns into a chrysalis.

"If you leave them for another three weeks, moths will come out of the cocoons; and each female moth will lay 250 to 350 eggs. But it is not a good idea to try to hatch your own eggs because the moths from one cluster of eggs would all be brothers and sisters and if they mate with each other—this is called inbreeding —their bodies are not very strong and easily catch a disease which can kill silkworms in thousands. So it is best to leave the breeding to experts who know how to protect the eggs against this disease.

Aquamarine Beryl

Agate
(sliced, stained and polished)

Fluorite

Sulphur

Amethyst in quartz
(broken open)

Quartz or Rock Crystal

Onyx
(stained and polished)

Blue Agate
(sliced and polished)

Rose Agate
(cut and polished)

Smoky Quartz or Cairngorm

Crocidolite or Tiger Eye
(sliced and polished)

Rubellite

MINERALS, PARTLY IN THEIR NATURAL STATE AND PARTLY POLISHED

from the Amazon

from Peru

from French Guiana

from the Amazon

from Colombia

from Bolivia (underside)

from Paraguay

from India

SOME BEAUTIFUL BUTTERFLIES FROM TROPICAL COUNTRIES

Tortoiseshell

Painted Lady

Comma

White Admiral

Peacock

Red Admiral

Common Blue (male)

Small Copper

Orange Tip (male)

Swallowtail

Chalkhill Blue (male)

BUTTERFLIES FROM GREAT BRITAIN AND NORTH AMERICA

Green Turbo
(Pacific)

Ear Shell
(English Channel)

Bleeding Tooth
(Atlantic)

Orange Spire
(Atlantic)

Top Shell
(Madeira)

Orange Strombus
(Indian Ocean)

Zebra Cone
(Torrid Zone)

Tiger Cowrie
(Indian Ocean)

Pink Eared Murex
(Australia)

Spider Shell
(Indian Ocean)

Pectens (2)
(English Channel)

SEA-SHELLS OF ALL SHAPES AND COLOURS FROM MANY SEASHORES

"What we really want are the cocoons, because the thread the worm has spun round itself is *pure silk*! If you unwind it, you can get nearly half a mile of unbroken silk thread from each cocoon. You can do this yourself by softening the cocoon in a cup of warm water, and winding the thread on to a piece of card. As you may not be able to unwind all your cocoons before the moths come out—which spoils them for winding—you should kill the chrysalis inside the cocoon ten days after it has been formed, by baking the cocoons on the bottom shelf of a very low oven (180 degrees Fahrenheit) for four hours.

"Actually I don't try to unwind my cocoons, because I can't use the silk thread properly; but I send them to a silk farm, which buys them if they are up to standard, and the money I get is a very useful addition to my pocket money. From the farm they send the raw silk to 'throwsters' who twist it into threads, and dye it different colours, and to weavers who weave the threads into lengths of silk."

Silkworm moths emerging from their cocoons.

Queen Elizabeth II in her coronation robe of pure silk, spun by silkworms that were bred in England.

74

SHELLS FROM THE SHORE

A whelk shell.

A GIRL now came to the table with a shallow wooden box, and when she had opened it the children saw that it was divided into square compartments, in each of which lay a brightly coloured shell.

"I've been collecting shells for three years," she said. "Every year we go to a different seaside place for our holiday, and I bring home a good assortment of different kinds each time. I suppose everyone knows that shells are not like stones, but that every shell was once the house in which a little creature called a mollusc lived. There are two kinds of shells; single shells, called univalves, which generally grow in a spiral shape, with the number of whorls, or turns, increasing each year the creature lives; and hinged shells, or bivalves, which can close up tight, so that you can't possibly open them with your fingers. Common univalves are winkles, whelks, limpets, and cowries; common bivalves are mussels, scallops, cockles, oysters, and razor fish.

Dredging for shells on the seashore.

A cockle shell.

"You can find hundreds of broken or chipped shells on any sea shore at low tide, but it's only worth while collecting perfect specimens; the halves of bivalves, with their hinges broken, are not worth picking up. If possible it's always worth looking for the actual living mollusc by digging in the sand or dredging in pools. They can be killed instantly by pouring boiling water over them. Of course, the mollusc should always be cleaned out of any shell you want to keep, and the inside thoroughly washed out.

"When I get a selection of shells home I identify what kind they are by finding them in a book I have; then I write a card with the name, and the date and place where I found it, and put it in a cabinet like this one. There are lots of lovely shapes and colours in shells, and my mother lets me use a little of her manicure powder for polishing them when they're dry.

"So far I've only collected sea shells, but, of course, there are lots of different kinds of snails, found on land and in ponds, each with its own kind of shell, and I'm going to start a new cabinet for these next."

(75)

FOSSILS

"Why, I've got a collection of shells, too," said a boy, jumping up, "but mine are millions of years old!"

There was quite a gasp all round the room.

"They're what are called fossils," the boy went on. "They're found in rocks. What happened was that in the ages when the earth was new, long before there were any men on it, animals died and their flesh rotted away and their skeletons sank into the oozy mud. Then gradually the mud hardened and after perhaps hundreds of thousands of years turned into hard rock. And then, perhaps a million years

Three types of animal fossils. The top drawing shows how univalve shells may be found embedded in rock together with traces of many other sea creatures. The two lower drawings show parts of molluscs that once lived on earth.

323

Scraping fossils from a chalk cliff
with a penknife.

later, the rock was heaved up out of the seas and valleys into mountains and hills. All this time the skeletons were still there in the rock, but by this time they had been turned into something like stone themselves. But they still kept their shapes, and you can still find them today.

"The best place to look is in chalk, especially in a quarry or along a cliff. Our chalk downs were once ooze at the bottom of the sea and lots of fossilized shells can be found embedded in them. I take a strong penknife and a hammer with a sharp point on one side with me when I go out looking for fossils; whenever I see any unusual kind of marking in the chalk I carefully chip a block of it away, and then even more carefully scrape it, until I can get an idea of what shape the thing is. For some delicate fossils, like sea urchins, I use an old tooth brush, with the bristles cut down, for brushing the chalk away; and I keep them in an empty matchbox to save damage. Of course, there are lots of fossils in other kinds of rock too; but these are sometimes too hard to cut away, and you can only see their shape in the stone. I've got a book on fossils now, which is teaching me a lot."

324

(76)

ROCK-COLLECTING

"I go out with a pointed hammer too," said another boy, "but I don't only look for fossils; I'm making a geological collection—you know, different kinds of rocks. I've been on all kinds of expeditions with my father to places where different rocks are found.

"You really need a proper geological hammer, with one end square and the other shaped like a chisel, but you can manage with an ordinary hammer and a cold chisel. When you find an exposed rock of which you would like a specimen it is best to knock a piece off a projecting edge, or corner, with the square end of the hammer; heavy blows are not needed, but sharp taps in the right place. Then you should trim the piece with the pointed end of the hammer to a convenient size, about 3 inches by 2 inches. Don't collect bits of rock that have been worn away by the weather, as this gives a wrong idea of their usual shape. Finally wrap your specimen up in a bit of old newspaper, and put it in your haversack. When you get home you should wash

Collecting specimens of different kinds of rock with a geological hammer.

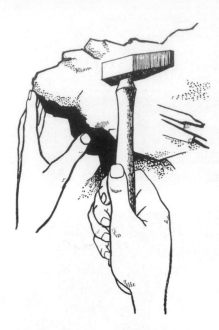

Using a geological hammer to knock off a projecting piece of rock.

Using the hammer to trim a specimen to a convenient size and shape.

it, and gum a small label on it, giving the name of the rock and the place where it was found, with the date. My dad's got a book which helps us to tell what kind it is, and there are some jolly useful geological maps you can get, too.

"There are two main types of rocks: what are called 'sedimentary' rocks were formed by deposits gradually settling during millions of years, like chalk on the bed of the sea, or coal which was once forests that have fallen and rotted away; 'igneous' rocks on the other hand, were once so hot that they melted fifty miles inside the earth's surface, and were thrown up like lava out of a volcano to run like treacle until they cooled hard, into granite for instance. That's why the sedimentary rocks are usually found in layers or seams, one above the other, and the igneous rocks in piles, like mountain ranges. There is a third kind called 'meta-morphic' rock, which is one of the first two kinds that has been changed into some other form; for instance, I've got a little loose sand in a jar, but if, as has sometimes happened, this sand gets pressed down very deep in the earth where it is terrifically hot, it gets turned into very hard rock called quartzite. I've got a piece of this too. Then I've got a lump of limestone, which is made up of millions of bits of broken sea shells all squashed together; but if this gets hot deep in the earth it turns into marble, and I've got some fine bits of marble with lovely veins and patterns in them.

"Sometimes I find a crystal, like a jewel or precious stone; I've never picked up a diamond or sapphire, I'm afraid, but I have got some serpentine and fluorspar which look just as good, even if they're not so valuable.

"I keep my specimens in a tray like the one used for shells, only with rather larger com-partments. I find that looking out for rocks makes a walk in the country much more interesting."

326

77

A TABLE-TOP GARDEN

A cactus garden in a bowl is ideal for indoors.

"WE live in a flat," said the girl who spoke next, "but I'm very keen on gardening, and I've made an indoor garden in an old meat tin. It's just like a real garden, with growing plants, but everything is in miniature; I've even got two trees and a lake !"

"However do you do that?" someone asked.

"Well, it's all a matter of choosing the right plants," the girl answered, "and of planning a nice arrangement. You can use a bowl or anything you like for the garden, as long as it's three or four inches deep; you should fill it with soil to about an inch from the top. If you're going to have a lake this can be an empty shaving bowl, such as my daddy uses, or any other small round bowl, buried to its rim in the earth. It looks best if it's put not right in the middle, but a bit to one side. You can keep it

Looking after a miniature garden indoors.

327

A dwarf oriental evergreen tree, 45 years old and 24 inches high. The Japanese are masters at rearing dwarf trees.

filled with water, and build a little bridge over it, and buy ducks to float on it if you like. Then you should arrange small pieces of stone making a footpath to the lake, and you might be able to buy a miniature pagoda, or make a little summer house, to go at the other end of the path.

"Here are some of the plants that look well in a miniature garden. First of all, for some greenery: *helxine* grows almost everywhere and spreads so quickly that its nickname is 'Mind Your Own Business'; it makes a thick mat of bright green, and is useful for covering up any bare patches; you have to keep it under control by cutting it back with scissors. *Selaginella* is another tiny creeping green plant that spreads easily, and patches of *moss* look well among the stones. *Ferns* always grow well in shady spots, and there are small and tiny varieties that are excellent for a miniature garden.

"For flowering plants, *stonecrop* is very useful; it comes up every year and grows up to four inches high; it has either yellow, white or pink flowers, which blossom all through the spring and summer. Another pretty little flower is the dwarf *sweet alyssum*, which can be planted in spring and will blossom to the very end of summer; it's a good idea to keep a reserve stock of this in a pot on the window sill, and transfer small pieces, with their roots, to the miniature garden as they are needed. Then you can get a kind of *sempervivum* called the cobweb houseleek, which grows a stalk about four inches long with a red flower in June; and lots of common garden flowers—like thyme, viola, daffodils, and roses— can be bought in special dwarf varieties for indoor gardens."

"How do you get trees to grow?" a boy asked.

"There is quite an art in this," the girl answered. "You must start with the seed or a very tiny shoot. Some gardeners prune the roots every November; others moisten the roots and tie each one into a knot near the main

This pine tree is 50 years old, and yet has grown to a height of only 30 inches.

MAKING A MINIATURE GARDEN IN AN OLD KITCHEN SINK

driven by a
rubber band

glider

engine-driven
on a control
line

engine-driven
for free flight

THESE BOYS ARE HAPPY WITH THEIR VARIOUS MODEL AIRCRAFT

trunk; others use very slow-growing trees which will keep small for five or ten years. The tree must be kept in a pot to prevent its roots stretching out. You can grow a dwarf oak tree from an acorn, or a dwarf chestnut from a conker in this way. I've seen a pine tree that was fifty years old, and only 30 inches high. These dwarf trees are rather delicate though, and they do need to be looked after carefully; they should be kept away from gas fumes and the dry heat of a fire, and out of cold draughts; they should also be sprayed from time to time with luke-warm water to wash dust off their leaves.

"If you want to have a dwarf tree in your miniature garden you should still keep it in its pot—otherwise it will start to grow too big, but you can sink the pot in the soil and then build up a little hill round it covered with moss."

"Do you have to water an indoor garden?"

"Yes, but not too much. The moss is a good guide; if this is green and fresh-looking, the soil

A dwarf chestnut tree, grown from a "conker."

is almost certainly moist enough. You should never get the bowl swimming in water."

"Do you have to put the bowl in a window box?" asked Mr. Woodford.

"No. You can keep it on the top of a table near the window. It's a good idea to turn it round from time to time so that the flowers don't all lean in one direction to face the light. But, of course, you can have a miniature garden out of doors on a balcony or in a yard; a good thing for this is an old-fashioned shallow kitchen sink; you can often find these lying about in builders' yards; if possible it should be of stone, not of glazed earthenware; it should be raised off the ground on bricks or blocks of wood, so that any water in it will drain out of the sink hole. The drainage hole should be covered with a layer of broken flower pot that will let the water out but keep the soil in; then a layer of cinders should be spread all over the bottom before the soil is put in."

A miniature orange tree, grown from a pip. Lemon and grapefruit trees can be sown in the same way.

78

MAKING A MUSEUM

Mr. Woodford now stood up. "I'm afraid it's time to end the meeting for today," he said. "But before we go home there's one idea I've had. We've heard of so many different interesting hobbies, and so many things to collect, and I thought it might be a good idea to make our own museum. Perhaps every boy and girl who has spoken about their hobbies would like to give just a few specimens of them to the museum. That would make a start. And then I expect that many of us have some old or interesting things tucked away at home that we'd be glad to lend."

"I have some old coins," said one boy straight away; "my uncle found them in a field last year just after it had been ploughed. He took them to the museum, and they told him they were Roman coins."

"And I have some coins too," said a girl. "They are dated 1815, the year of the battle of Waterloo; my grandmother gave them to me; she said they had lain in a purse that belonged to her great-great-great grandmother."

"I have an interesting bank note," said another girl, "it's a German note issued in 1922 for 100,000 marks. You might think it was worth a lot of money, but its value was only about a penny because of the inflation of money in Germany at that time after the Great War."

"I have a German bank note issued by the Allies after the second war," said a boy; "my dad brought it home. We could put those two side by side."

"I have some sharp little flints," said the boy who collected fossils; "I found them out in the hills, and the man at the museum said that they were the heads of arrows or spears, used by cave-men in the Stone Age."

coins

medals

regimental cap badges

prehistoric flints

Some of the objects that you can collect for a school museum. You might also have some curios from foreign countries.

Visiting the local museum.

"What about medals?" asked another boy. "I have some medals given to my great-grandfather for fighting in Egypt; they've got Queen Victoria's portrait on them."

"I have a medal for the Crimean War," said another boy.

"If you're going to show army things," said a third, "my dad made a collection of cap badges of famous regiments; he's given it to me now, and I'm trying to bring it up to date."

"I see that we're going to get plenty for our museum," said Mr. Woodford. "I must arrange for some glass cases to show it all in. Then we must write little notices under the objects explaining what they are. We can get some ideas by studying the display in our own town museum, which we ought to visit regularly. Now we've no more time today, but next week we will have another meeting, and I would like **any** boys or girls who make and do things themselves to come ready to tell us all about it."

333

79

MODEL AIRCRAFT

A glider. This is the best model to start with, to learn the principles of building, trimming and flying. The wings and tail are fastened to the fuselage with rubber bands, which may be seen in the photograph. The glider is launched into the wind with a smooth, steady over-arm throw. A good spot from which to launch it is a mound or small hill; in suitable conditions it is amazing how far it can fly before grounding.

At the next meeting of the Hobby Club there was an even larger attendance than before. After a little pause a boy called John came forward who had brought with him several kinds of model aeroplanes in various stages of construction and now put them in front of him on the table.

"I think that making model aircraft is the most interesting hobby you can have," John said, "and it is certainly very popular nowadays. There's lots to learn; in fact you never stop learning if you go on making them all your life, but it's quite easy to start with simple models. Another good thing is that it's very cheap, at the beginning stage anyhow; the smallest kit costs about one and sixpence and there are lots of very good models at under ten shillings."

"Do you make the aeroplanes, or buy them ready-made?" Billy asked.

"You can buy one or two models ready-made, but the interesting thing is making them yourself," John answered. "There are four ways of doing this : you can buy a kit of parts that are already all cut out, and all you have to do is to put them together; or you can buy the kit with the parts 'die cut,' which means all you have to do is to push them out of the wood and you have the right shapes; or, thirdly, you can buy kits with the shapes marked on the wood, which you have to cut out yourself; and, lastly, you can just get a plan, and then buy what materials you need to make it up."

"What materials are model aircraft made of?" Billy asked.

"They're almost all made of balsa wood. This is a very light wood, easy to cut out and ideal for the job. There are two main types of construction : the solid model, which is made of

A rubber-driven model. This is cheap to build, and ideal for gaining experience for more advanced flying.

balsa wood throughout; and the built up model which is made of a framework of balsa strips, over which a paper cover is stretched. The built up models are lighter and larger, and are the most common."

"How do you make the aircraft fly?" another boy asked.

"The simplest kind are gliders: that's the best model to start with. They just glide through the air, of course, for a short distance. An ordinary home-made glider may fly for a minute, or even longer. But you can make a model fitted with a propeller and it really will fly all by itself."

"What sort of engine do you need?"

"There are three kinds. The cheapest and simplest is india-rubber. You just turn the propeller round and round, twisting the rubber band that is fastened to it, and then when you let go it will spin back rapidly till it's straight. The best rubber models can fly for about four

A control-line model. This is the fastest type of model aircraft, and is flown in circles round the operator; you can see where the two controlling wires pass under the wing. This is the only type of model aircraft to have a hinged elevator, governing climbing and diving.

minutes, which is quite long enough to take them out of sight before they land. Then you can get tiny internal combustion engines, either diesel or glow plug; these are really wonderful examples of engineering, and of course quite expensive. And lastly, the latest in engines is a jet engine, which burns solid fuel and is in some ways simpler to use than the internal combustion motors, especially for small models. With some of these engines you can get speeds of up to 100 miles an hour, and the world record for a model aeroplane is 179 miles per hour."

"But whatever happens if one of these aircraft goes hurtling off at high speed with nobody in it?" asked Barbara. "It might kill somebody."

"Ah! You never let it do that, of course. There are three kinds of flying. First, what are called duration flights; you can use rubber-driven or petrol models for this, but you only put enough fuel in the engine to last for 20 or 30 seconds; in that time the aircraft should

One of the simpler free flight models, fitted with a diesel engine.

climb to a height of about 500 feet; when the rubber has spun straight or the engine has stopped, the model should settle into a flat, slow glide, which can last for five minutes or longer. For faster engines than this you use what's called a control line. This really consists of two steel lines held in a control by the flyer, and attached to a control plate or bellcrank on the aircraft; according to the way the control is held the hinged elevator of the model is either raised or lowered; this causes the aircraft to climb or dive; the model circles round the flyer, who stands in the middle, and it can be made to loop the loop, do figures of eight and all kinds of aerobatics at very high speed. Finally, the very last word in model aircraft flying is by radio control, when you can make an aeroplane twist about in the air as you like by turning a control knob on a special radio transmitter."

"I'm afraid that sort of thing would be beyond most of us," said Mr. Woodford, "but what kind of aircraft do you think we could make and fly ourselves?"

"I have all the parts of a simple glider here," said John, "would you like to watch me put them together?"

They all said they would, so he began straight away by stretching out a full-scale plan of the model on a work table. They were curious to see him rub over it with soap, and he explained that this was to stop the paper sticking to the wood later on; then they saw that he had pieces of balsa wood already cut out for every part shown on the plan, and he laid the pieces exactly over the place where they were printed on the plan, holding them on a curve, where necessary, by rows of pins on either side. It was a built-up model, and when one side of the fuselage was laid out correctly he stuck all the longerons and spacers together at every join with a blob of liquid cement from a tube.

He then constructed the other side of the

The kit of parts.

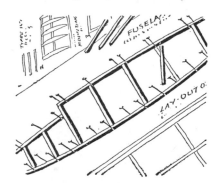

Rubbing the plan with soap.

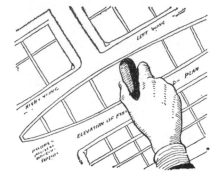

Pinning out the fuselage.

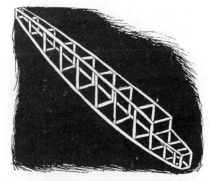

The fuselage assembled.

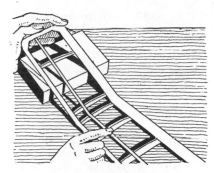

Assembling the wings.

The framework completed.

Covering the skeleton.

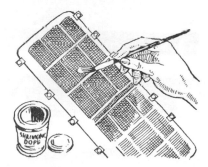

Putting on the dope.

fuselage, and joined the two halves together with cross pieces as shown on the plan. While that was drying he did exactly the same thing with the wings and the tail, and when he had finished he had three separate skeleton frameworks of balsa wood; finally he smoothed them with a rub with some fine sandpaper.

Then came the covering. He used some special paper for this, first sticking a sheet, cut roughly to size, over each side of the skeletons with tissue paste. Then he trimmed off the surplus paper with a razor blade, and then came what he called "putting on the dope." Dope is a kind of cellulose lacquer that makes the paper shrink so as to fit over the skeleton very closely, and also makes the paper wind-proof and weather-proof; he painted it on with a soft brush. The boy explained that the flat wings and tail needed to be held flat while they were drying, so that they wouldn't be twisted out of shape by the shrinkage. If there were any solid pieces of wood in the model they also needed this treatment, either by pasting paper over them and doping it, or by painting the dope straight on to the wood but in this case you had to rub a special "filler" over the wood first to fill the grain and leave it quite smooth. Several coats of dope were sometimes needed, and it could be obtained in colours to give the model a bright and distinctive finish.

Then he showed how the wings and tail were fastened to the fuselage with rubber bands, how the model was tested for trim and balance, and how weights of lead shot were added to the nose of the model until it exactly balanced itself on its centre of gravity, somewhere near the centre of its wings.

Finally, as it was a quiet, still evening with hardly any wind, all the members of the hobby club trooped out into the school playground to see a glider make a flight. John showed how to hold it, slightly behind the point of balance,

337

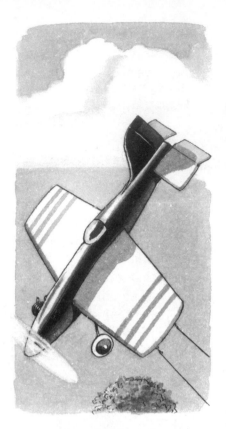

A control-line model in a power dive.

facing into the wind, and pointing a little downwards; then he launched it smoothly, "following through" with his arm as if he was bowling, and they were delighted to see it soar through the air for twenty or thirty feet before landing on the other side of the playground.

When some of the other children tried, the glider tended to point its nose up in the air and then dive to the ground, but John explained that this was because they had launched it too fast. "You get the same result," he said, "if there's too much wind, or not enough weight in the nose. But if it dives immediately after launching, the nose is too heavy, and you should take a little weight out.

"There's lots more I could tell you," John said when they had gone back indoors, "but the best way to learn is to make up a simple kit yourself, and then to get a good book about model aircraft and study it at home. Once you start I'll be very surprised if you don't go on; a rubber-driven aircraft is not much more difficult than a glider and there are dozens of different kinds to experiment with."

(80)

KITES

"I'm also interested in flying," said the boy who came next, "but my hobby is making and flying kites. There are quite a variety of designs that you can have, but the main types are kites with tails, and box kites. For flying you should choose an open space, the top of a hill, or the seaside, where the wind can blow freely, and a fairly breezy day. One boy must hold the kite as high as he can in his arms, in the direction that the wind will blow it, while the other stands ready with the winder. At a signal the boy with the kite throws it in the air, and the boy with the winder, who has the job of

338

making it fly, pulls sharply on his line to make the kite rise still higher. Once you get the feel of the thing you can soon discover the knack of pulling on the string to make the kite rise high, and letting it out to make the kite go farther away.

"If the kite won't rise at all in the air it probably means that it has too much tail, and you should cut a little off; but if it plunges about in the air and won't keep steady, it needs a longer tail, and you should tie a bit more on, or tie a few more paper twists on to the bit you have.

"Once it gets going you can let out the string steadily, and the kite will go on sailing up into the sky. I've seen kites go so high that one can hardly see them: they look so small. It's fun to cut a piece of cardboard or paper with a good sized hole in it and slip it over the winder; it will be carried by the wind right up the string to the kite; these are called messengers. Another thing that's fun is to fly a kite at night with a light torch or candle burning in a Chinese lantern hanging from the tail; this looks very

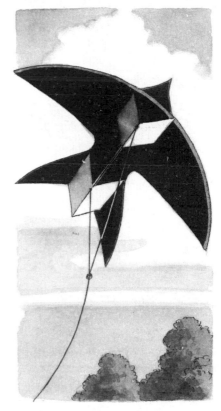

A bird kite in flight.

mysterious shining in the darkness, and, of course, no one can see what's holding it up.

"You can make your own kite at home for very little money. Here's a very easy way. Take two laths of wood, like the ones builders use, one three feet long and the other two; screw the middle of the shorter one to a point one foot from the end of the longer. Then make a small groove at the ends of each lath, and make the outline of the kite by stretching a length of strong string to join the four ends together, tying it securely in each of the grooves.

"That's the skeleton. To cover it, you can use strong light paper, but thin glazed calico or any cotton material is better. Lay the skeleton over a piece of the material, and cut it out a little larger, so as to allow an overlap all round. Bend this over, and sew it down. If you're using paper

339

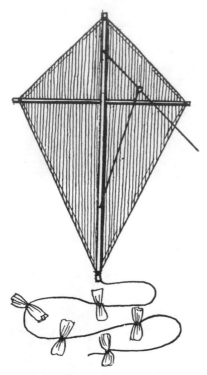

A simple "peg top" kite.

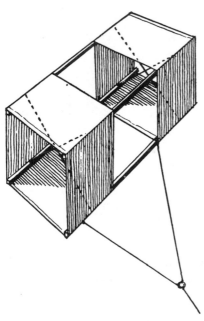

A simple box kite. The dotted lines show where the cross-bars should be placed.

you can stick it, of course. Then fix a loop of cord to two spots on the longer lath, like this." And he held up a kite so that everyone could see that one end of the cord went through a hole about six inches from the top of the kite, and the other through a hole about nine inches from the bottom; each was tied in a knot on the far side so that it could not slip through, and the total length of the cord was two and a half feet.

"This is called the bridle," he said. "Somewhere in the bridle a ring is tied; this should be nearer the top than the bottom, and you can adjust its exact position; if it's very windy move it down towards the half-way mark, and if the wind is light move it up nearer the top.

"A kite like this needs a tail. This is just a length of string with twists of tightly rolled paper tied to it every foot or so; the tail should be about five times the height of the kite, so for this kite you would need fifteen feet of it.

"All you have to do now is to fasten one end of your flying line to the ring on the bridle, and the other end to a wooden stick, or reel, round which the line can be wound. Any strong light string will do for a flying line. The kite is now ready for flying.

"Box kites are not much more difficult to make. You need four 'stretchers' of light wood, and four thinner cross-pieces of bendable cane or ash. The stretchers should be marked into three equal lengths, but you only put the covering round the two outer ones. The bridle is fastened to points one-third of the way down one of the stretchers and about three inches from its other end. This kind doesn't need a tail. You can get kites fitted with wings, or with fins, or made in the shapes of birds; you can make them four-sided, or five-sided, or completely round. I have several of these different kinds at home and if anyone likes to come out on the common one breezy afternoon with me, you can see how they fly."

MOBILES

Six underwater figures.

"I'VE made something that floats in the air, too," said a girl. "It's called a Mobile, because it moves so easily, and we hang it up in my bedroom at home as an unusual kind of decoration. All you need are thin galvanized wire, thread, cardboard and paints.

"An underwater scene provides a good subject. Draw six figures on cardboard. Fishes should be about 6 inches long and a mermaid, frogman and sea horse slightly larger. Cut out the shapes and paint them *both* sides in bright colours. Discover the point from which the shapes hang best by making tiny trial holes with a pin. At this spot, make a slightly larger hole and tie on a short length of thread.

The mermaid balanced against two fish.

"With pliers, cut the wire into two lengths of 10 inches, two lengths of 11 inches and one length of 15 inches. At each end of the wires make small loops. To each loop on a 10 inch wire tie a thread from a fish. By placing the wire across a finger find the point at which the fish just balance each other. Give the wire a complete twist at this point, making a small loop.

"Take an 11-inch wire and to one end attach the mermaid and at the other end loosely tie the loop in the wire supporting the **two** fish. As before, find the best point of balance and give the wire a complete twist to make a small loop.

"Attach the remaining three shapes to 10-inch and 11-inch wires in exactly the same way. The two sets of three shapes are then tied loosely to the loops at each end of the 15-inch wire. Find the point of balance between the two sets of shapes and make a complete twist. Tie a piece of thread to the resulting loop and hang the finished mobile from the ceiling. If necessary, adjust the lengths of thread and bend the wires so that the shapes move perfectly freely."

The mobile completed, and ready for hanging.

341

"Once you know the method of construction, you can make a moving picture of almost any scene in this way. It's fascinating to watch a mobile gently spinning round and round in slight air currents as it hangs from the ceiling."

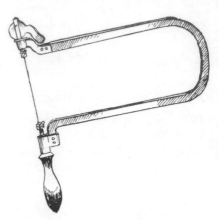

A fretsaw frame and blade.

(82)

FRETWORK

A BOY now came to the table, and put on it all the pieces of a jig-saw puzzle. "I made this myself," he said, "with a fretsaw.

"A fretsaw is really a very, very thin saw blade, fitted in a specially shaped frame. With an ordinary saw you can only cut straight lines, but with a fretsaw you can cut curves and circles as well. If you want to cut a shape out of the middle of a piece of wood you can drill a small hole and thread the blade through it. The blades have teeth of varying thicknesses, and can be changed as required; it's very important that they are adjusted to just the right tension in the frame; they ought to be tight enough to give off a high 'ping' if plucked.

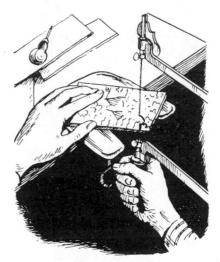

On the cutting board.

"You can make lots of patterns and shapes in fretwork, but I find the most interesting thing to do is to make jig-saw puzzles. When I see a good coloured picture in a magazine, I cut it out and glue it on to a piece of three-ply wood. Then I mark on it in pencil the pattern that I want to cut; you can make up any pattern you like, but the best way is to draw a number of wavy lines across the picture, up and down. I hold the wood on what's called the cutting board, which can be screwed on to the edge of any ordinary table, and begin to saw carefully along my lines, holding the saw upright all the time. I start at one corner, and work my way across the picture to the opposite corner, shifting the wood as necessary. Then you need a rub with a file to trim the under-edges quite smooth.

A jig-saw marked for cutting.

How to hold a camera.

Bad photo. Camera not straight.

Good photo. A happy subject well arranged.

"When I've finished I shake the pieces up in a box, and get a lot of fun out of putting them back in their right positions. It's a jolly good occupation for a rainy day. When the puzzle has been all round the family I give it to our local hospital."

(83)

PHOTOGRAPHY

"My great interest is photography," said the boy whose turn came next. "I've got a small camera which is easy to use, and I can take reasonable pictures with it. Loading the camera is simple; all you have to do is place a cartridge of film in and wind it on until it stops. Then you are ready to take your first photograph.

"When taking a photograph look at your subject through the viewfinder, hold the camera firmly and press the shutter release gently; this will prevent camera shake, which causes blurred pictures. Once you have taken a photograph you must remember to wind the film on to the next frame, otherwise you will have two pictures on one frame of film and both will be ruined.

"You must never point your camera towards the sun; it is usually best to have the sun at your side or behind you. Weather conditions can also affect the quality of your pictures. On simple cameras there is normally a dial which can be moved for sunny or dull lighting. With these types of cameras it is difficult to photograph subjects which are moving fast.

"Indoors where there is little daylight you can use a flashcube, which clips on the top of the camera to provide enough light to take a photograph by. The flashcube is connected to the shutter system and fires when you press the release.

343

Changing the film.

Bad photo. No composition; the camera is carelessly pointed.

Good photo. The objects are arranged in a pleasing composition.

"When you have taken your last photograph you must wind the film completely into the cartridge. However, if you are using a camera which takes roll films and not cartridges, the film must be fully wound on to the take-up spool. When you have carefully removed the film from the camera you can once again reload with new film and start again.

"Next Christmas I hope to get a better camera, with varying shutter speeds, and with a pointer that changes the size of the opening of the lens; it will also have a focusing arrangement, so that I can get clear pictures of anything very close, which the simple camera cannot do. There is a lot to be learnt about handling a camera like that properly, but by taking care to arrange your subject to make a pleasing 'composition,' even simple cameras can produce good photograph.

"To process your own black-and-white films you must use a darkroom, which enables you to load your film into a light-tight developing tank. First of all you pour developer into the tank, which produces an image on the film. After this stage the developer is replaced with a fixer, which makes the image permanent; after washing in water, the film is taken from the tank and allowed to dry. When dry, your film is ready for printing. To make prints, you lay the negatives on some printing paper and let a light shine through them. The print is processed in a similar manner to the film, but in a processing dish. Colour films must be sent to a processing laboratory because the stages of development have to be very carefully controlled and involve many different chemical solutions. Colour materials come in two types: colour negative film which produces prints, and reversal colour film which produces colour slides that can be shown on a screen or seen in a viewer.

"If you have an enlarger, you can make bigger black-and-white prints."

COOKING

"I HAVEN'T brought any exhibits to show you," said a girl who now spoke, "but I'm sure you'll agree that my hobby is a jolly useful one. I like cooking and making nice things to eat."

"We're certainly sorry you haven't brought any exhibits," said a boy at the back.

"Yes, do bring some next week," said another boy. "You won't have to bother about carrying them home again !"

Everyone laughed at this.

"Don't be so greedy," said the girl. "If you listen to what I tell you you'll be able to cook something for yourselves at home. But there are two rules that you must keep. The first is that the kitchen belongs to Mother, and no one should start taking things from it or using the oven without asking her first—especially as most cooking needs boiling water or fat, which can burn you terribly if you spill it over yourself. She will probably want to stand by while you're cooking to keep an eye on things. The second rule is *always* to wash your hands before you start to handle any food, and to put an apron on to keep your clothes clean. Chefs always wear a white coat and hat, so the rule is just the same for boys.

"Now here's a cold sweet you can make for a tea party that doesn't need any cooking at all. It's called Blackcurrant Cream, and you need a tin of blackcurrant purée, a small tin of evaporated milk and some granulated sugar."

"We have a bottle of concentrated blackcurrant juice at home," said Barbara, "and some condensed milk, too. Can we use those instead?"

"No, I'm afraid not," the girl said, "it must be just what I've said. Now, you mix the purée and the sugar together with a wooden spoon, beating them into a nice mixture and adding

How to make tea. Fill the kettle with cold drinking water.

Warm the tea pot with hot water.

Empty it, and put in tea leaves— one teaspoonful or one teabag for each person.

a little milk gradually as you go, until you have the colour and sweetness and flavour that you want. This means you can taste it several times until you get it right! But keep a different spoon for this purpose, and a bowl of hot water to put it in between tastes.

"The more you beat the mixture the thicker it becomes. When it looks right pour it off into individual fruit glasses; this makes enough for four; it's very rich, so you need only give small helpings."

"I'd like a large helping, please," said the boy from the back of the room. When the laughter had died down, the girl went on.

"And now, here's a hot sweet that's lovely for tea in the winter. It's called Golden Apple Whip. You need three large cooking apples, which you must peel, cut the cores out, and slice into big chunks. Place these in a fireproof dish that you have greased by rubbing some butter wrapping paper round. Sprinkle over them about two tablespoonfuls of brown sugar, or a little less granulated sugar; put in three or four cloves if you like them; and on top of everything put two or three small knobs of butter."

"Will margarine do instead?" someone asked.

"No, I'm afraid not. If cooking with butter is not allowed you can leave this part out altogether. The dish is now ready; do not add any water, but cover it with a close-fitting lid and put it into a moderately hot oven. Leave it there until the apples are tender enough to mash, but not pulpy; this will take about twenty minutes.

"While the apples are cooking, break an egg into a bowl, and beat it with a wooden spoon until the white and the yolk are thoroughly mixed together. Then, when the apples are done, take the dish out of the oven and mash them with a wooden spoon; go on beating the apple, and *at the same time* pour in the beaten egg. Continue beating until the egg is thoroughly mixed with the apple; then put the dish back in the oven, and

Immediately the kettle boils take the tea pot to it, and fill it with freshly boiling water. Do not leave the kettle boiling, or carry it across the room to the tea pot.

Let the pot stand for five minutes to "draw" before pouring out the tea. For a change, try China tea, or Russian tea with a slice of lemon instead of milk.

346

This decorated cart horse, drawn by a girl of eleven, looks splendidly vigorous. But she didn't allow enough room for its head.

A Partridge in a Pear Tree, by a twelve-year-old artist.

SOME PAINTINGS FROM THE NATIONAL EXHIBITION OF CHILDREN'S ART

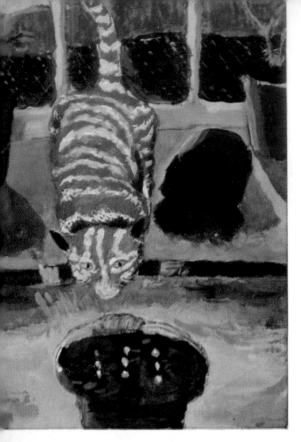

The Cat in the Greenhouse,
by a child of eleven.

A Portrait of a friend, by a girl of
fifteen. Children often find faces
the most difficult things to draw;
a common mistake is to put the
eyes too near the top of the head;
actually they come about the
middle. Notice, too, that people's
heads are not round but oval
in shape.

MORE EXHIBITS SHOWN AT THE NATIONAL EXHIBITION OF CHILDREN'S ART

cook for a few minutes longer. You will have a delicious golden sweet, enough for two; serve it with cream from the top of the milk.

"There are many more recipes I could tell you of; I've got a book of them at home. The best thing about cooking is that you can enjoy making the food, but every one in the house can enjoy eating it."

(85)

PAINTING

"I get a lot of fun out of painting," said another boy.

"So do I! I painted the garden shed last summer," said Alan.

"Not that sort of painting, silly," the boy answered; "I mean painting pictures. Some people think this is very difficult, but it isn't at all hard, really. Anyone can paint pictures; they may not be good enough for the Royal Academy but they're lots of fun to do.

"It's important to have the right kind of paper and paints. Big sheets of sugar paper are best— you can get them from art shops; and for paints many people buy those little paint boxes with watercolour squares, but most art teachers think it's better to use what are called tempera or powder paints; it's easiest to buy these made up into blocks, but if you buy the powder loose you have to mix a little of it at a time with some water in a saucer to make your colours; a useful thing to use for this is a deep bun tin with six or nine round compartments—each for a different colour; your mother may have one in the kitchen she can spare. Then for brushes, the large hog's hair ones are best; you need two or three of different thicknesses. And, of course, you will want a jam jar full of clean water, in which to wash your brush out every time you use a fresh colour.

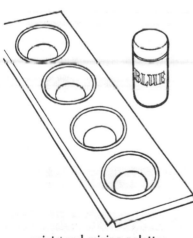

jar of clean water

Hog's hair
paint brushes

paints and mixing palettes

Paints, brushes and water. With these, and a large sheet of paper, you can start to paint.

A half-finished painting. Sketch in the outline with charcoal, and then put the colours on with broad easy strokes of the brush.

Mixing the powder paints.

"Before painting it's sometimes a good idea to sketch out on the paper with a stick of charcoal the shape of what you're going to paint. There's no end to the subjects you can choose. I like to shut my eyes for a minute and 'see' the picture in my mind before painting anything; then I plan out the general shape with charcoal and go right ahead. Of course, you're not limited to the colours you have bought; by mixing them together you can get every shade that there is—you know, blue and yellow make green; yellow and red make orange; blue and red make purple, and so on; but you can also experiment with mixing three or more colours in a saucer to make tints that are less bright than the powders that you have, and these are

350

very useful as backgrounds and for contrast.

"There are lots of other ways of making pictures : sketching with pencil or ink; with pastels or crayons on tinted paper; with poster colours; with water colours; with oil paints on canvas, and so on. If you enjoy painting with the powder colours, as I've described, you will probably want to try out all of these methods later on."

(86)

LINO-CUTS

"I MAKE pictures, too," another boy said, "but I print mine from lino-cuts. All you need are some pieces of fairly thick lino, a box of cutting tools, a tube of printing ink, a tile or piece of glass, and two rubber squeegee rollers. You can buy all these things from an art shop, and they will cost a pound or two."

"What are lino-cutting tools like?" somebody asked.

"Well, I've got my case here, if you'd like to see them," said the boy, as he brought them out.

The children could see that there were five pointed nibs or gouges—rather like the end of a potato-peeler, but much sharper—in various widths and shapes; the nibs could be fitted into a wooden handle, as required. The boy showed how to hold the tools, firmly pressing them away from his body into the lino, and how each tool cut a thin sliver of lino away as it went.

"When cutting the block," he said, "you have to remember that the print will come out in reverse—any letters, for instance, will appear the wrong way round, as if in a mirror. And a lino-cut is not at all like an ordinary drawing; it isn't much good trying to copy a picture, but you must work it out as a new idea. Remember that where you cut a line it will come out

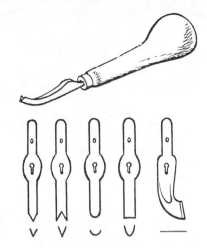

A lino-cutting tool, with some of the different shaped nibs that will fit it, and the cuts they make.

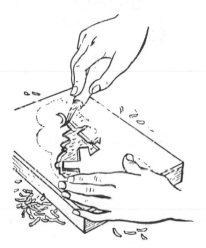

Cutting away the surface of the lino.

The finished block, ready for inking.

351

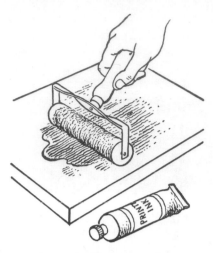

Inking the roller on a smooth tile.

Rubbing the paper with a spoon to make a print.

Peeling a print off the block. Once the block is made you can print as many lino-cuts as you like.

white in the print, and where you leave the lino alone it will come out black. Little thin fussy lines aren't much good; what's wanted are bold shapes of black standing out against a white background; or white shapes against black. One way of testing your ideas before you start is to paint the whole block white, and ink over the parts that you want to show black. Then, if you cut wherever the white is left you will get the same effect on your print."

"How do you do the printing?" he was asked.

"When the block is cut you squeeze some printing ink over the tile, and roll it smooth with one of the rollers; then roll the roller across the block, thus inking all the lino that has not been cut away. Now lay a clean sheet of printing paper—thin kitchen paper is quite good—over the block, and roll the other clean roller over this with a good pressure several times; or you can rub the back of the sheet with the bowl of a spoon. Carefully peel the paper off, and you've made a print. You can repeat this as often as you like, inking the block again before each printing. Remember to spread plenty of newspaper over the table, and it's a good idea to wear an apron, as the printing ink is messy; the roller must always be cleaned with turps before putting it away unless you are using special water-colour printing inks; these can be washed off with water and dry quicker, and are the best to start with.

"Of course, you don't have to use black ink and white paper for printing. You can use any colour you like; a bright red often looks very good. When you get fairly expert you can print lino-cuts in two or three different colours on the same print. The great thing about lino-cuts is that you can print as many copies of your picture as you like. I make my own Christmas Card every year with a lino-cut, and send a copy to each of my friends."

A lino-cut by a child of twelve, with good contrast of black and white.

A lino-cut by an older boy, showing the use of many different nibs.

APPLIQUÉ PICTURES

Cutting out the shape.

Sticking the pieces on to hessian.

Sewing the picture into position. You usually use a thread of the same colour as the material, but sometimes a good effect can be got by using a contrasting colour.

A GIRL now stood up, and said: "I make pictures too, but in quite a different way. I make them with sewing and embroidery. It's called appliqué work. The idea is that you cut the shapes of what you want out of all kinds of materials, and then sew them on to a strong plain background, like a piece of hessian."

"Do you trace the shapes from a picture?" someone asked.

"No," the girl said. "Appliqué pictures are rather like lino-cuts in a way. You can't just copy an ordinary painting—you have to think the idea out afresh, and use bold, simple outlines, with very little background decoration. And it isn't really necessary even to draw your outlines, as you can cut quite good shapes straight from the material with a pair of scissors."

"What sort of materials do you use?" she was asked.

"Any kind of material—cotton, wool, silk, net, American cloth—anything you can dig out of Mother's rag bag. The more varied the materials are, the more interesting the picture is and the art is in choosing suitable materials for what you want to show. A girl holding a shopping bag and taking her dog for a walk, for instance, might have a piece of felt for her face and hands, a gaily striped cotton for her frock, some thin plastic material for the shopping bag, strands of knitting wool for her hair, a rough woollen cloth for the dog, and a scrap of leather for the dog's collar."

"How do you sew the bits on?"

"First of all I just stick them on with a dab of fairly dry paste. That gives the right position, and then if I want to make a neat job of it I go round each piece of material, stitching it down with one of the needlework stitches I've learnt.

354

Details like eyes and mouths, or stems of flowers, or clouds in the sky, can be put in by stitching and embroidery too, and you can add beads, shells, and all kinds of spangles to make the picture more exciting. You'd never guess what lovely pictures can be made in this way until you've tried it yourself !"

(88)

PASTY PAPERS

Making a pattern with a brush.

"I've noticed that a lot of the hobbies that we have been told about need an album to mount specimens in," said a girl who stood up in her place. "I wonder if you'd be interested to know how I make patterns for covering books and albums."

The children were certainly interested to know about this, so the girl came up to the table and they could see that she had brought a folder of brightly patterned paper sheets with her.

"They're what are called pasty papers," she said. "You make them by mixing colours with paste. You can get some paste made at home by mixing three teaspoonfuls of powdered starch in a little cold water and then pouring half a pint of boiling water over the creamy mixture; you may need to boil the paste for a minute to make it thicken. You can use household flour or paper-hanger's paste instead of the starch if you like. This paste won't keep for very long, but a clove will help to preserve it.

Using a pointed stick.

"Now mix some powder colour thickly in a little water in a saucer, and add this to the paste, mixing the two together in a bowl with a stiff brush until you have the colour you want. You are now ready to begin. Take a sheet of fairly stiff and non-absorbent paper, damp it and pin it with drawing pins on to a board or table. Then spread the coloured paste all over it with a broad soft brush till it forms an even level

Patterns from a piece of cut card.

355

coating. Now, before it dries hard, you must make the pattern. You can use your fingers, or an old comb, or a stiff brush, or a stick, or anything you think of; you can make wavy lines, or zig-zags, or spirals, or any kind of pattern that comes into your head. When it's finished, leave the sheet to dry, and just before it is quite dry put it under pressure to keep it flat. To make the pattern fairly firm, so that it won't rub off, you can rub a little white polish over it.

"Another method is to spread the natural paste over the paper, and then to squeeze drops of water-colour paint on to it from a tube; these can be in different colours, and if you brush them out with straight strokes across the paper you will get stripes of colour merging into each other.

"Pasty papers can also be used for covering boxes or lining the drawers of cabinets. I hope you will find them as much fun to make as I have done."

An album with patterned covers. The spine, or hinged part of the book, should be covered with something stronger than paper; a book cloth or buckram is ideal. Bookbinding itself is a most interesting craft. Perhaps you learn it at school.

(89)

PATTERN PRINTING

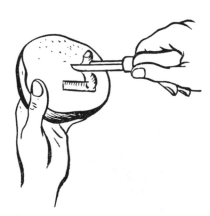

Cutting a pattern in the smooth side of a half potato. A potato-peeler is the only tool you need.

"THAT sounds a jolly good idea," said another girl, "but I've made album covers in a different way, by printing them." And she, too, spread out a lot of gay paper patterns on the table in front of her.

"They're printed from potatoes," she explained. "It's very easy; you just cut a potato in half, and then on one half you cut some simple pattern with a potato-peeler to make a printing 'block.' To print with it you can either paint the block with a brush dipped in paint—powder paints are best—or, better still, press it on to a pad made out of pieces of felt well-soaked in paint and kept in something like the lid of a cocoa tin; in either case you need to put fresh colour on to the block for every new printing.

SOME ATTRACTIVE PATTERNS MADE WITH PASTY PAPERS

LILIAN KING

V   R'ump

APPLIQUÉ PICTURES MADE BY CHILDREN AGED SEVEN TO NINE

AN APPLIQUÉ PORTRAIT BY AN OLDER GIRL AGED TWELVE

SOME DESIGNS PRINTED FROM POTATO CUTS

A print from a half potato in its natural state.

A print from a potato with one circle cut in its face.

A print showing a more elaborate pattern cut in the potato.

The best paper to use is thin and absorbent; cheap kitchen paper is excellent, and you can practise on sheets of newspaper.

"Just one print from the potato doesn't look like anything, but the thing is to cover the paper with them, close together, in lines running up and down. Sometimes you can vary the design by printing alternate lines upside down, or with a different pattern or in a different colour. You'll be surprised what a bright jolly pattern you can make in this way, and you can easily paste it on the covers of your albums."

"I've done that, too," said a boy, "at the first school I went to. But we didn't use only potatoes; we cut turnips and carrots as well; we carved patterns on cotton reels; we made designs with spirals of string glued on to the end of a stick; and we even printed patterns with our finger tips."

"And you can use lino-cuts, too," said the girl. "Another thing is that you can print on fabrics with these blocks. The best materials are thin, like muslin or cotton, and instead of paint it's better to use printing inks; if you want the colours to stand up to washing you can get special dyes, though these are rather expensive. You stamp the block on the pad and press it on the material in just the same way as if it was paper. I've made some lovely head scarves and aprons like this, and my sister goes to an art school and has made curtains and dress lengths."

"Well, we've certainly had some good ideas of things to make," said Mr. Woodford. "It's a splendid thing to do something creative with one's hands, and we all ought to practise some kind of hand craft, now that almost everything we have comes from factories. It's only by making things that one can really appreciate them. There's no time for any more now, I'm afraid, but next week I'd like any children who give shows or entertainments at home to tell us something about them."

90

TOY THEATRES

AT the next meeting of the Hobby Club the children found a beautiful model stage arranged on the table when they arrived As soon as they were ready a boy stood up beside it, and began: "I've had a lot of fun from making and playing with toy theatres. Once you've become interested in this hobby your theatre may develop into something quite large and elaborate, but you can make a start with a cardboard box.

"The simplest kind of all may be made from the sort of box shops deliver groceries in. Cut a large hole in one side for the stage, or proscenium opening, as it's called; cut holes in the two sides for the characters to come in and out by; fix side pieces on either side of the proscenium opening to mask the entrance and exits; and paint the whole thing in nice bright patterns. The curtain can be a piece of card that is lowered and raised; the scenery, other pieces

TO-NIGHT AT
6 30 PM
A GRAND PERFORMANCE OF
ROBIN HOOD
OR
THE MERRY MEN OF
SHERWOOD FOREST
AT THE TOY THEATRE

ADMISSION 1p.

It is fun to write out posters and tickets for your toy theatre shows.

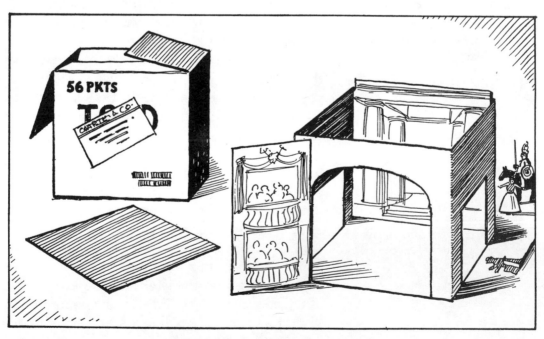

A simple theatre made from a grocer's box.

A more elaborate theatre can be made from a dressmaker's box.

of card, fitting into the back of the box; and the characters, cut-out figures four or five inches high, stuck on to small blocks of wood, or empty match boxes, and pushed on and off with strips or slides of cardboard.

"A more elaborate model theatre can be made from a ladies' dress-box or similar box; you know, one of those flat oblong boxes, about 12 inches by 18 inches by 3 inches. The box part turned upside down becomes the stage floor; this fits into the lid, stood on its side, which has a hole cut in it for the proscenium opening; the lid of another box—or strips of card stuck together with gummed paper—makes the back of the theatre; and the top corners of the lids are joined together by two strips of cardboard, called grid pieces, with slots cut along their undersides. All these parts are fastened to each other by brass paperclips of the split-pin type, which can be quite easily taken out and the whole stage packed neatly away.

"Instead of a flat 'Safety Curtain' you can make one of cotton or calico rolled round a

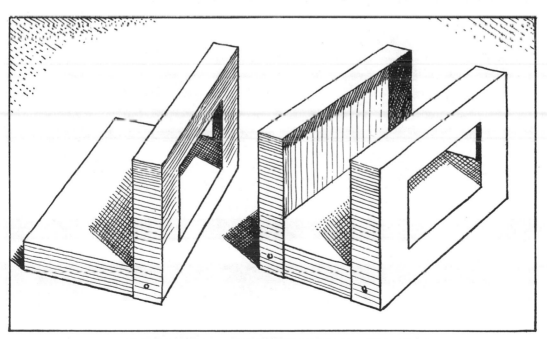

The first two stages in making a dress-box theatre.

363

round wooden stick. The scenery and wings either side should just fit into the slots in the grid pieces, and the whole stage will stand up and look very well.

"But if you become keen on model theatres you will want a wooden one, which is much stronger than anything you can make on cardboard. You can still buy small toy theatres, of the original old design, with metal slides and so on, or you can make one for yourself with a little very simple carpentry. If you look at mine you will see how the grids are made." And the boy pointed to the gaily decorated little stage on the table before him.

"What do you do for lighting?" someone asked.

"The simplest thing is to arrange a reading lamp in front of the stage, shining into it like a spotlight from the audience. Or a very good light can be got from a strip-light resting over the stage, in front of which you can place strips of gelatine for coloured lighting effects; but you must remember that anything working off the

The Sheriff of Nottingham, as he might be drawn for a toy theatre production of *Robin Hood*.

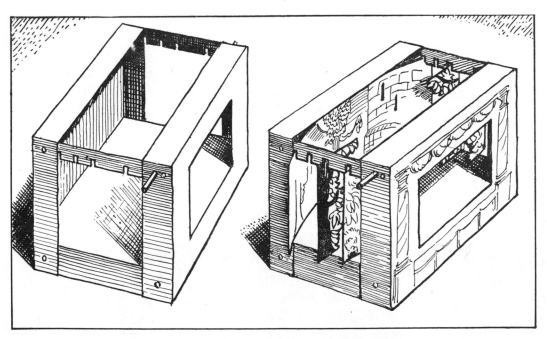

The last two stages in making a dress-box theatre.

364

A performance in progress on the finished stage.

Robin Hood as a toy theatre character. It is best not to try to cut out the space between the legs.

electric mains is at a high voltage which may be dangerous, and you should always have it fitted up by a qualified electrician. The other way is to use small torch bulbs working off a battery, or transformer, and if you understand about electric circuits you will find it most interesting to wire up a model lighting system with dimmers, just like a real theatre."

"How do you get plays for your theatre?" a girl asked.

"You can buy special toy theatre plays, or you can write your own and draw your own scenery and characters."

"I'd never be able to draw the characters well enough," the girl said.

"Oh yes, you would. It doesn't matter if you can't draw faces very well, because they're not seen close up, and if you give the figures good attitudes, with one arm raised and bold easily recognized costume, people will know who they are."

"How do you choose your plays?" the girl asked again.

365

"Some people think of a story, perhaps one out of a book or one they've made up, and draw characters and scenery for it; another way, especially when you're starting, is to draw a few characters out of your head, or cut some out of a magazine, and then make up a story to suit them. You don't need much talking, and each scene can be quite short. You should have all the characters waiting on their slides at the side of the stage before you begin, and you can show which figure is supposed to be speaking by gently jigging its slide. You can easily do a whole play by yourself, but if there are two or three others they can each speak for a different character.

"A toy theatre can start as a very simple affair, but there's no end to making it more elaborate, with beautiful scenery and artistic lighting effects, and entertaining your family and friends with it when your show is well rehearsed."

Characters can be made to stand and move with half match box trays stuck on to cardboard slides.

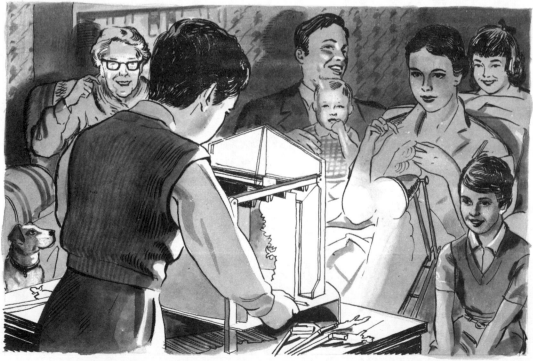

The backstage view of a toy theatre performance.

SHADOW SHOWS

Shadow figures. The child's arms can be hinged, so that the mouse gets a sprinkling from the watering can.

"I ALSO have a theatre at home," said a girl, "but mine is rather different because the audience only see the *shadows* of the characters. The whole idea is to have a frame covered with some material that lets the light shine through; then behind the screen a bright light is fixed, and the characters are moved close against the screen, so that the audience sees their shadows on the other side. It looks very mysterious and pretty.

"You can make your own frame out of strips of wood, properly joined at the corners, but it is possible to use a real picture frame. A good size would be about 36 inches by 20 inches, or even larger, and you can often pick up nice old gilt frames in junk shops for very little money. It doesn't matter if the glass is broken as you

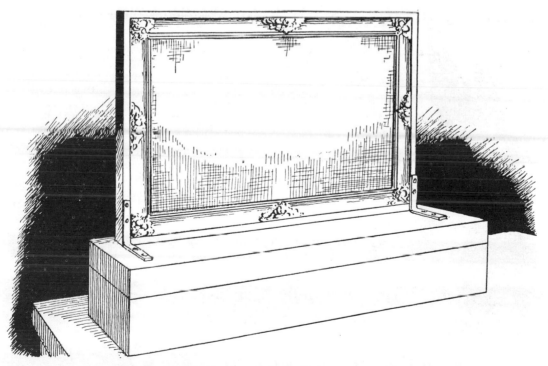

A completed shadow theatre, made from an old picture frame.

don't need this, nor the wooden backing.

"For the screen you can use lampshade parchment, or tracing linen, or any material that lets the light through. A piece of an old cotton or linen sheet would do very well. It should be stretched as tightly as possible across the frame, and fastened down with tacks or drawing pins.

"To make the screen stand up by itself, the easiest way is to screw angle brackets to the bottom corners on the audience side of the frame. These can now be screwed into a box, or block of wood, about eight inches high, on which the frame can stand; and the whole thing can be put on a table.

"The simplest kind of figure is just like a toy theatre character, cut out of cardboard, but to be clearly seen it is best to make it at least six inches high. It's usually best to draw it in side view, and rather to exaggerate things like curly hair, and the thickness of collars, socks

The parts of a gnome.

and shoes. Of course, you don't need to paint it at all, as only the outline will show.

"A figure like this can be pushed from one side of the screen to the other by a strip of cardboard fastened to its feet, and it can gradually grow bigger and fainter, until it disappears into a kind of cloud, if you gently draw it away from the screen towards the light.

"Probably you will want to make your figures move their legs and arms about, and this can be done if you cut them out in a special way, and then join them together. For a simple jointed character you might make one arm and both legs move. It will be best to draw the figure with one arm fixed, perhaps with the hand resting on the hip. You do not draw the other hand at all on the figure, but on a separate piece of card altogether; unless you want it to look like a stiff toy soldier you must cut the arm in two pieces, with a joint at the elbow, and it will look much better if you give it a wrist joint as well,

The shadow of a witch.

368

The shadow of the gnome.

and better still if you put in a couple of extra joints in the arm so that it can bend almost like a snake. Every joint should overlap the next where it joins. Each leg can be cut out in the same way, with knee and ankle joints if you think they're necessary, and hinged—not right to the waist—but to the bottom of the coat, or skirt of the figure. A waist joint will often make the figure move much better, too. If you look at these you will see how it's done."

And at that the girl put a number of cut-out cardboard figures on the table for all to see.

"I use split-pin paper clips for the hinges," she said. "Of course, they should be pushed through so that their heads—not their points—are against the screen, and the arms and legs should be attached to the side of the body that is away from the screen."

"How do you move jointed figures like these," somebody asked.

"I use thin wires," she answered. "They are twisted into a loop at the end, and this is sewn on to the figure with thread. It's more comfortable if you fix the wire into a bamboo handle for you to hold. A simple shadow figure can be moved with two wires—one to the head or shoulder, and one to the moving arm. To work the figure you hold it against the screen which should be just above the level of your head. At the bottom of the screen it is a good idea to fix a strip of wood half an inch wide for the puppets' feet to rest on; and the screen itself should be raised about one foot above the table. If you have some heaps of plasticine on the table behind the screen you will find that you can stick the wires holding the figures in it, and they will then stand up on the screen without you having to hold them. In this way you can get quite a crowd on to the stage. Of course, you can't help the shadows of the wires being seen on the screen, but the audience soon gets used to this and hardly notices them.

The parts of the witch.

A shadow show from the back.

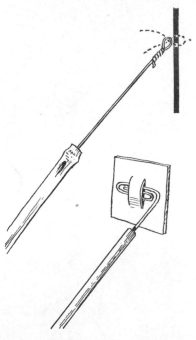

Two ways of fastening the rods to the figures.

"For scenery, it looks good if you cut out a large piece of cardboard the same size as the screen into various openings; or you can fix side wings and small pieces of cut-out scenery on to the screen with adhesive transparent tape. When you get expert you can get some good effects by hanging cut-outs of distant hills or buildings about three or four inches back from the screen; these will look grey to the audience.

"Finally, you must fix your light a few feet away from the screen, and high enough not to cast the shadow of your head or hands on to it. A strong electric bulb does quite well, but if you can put a tin round it so that all the light is thrown in one direction it's much better, and then you can put slides of different coloured gelatine in front to make coloured light.

"Last of all, the frame of the screen must be 'masked' round with curtains on all sides so that no light shines through and all the audience can see is the lighted screen of your

shadow theatre shining in the darkness. You can sometimes fix the screen up very well in the doorway between two rooms.

What the audience sees at a shadow show.

"Though it may sound complicated, shadow figures are very quick and easy to make. After a little practice you will find all kinds of elaborations, like using gelatine sheets to make coloured figures, or 'insetting' them in scenery for stained-glass windows. You can make some lovely pictures in this way.

"To give a performance I find that we need at least three people : two to work the figures, and one to read the story and make the music. There are lots of splendid stories that can be told with shadows, especially fairy tales and anything a bit fanciful or weird with visions in it."

"That sounds splendid," said Mr. Woodford. "You must come and give us a performance with your Shadow Theatre one evening. But I hope we won't all have nightmares afterwards."

Jack Horner pulls out a plum.

371

92

GLOVE PUPPETS

"I've got another kind of puppet show," said a boy. "It's like Punch and Judy. The figures are called glove puppets, because they fit on your fingers like a glove. Look at them."

A glove puppet made by a young child aged seven.

And at that, the boy put some puppets on the table. As they lay there they looked very lifeless and flat, but as soon as he fitted one on to his hand the children roared with laughter as they saw it "come alive" before their eyes, turning and twisting in every direction, and then putting its hands out and pinching the nose of the boy who was working it.

"As you can see, the dress is just hollow," he said. "There are various ways of holding a glove puppet, but I find the best way is to put my first two fingers up its neck, my thumb into one arm, and my other two fingers into the other."

"How do you make the head?" someone asked.

Making the paper pulp.

"There are lots of different methods," he said. "One of the simplest is to use a potato. Just scoop out a hole in which to insert a cardboard tube for its neck, and carve the features. Another easy way is to use an old tennis ball; you can stick in pins and buttons for the eyes and mouth, and you'll be surprised how good it looks with a hat on and a dress over your hand. But for a head that can be modelled to any shape you want, and that will be strong and light, I use some paper pulp.

"First of all I have to make the tube into which my fingers will fit, so I roll a postcard round my first two fingers and stick it down with some sticky paper. Then I wedge it over the neck of a bottle to make a stand. Lastly, I have to model the head over the cardboard tube with some suitable material.

Shaping the head.

Another child's puppet made from paper pulp.

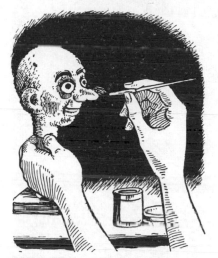

Painting the head.

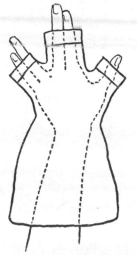

How to place the fingers.

"I make a special pulp for this, by tearing up an old newspaper into very small pieces, about the size of confetti. Then I put a little water into a jam jar, and half fill it with the paper bits. Now comes the hard work. I have to pound the paper up in the jar until it becomes one grey mass. A round stick like the end of a broom handle is good for this job, and the paper may need turning out and putting back again several times until it's properly mixed. One jar only makes enough pulp for one head, so it's a good idea to mash several jarfuls at a time and get all the family to help. When I've made enough pulp, I spread it out on a board or old table and add some cold-water paste, like paperhangers use, which is sold as a dry powder in packets. You need plenty of this—half as much paste as you have pulp. Now there comes a lovely messy job, mixing the paste in with the pulp with your fingers ! You can stir it up in an old bucket if you like, adding a little water if it seems to need it. When it's all thoroughly mixed up, the paper pulp will feel like soft soap, and it's ready for modelling.

"The first stage is to model the neck, by pressing small pieces of pulp round the bottom part of the cardboard tube, remembering to build up a small ridge round the bottom for the dress to fasten over. When the neck has dried, you can model the face, building it up with small pieces of pulp, pressed firmly in, and shaped sometimes with a penknife or a flat piece of wood. The secret is to make the features very bold, not lifelike but greatly exaggerated.

"When the head is finished, put it in an oven at a very low heat to dry slowly. When it's dry, you can smooth the face with sandpaper and fill in any cracks with some more pulp.

"Then comes painting. Poster colours are best. Paint the head all over white, and let this dry before you add anything else. Then paint it as bright as you like, but let each colour dry

373

A glove puppet performance of
Alice In Wonderland.

before you put the next on. Lengths of string or wool gummed to the head look very good for hair.

"There are lots of other ways of making puppet heads, and you can get a book out of the public library that tells you about them.

"Making the costumes for a glove puppet is easy. You cut out two pieces of material in a simple shape, and then sew them together down the sides. The top is glued round the neck of the puppet, little hollow felt hands are fitted into either sleeve, and the bottom, of course, is left open for you to put your hand in. All sorts of trimmings and specially designed clothes can

374

be put on later, but that's the general idea.

"There's no need to have any special stage for a
a glove puppet show. I make my puppets pop up
from behind tables or chairs. When I had a few
figures ready I made up a story for them; I didn't
write it down; I just make up the words in my
own head as I go along. There are lots of things
glove puppets are very good at doing, like
picking things up, and having fights. Of course,
if you're doing the show yourself you can only
have two figures in view at a time, but if there
are three or four children working together you
can have six or eight puppets up at once, and
give quite a performance."

Behind the scenes in a glove
puppet booth.

93

MUSIC FOR HOME SHOWS

"ALL these shows seem to need some music and sound effects," said Mr. Woodford. "I wonder whether anyone can tell us how these are best arranged."

"I can," said a girl called Jane, jumping up, "I do all the backstage music and noises for Margaret's shadow show. They're just as important as moving the figures or lighting the stage. We generally use a gramophone. Now that practically every sound from bird song to a thunderstorm has been recorded, it is the most convenient way."

"But isn't that rather a costly business, Jane?" asked Mr. Woodford. "I thought that records, especially long-playing ones, were getting more and more expensive."

"That's quite true, Mr. Woodford," was the answer. "I was coming to that. But we don't need long-playing ones, really, and besides, the public library will lend to anyone responsible"—there was general laughter at this—"and occasionally we get presents of records."

"And you want someone careful to handle them, too, I'm sure," went on Mr. Woodford.

Margaret agreed. "Yes, and we make it a rule that the records must be put away directly they are taken off the gramophone, before anyone has time to step on them. Of course, a really professional outfit always has two turntables so that one record can be faded out and another faded in with a volume control. It makes a very good effect to bring the sound up or take it down gradually, and incidentally, a radio gramophone always has this volume control already fitted. You often don't need to play the whole of a record, and if you want to start in the middle you can mark the spot with a crayon."

"Well, you've told us quite a lot about

Some simple musical instruments that you can buy in toy shops and use for home shows.

records," said Mr. Woodford, "but do you ever make your own music for your shows?"

"Oh yes," Jane said. "Our class made bamboo pipes at school last term, and we played these; they gave just the right atmosphere for a Nativity Play. Or, if we know anyone who plays the oboe (not too near a miniature stage, because it could seem rather out of proportion close at hand), a phrase or two on that instrument somehow seems to make you think of a clear frosty night, and the shepherds sitting round their fire on the hills of Bethlehem."

"Good!" said Mr. Woodford. "Now, does anyone want to ask a question?"

"Yes, I do," said a boy called Nicholas; "I want to put on a rough-stuff-tough-guy play for my next show. What would Jane suggest?"

"Kitchen music," answered Jane without hesitation.

"What exactly is that?" asked Nicholas.

"If you have a piano, let somebody play a good tune, like 'The British Grenadiers'—with one finger will do, as you only want a melody with a good rhythm—while somebody shakes nails, forks, spoons, in a can, somebody else beats a brass tray or a gong and a third taps lightly on a drum; but all must keep to the rhythm set by the piano. There you have your 'kitchen music.'"

"It sounds to me a bit like 'noises off,'" said Mr. Woodford. "Now, what about *those*?"

"Well, there's horses' hoofs," she said. "That's two inverted halves of a coconut shell tapped gently on a board or a box of gravel or a slab of concrete. Most people know that one. They still use it sometimes on the B.B.C., so I've been told, though they've got records of everything. And, of course, shaking a big piece of thin cardboard makes a noise like thunder."

"And what others?" went on the question-master.

"The sounds of rain and waves—you need

horse's hoofs

waves

thunder

How three common sound effects can be produced behind the scenes in the home.

377

an ounce or two of lead shot and a drum face; for rain, it is simply poured on to the parchment. Then there's something you can do to make a noise like rats and mice squeaking, supposing you wanted to do a scene from 'The Pied Piper of Hamelin.' You take a bottle and a cork; damp the cork (*really* damp it) and rub it up and down the surface of the bottle. But you'll have to practise it over and over again before you get it perfect—the same with the others too."

"Yes, I can well believe that," said Mr. Woodford, "and I expect you have to listen to the actual noises themselves a lot first?"

"Can you give us any help in choosing suitable records?" another girl asked. "We get up shows at home, and I love acting in them, but I never know what music to play."

"I've got a list here," Jane said, "of useful music for lots of the kinds of situations that come in plays. You might like to copy it. But remember that if you play any records in public—outside your home—you must get permission and pay a small fee."

And this was the list that Jane handed round.

Triumphal Procession
   "Pomp and Circumstance" March No. 1 (Elgar).
   "Knightsbridge" from *London Suite* (Eric Coates).
   Grand March from *Aida* (Verdi).
   March from *Tannhäuser* (Wagner).
Wedding Procession
   Wedding March from *A Midsummer Night's Dream* (Mendelssohn).
   Fanfares for the Royal Wedding of T.R.H. The Princess Elizabeth and the Duke of Edinburgh.
   Bells of St. Margaret's, Westminster.
Church Music
   Trumpet Voluntary (Jeremiah Clarke).
   Hallelujah Chorus from *Messiah* (Handel).

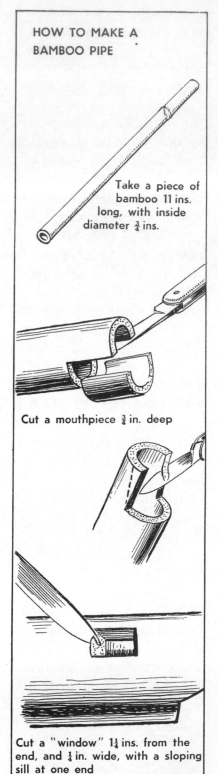

HOW TO MAKE A BAMBOO PIPE

Take a piece of bamboo 11 ins. long, with inside diameter ¾ ins.

Cut a mouthpiece ¾ in. deep

Cut a "window" 1¼ ins. from the end, and ¼ in. wide, with a sloping sill at one end

Join the window and the mouthpiece with a very shallow channel inside the pipe

Choose a cork that just fits the mouthpiece and trim to the same shape. Cut a straight side where it fits over the channel

The view down the pipe from the mouthpiece, showing the channel as a black crescent

Make 6 holes in the window side, and 1 on the opposite side. By blowing gently down, and covering different holes with your fingers, you can produce a range of notes

Ballet
    Swan Lake (Tchaikovsky):
        Act I, No. 4, Waltz.
        Act II, No. 12, Dance of the Swans.
           No. 14, Dance of the Cygnets.
    Casse-Noisette (Nutcracker) Suite (Tchaikovsky).
Court Ball
    Minuet from *Berenice* (Handel).
    Gavotte (Handel).
Country Dancing
    "Goddesses" from Playford's Collection.
    "Haste to the Wedding" (Traditional Devon).
Pastoral Atmosphere
    Pastoral Symphony (Beethoven), 1st, 3rd and 5th movements.
    "Sheep may safely graze" (Bach).
Spanish Atmosphere
    Dansa Española (de Falla).
Oriental Atmosphere
    Polovtsian Dances from *Prince Igor* (Borodin).

(94)

CONJURING

"I'm a magician," said the next boy, "And I'll show you some tricks."

He took a pack of cards, spread them out face downwards like a fan, and asked anyone to choose a card. Barbara picked one, looked at it carefully (it was the ten of spades) and put it back in the pack. She was quite certain that the boy could not possibly have seen what it was. Yet he laid the cards down on the table, one by one, until he came to the ten of spades and said "That's the one." Everyone was astonished, and asked how he did it.

The boy said it was a secret, but this time Billy laughed, and said he knew how it was done. "When you put the chosen card back into the

379

The card that Barbara chose.

pack," he said, "you cut the pack into two halves, and you secretly take a quick look at the bottom card of the top half. Then you put the two halves together, and the chosen card is in between them, so that if you deal the cards out the chosen card will come immediately after the card at which you have just looked."

"He couldn't do the trick if somebody shuffled the cards, and changed their order after the card was put back," said Barbara.

"Oh couldn't I," answered the boy conjurer, "you just see ! And to make it more difficult I will let you choose two cards this time, and shuffle the packs as much as you like."

He sorted out the cards into two piles, and then asked Billy to choose a card from one pile and Barbara to choose one from another. They both picked a card and looked at it carefully, showing it to the audience without letting the conjurer see it. Barbara had the three of diamonds and Billy the seven of clubs. Then the boy invited them to put their cards back, each into a different pile, anywhere they liked, and to shuffle the cards thoroughly. When they had finished they were both sure that the boy could never have seen the cards they had chosen, and could never discover whereabouts they were buried.

Yet he merely took a quick glance through each pile, and immediately threw down the three of diamonds and the seven of clubs !

No one had any idea how this trick was done. At last the boy conjurer laughed: "This is so easy, you'll kick yourselves when you hear how you've been misled ! All I do is to sort the pack into two piles, the red suits—the hearts and diamonds—in one pile and the black suits—the spades and clubs—in the other. Barbara chose a card from the red pile and Billy one from the black pile. While you were examining your cards I changed the two piles round, so that Barbara put her red card into a pile that was all

DO THIS

This is a trick in which the conjurer pretends that he can read people's thoughts; it needs an assistant "in the know." While the conjurer goes out, the rest of the party decide on an object that is in the room; on his return the conjurer asks every one to think hard of the object chosen, while his assistant points to a number of objects in turn. Not a word need be spoken. At each object the conjurer says "No," until the chosen object is pointed at, which he always recognizes.

380

black, and Billy put his black card into a pile that was all red. Of course, both piles look exactly the same from their backs, and no one is allowed to see their faces. You can shuffle the cards as long as you like, but it only takes one glance from me to know which cards have been chosen."

The children certainly did feel like kicking themselves when they heard how easy it was!

"Now I'll do another trick," said the boy, "if anyone will lend me a 10p coin."

Billy produced one, and the boy showed a small round pill box, which he passed round the room for everyone to examine. There was certainly nothing wrong with it. Then the boy put the coin in the box, which it just fitted, put the lid on it, and shook it about to show the coin was still there. Then he stood the box on the table, tapped it with a pencil and said, "Coin, coin, fly away in to the silver cup on the mantelpiece." Sure enough, when he lifted

Placing a coin in a matchbox

the lid off the box it was empty inside, and there was a 10p coin in the School Sports' Trophy on the mantelpiece.

But once again Billy was too smart. "It's not the same coin," he said: "I looked at the date of mine before I gave it to you. Mine was 1968, and this is 1969."

The boy conjurer had to admit he had been found out. "As you've discovered that, I'll tell you how it was done. Of course, I put the coin in the silver cup as soon as I came here this evening; it was just bad luck you noticed the date. Here's your coin, in my pocket all the time! The coin I put in the box was a special one, with dark paper stuck over one side, the same colour as the inside of the box. I didn't let you see the papered side, but I arranged it so that the paper was on top when it was lying in the box, and it looks as if there's nothing there at all. While you were looking in the silver cup I slipped the trick coin into my pocket, so that

HOW IT IS DONE

Immediately before the chosen object, the assistant points to something round (ash tray, vase, etc.). This warns the conjurer that the next object is "it." To vary the clue, they can use something with legs (chair, table, person, etc.).

381

you could examine the box carefully and not find anything wrong with it at the end."

Billy felt very pleased at catching the conjurer out again, but the boy said, "Perhaps you'd like me to do the trick again; I may manage better this time."

So once again Billy lent him a 10p piece, not only carefully noting the date but scratching a little cross on it with his penknife. This time the boy took a matchbox, emptied the matches out of it, and put the coin inside it—holding it up so that everyone could see it was the same coin that Billy had marked. Then he put the matchbox on the table, stood well away from it and said, "When I tap the matchbox the coin will fall through the table into this hat," which he then put on the floor underneath. "If you look carefully you may see it fall."

They all looked hard. He tapped the box, and said "Presto." No one actually saw the coin fly through the air, but when the boy

invited Billy to pick the hat up, there was his own coin, with the cross on it, sure enough, lying inside.

Even Billy could not suggest how that trick was done, so at last the conjurer said, "I used a trick box that time." And he showed them that the matchbox had a slit cut away in one end of the drawer big enough for a 10p coin to slide through. "As soon as I had put your coin in the box," he said, "I tilted it so that the coin slid through the slit into my hand. When I put the box on the table it was already empty. I just slipped the coin into the hat myself as I put it under the table."

"I never thought of examining the matchbox that time," said Billy.

"And now here's one more trick, to make you laugh," said the conjurer, as he took a glass of water, put it on the table, and covered it up with a hat. "I'm going to drink the water in that glass without touching the hat." Then he knelt

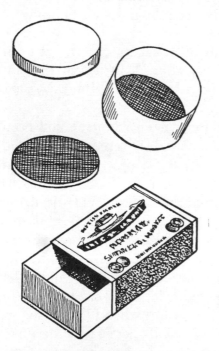

The trick coin and the slit matchbox.

A copper coin will become quite hot if it is held tightly in one's hand. As long as all the coins are cold to start with, the chosen coin will feel distinctly warm when the conjuror touches it.

down under the table, put his mouth up against it, and made loud sucking noises.

"There you are," he said, when he came out.

"Don't be silly, you haven't drunk the water," cried Billy, picking up the hat and showing the glass still full of water underneath.

"I have now," cried the boy, as he quickly drank it up, "and *I* didn't touch the hat either !"

Everyone laughed at that, and Billy, who had really been very clever at discovering how the tricks were done, had to agree that the conjurer had had the best of it.

"I've got lots more tricks," the boy said. "Some of them I've read in books, and made my own apparatus; and I've been given a box of conjuring tricks too. I often give shows at parties.

"You must give us a show at my birthday party," said Barbara, "as long as you don't try to saw me in half !"

"Well, there's no time for any more tonight," said Mr. Woodford. "We've had lots of exciting suggestions, and I'm sure that you are all itching to get together and practise doing some of the things we've heard about. And when you've had a go at making or doing these things, there are plenty more fascinating activities to go on to—carpentry, for instance; marionettes; sewing and embroidery; hand weaving and spinning. There are books about all these subjects—and the ones we've already heard something about—at the public library. Get them out and study them, and it's well worth buying the best one on the subject you're interested in, as you will always be wanting to refer to it. Life is never dull or empty for any one who has a hobby."

The meeting of the Hobby Club came to an end, and Billy and Barbara walked quickly home, talking of the hobbies they looked forward to enjoying in the future.

ACKNOWLEDGEMENTS

The publishers wish to thank the many organizations who have helped them with advice in the preparation of this book; they also wish to thank the following for their courtesy in allowing their copyright photographs or other material to be reproduced on the pages indicated:

Aerofilms Ltd. (101 bottom, 191 top); Associated British-Pathé Ltd. (30 bottom); Austrian State Tourist Department (33); Baron Studios: Photo Centre Ltd. (270, 273, 280, 281 bottom, 282 bottom); Jack Blake (284 bottom); Bodleian Library, Oxford (16 bottom); Boymans Museum, Rotterdam (139 bottom, 140 bottom); British Broadcasting Corporation (238 bottom, 251 bottom); British Matchbox Label and Booklet Society (290); British Museum (15 bottom, 38, 42 bottom, 43 top, 44 top, 47 top, 80–81 top, 94 bottom, 111 bottom, 115 bottom, 116–117 bottom, 119 top, 162 top, 171 top); British Tourist Authority (211, 212, 285); Brookite Ltd. (339, 340); Burlington House (129 top); Burrell Collection, Glasgow (113); Camera Press (219 top); Central Press (254 top); J. Chettleburgh (281 bottom); Lucy Clause (367 top, 371 bottom); Condé Museum, France (118 top); Anthony Crickmay (272 top); Dance News Ltd. (253 bottom); Mrs. Denholme (153 bottom); Dresden Art Gallery, Germany (140 top); Egyptian Museum, Turin (167 top); Former State Museum, Berlin (168 bottom, 169 bottom); Galleria Capitolina, Rome (131 bottom); Ganymed Press London Ltd. (152, 153 bottom); John Gay (282 top); Stanley Gibbons Ltd. (288, 289); Gregory, Bottley & Co. (317); Hohner Concessionaires (259, 260 bottom, 261 top); Imperial Museum, Vienna (147 top); Karsh of Ottawa (72 top, 92 top); Mrs. A. Kessler (152 bottom); Keystone (44 bottom, 239 top, 241, 252 top, 253 top); John Lane & Bodley Head Ltd. (164 bottom); The Louvre, Paris (110 top, 127 bottom, 132 top, 139 top, 147 bottom, 179 bottom, 235 top); Lullingstone Silk Farm (316 bottom); Macmillan & Co. Ltd. (28 top, 166 top); Mansell Collection (232 bottom, 240 bottom, 246 bottom); Metropolitan Museum of Art, New York (111 top, 172 bottom, 178 top); Mary Mudd (305 top, 306, 357, 358, 359, 360, 361); Museum of Asiatic Art, Paris (159 bottom, 160 bottom); Museum of Fine Arts, Boston (162 bottom); Trustees of the National Gallery, London (112 top, 120, 123, 124–125, 126, 131 top, 132 bottom, 133 top, 135, 136, 137, 138, 142, 143 bottom, 144 bottom, 145 bottom, 146 top, 148, 232 top); National Museum of Anthropology, Mexico (166 bottom); National Portrait Gallery, London (141 bottom, 143 top, 144 top, 145 top, 149 bottom, 150 bottom); New York Historical Society (110 bottom, 153 top); Henry J. Nicholls (334, 335); Oriental Institute, Chicago (116 top); Pallas Gallery Ltd. (155 bottom, from the Hanfstaengl print); Pinakothek Art Gallery, Munich (121 bottom, 134 top, 141 top); Benjamin Pollock Ltd. (286 bottom, 366 bottom); Paul Popper Ltd. (163 bottom, 240 top, 252 bottom, 254 bottom); Prado Museum, Madrid (151); By gracious permission of H.M. The Queen (129 bottom); *Radio Times* Hulton Picture Library (53 top, 70 bottom); Rijksmuseum, Amsterdam (146 bottom); Houston Rogers (242-3, 244-5, 271); Rovex Triang Ltd. (300 top and middle); Royal Academy of Art (122 top); Royal Festival Hall, London (224 bottom); Royal Institute of British Architects (217 bottom, 219 bottom, 220); Royal Library, Turin (128); Andrew F. Rutter (353 bottom); School Prints Ltd. (166 bottom, 168, 169, 171 top, 178 top); Sistine Chapel, Rome (130); Somerset Archaeological Society (185 top); Director of Information, South Africa House, London (115 top right); Peter Stuyvesant Foundation (156, 157); *Sunday Pictorial* National Exhibition of Children's Art (347, 348, 350 top); Surmondt Museum, Aachen, Germany (133 bottom); Trustees of the Tate Gallery, London (149 top, 154 top, 159 top, 179 top); *Daily Telegraph* (163 top); Uffizi Gallery, Florence (121 top, 134 bottom); United Press International (272 bottom); United States Information Service (52 top, 54 top); Victoria & Albert Museum, London, Crown Copyright (168 top, 169 top, 176, 302, 303 top); Watkins & Doncaster, The Naturalists, London and Welling (312, 313, 314, 318, 319, 320, 322, top, 323, 326); Mrs. L. Wertheim (152 top).